MW01469227

Transport and Its Place in History

Transport and mobility history is one of the most exciting areas of historical research at present. As its scope expands, it entices scholars working in fields as diverse as historical geography, management studies, sociology, industrial archaeology, cultural and literary studies, ethnography, and anthropology, as well as those working in various strands of historical research. Containing contributions exploring transport and mobility history after 1800, this volume of eclectic chapters shows how new subjects are explored, new sources are being encountered, considered and used, and how increasingly diverse and innovative methodological lenses are applied to both new and well-travelled subjects. From canals to Concorde, from freight to passengers, from screen to literature, the contents of this book will therefore not only demonstrate the cutting edge of research, and deliver valuable new insights into the role and position of transport and mobility in history, but it will also evidence the many and varied directions and possibilities that exist for the field's future development.

David A. Turner is Associate Lecturer in Railway Studies at the University of York and teaches at the Centre for Lifelong Learning and The York Management School's Masters in Railway Studies. He completed his PhD with the Institute of Railway Studies and Transport History, York, in 2013 and was awarded in 2016 the Business Archives Council's Bursary for Business History Research. He is also a book review editor for the *Journal of Transport History* and a co-convener of the Institute of Historical Research's Transport and Mobility History Seminar.

Routledge Studies in Modern British History

https://www.routledge.com/history/series/RSMBH

Transport and Its Place in History

Making the Connections

**Edited by
David A. Turner**

Routledge
Taylor & Francis Group

LONDON AND NEW YORK

First published 2020
by Routledge
2 Park Square, Milton Park, Abingdon, Oxon OX14 4RN

and by Routledge
52 Vanderbilt Avenue, New York, NY 10017

Routledge is an imprint of the Taylor & Francis Group, an informa business

British Library Cataloguing-in-Publication Data
A catalogue record for this book is available from the British Library

Library of Congress Cataloging-in-Publication Data
A catalog record has been requested for this book

ISBN: 978-0-815-39417-4 (hbk)
ISBN: 978-1-351-18663-6 (ebk)

Typeset in Times New Roman
by codeMantra

Contents

Figures

Tables

Contributors

Philip Batman MA, MD, FRCPath, was educated at Cambridge and Leicester Universities. He is a retired pathologist and originates from York. He is currently studying for a PhD at Leicester University, researching the migration of kinship families into York and out of Swaledale during the nineteenth century.

Oliver Betts is the Research Lead at the National Railway Museum. He completed his PhD at the University of York in 2014 focusing on the perceptions and realities of working-class life in three slum communities in late Victorian Britain. His current research interests cover the relationship between railways, cities and everyday life at the turn of the twentieth century.

Peter Cox is Professor of Sociology at the University of Chester. He chairs the international network, Scientists for Cycling, supporting the work of the European Cyclists' Federation and was a founder member of the Cycling and Society Research Group in 2004. Prior to academic life, he ran his own cycle business and still enjoys riding and fixing a variety of cycles, old and new.

Megan Doole is a building and historic site historian who trained at University of Cambridge after working for the National Trust at various historic sites around England. She has researched historic buildings and sites in north Nottinghamshire and is currently undertaking a PhD in History at University of Nottingham.

Mike Esbester is Senior Lecturer in History at the University of Portsmouth, UK, and is the originator and co-leader of the 'Railway Work, Life & Death' project. He has worked on a variety of topics relating to the history of transport and mobility, including the safety of railway workers and road safety. He is Deputy Editor of the *Journal of Transport History*.

Martin Higginson is an independent scholar and proprietor of Martin Higginson Transport Research & Consultancy. He is a public transport economist and historian whose career spans operational management, policy advice and academia. Positions he has held include London Transport Senior Lecturer at Birkbeck College, University of London, and Visiting Fellow, Transport Operations Research Group, at Newcastle University. He is a Fellow of the Chartered Institute of Logistics & Transport and is a member of the Transport Economics Commission of the International Public Transport Association.

Peter Lyth was a university teacher in tourism and transport history at Nottingham University Business School until his retirement in September 2014. His research focuses on both transport and tourism history, in particular, the history of air transport and civil aviation. He is a past editor of the *Journal of Transport History* and is the author (with Philip Bagwell) of *Transport in Britain*, and his latest book (with Richard Coopey) *Pay & Play: The Leisure Industry in Britain in the 20th century* is forthcoming with Routledge.

Susan Major completed a PhD with the Institute of Railway Studies & Transport History at the University of York in 2012. Her research focused on early railway excursion crowds during the period 1840–1860, from which followed her book *Early Victorian Railway Excursions: 'The Million Go Forth'* (2015). Her latest book, *Female Railway Workers in World War II* (2018), features the voices of wartime railway women recorded by the Friends of the National Railway Museum for the National Archive of Railway Oral History, set in the context of their representation in the wartime media.

Jodie Matthews is Senior Lecturer in English Literature at the University of Huddersfield and was appointed as the Canal & River Trust's first Honorary Research Fellow in 2016. As well as waterways, her research examines the representation of Romani people in Britain. She is the author of *The Gypsy Woman: Representations in Literature and Visual Culture*.

Kevin D. Tennent is Senior Lecturer in Management at The York Management School, University of York. His research focuses on the themes of governance and strategy in management history, across the fields of sport, international business, the music industry and transport. He is founding Chair of the Management and Business History Special Interest Group of the British Academy of Management and is active in the Management History Division at the Academy of Management.

David A. Turner is Associate Lecturer in Railway Studies at the University of York and teaches the Centre for Lifelong Learning and The York Management School's Masters in Railway Studies. He completed his PhD with the Institute of Railway Studies and Transport History, York, in 2013 and was awarded in 2016 the Business Archives Council's Bursary for Business History Research, which funded the research for his chapter. He is also a book review editor for the *Journal of Transport History* and a co-convener of the Institute of Historical Research's Transport and Mobility History Seminar.

Preface

In 2016, a one-day workshop was held at the University of York's King's Manor site. Academics, colleagues and friends all came together to hear about some of the latest research in transport and mobility history, to understand its new directions. This book is to a large extent the result of that workshop, and I hope it demonstrates to readers what an exciting and vibrant field transport and mobility history is and will be in the future.

The book would not have ended up in print without the dedication and hard work of all the contributors. I thank them for their generosity at various points, their receptiveness when I have returned chapters with suggestions, and their patience. It would have not have been possible without you!

I would also like to extend my thanks to the various anonymous individuals who provided comments on the chapters and contributions. My Particular thanks also goes to Mike Esbester and Kevin D. Tennent, who have been of huge emotional and academic support to me through the ups and downs of the project. I would also like to thank the team at Routledge, who have always been on hand to offer advice and support.

August 2019

Introduction

David A. Turner

This book is a celebration. Where other texts might want to address a single issue, subject or field, the objective of this text was never to show one thing, except the vibrancy and diversity of scholars working in the field of transport history. Throughout the text, you will encounter the richness and diversity that makes up the field. From canals to Concorde, from freight to passengers, from screen to literature, this book will serve not only to demonstrate the cutting edge of research, but will emphasise one of the field's major strengths; that it cannot really be defined as having one particular strand of research, of thought, of subject area, of evidence base or approach.

This plurality is partially rooted in the fact that over the last 25 years the field has changed. From the perspective of scholars working and writing in the 1990s and 2000s, there was much to justifiably criticise about how the field did or did not keep up with trends in the broader field of historical study. On the one hand, the writing of transport history had been perhaps overly focussed on the labour, economic or business aspects of transport, although with notable exceptions.[1] Moreover, the user of transport was usually side-lined or ignored completely, individual modes were studied in isolation, and those examined were for the most part inland navigation and, the usual star of the show, railways. Studies also focussed largely on transport in the global north in the nineteenth and twentieth centuries. Before the 2000s, moves towards the linguistic, cultural and social science orientated approaches that had been found throughout historical scholarship did not happen in transport history. Issues such as culture, identity and gender, for instance, were largely absent from the field. Consequently, Margaret Walsh argued in 2002 that transport history was 'ghettoised'.[2]

The apparent reticence to embrace ideas from elsewhere and advance the agenda of transport and mobility history was a point raised repeatedly from 1990 to the present day, especially in the pages of the leading journal in the field, *The Journal of Transport History (JTH)*. Over the last decades various scholars have emphasised a generalised dissatisfaction with the field's history up until that point, being concerned that, if change did not occur, the future might not be rosy and we might fail to be relevant. Gijs Mom argued nearly two decades ago that the *JTH* should endorse a wider scope of fields, ideas and subjects, moving beyond its traditional domains.[3] Similarly, John Walton argued that 'transport history ... needs to extend its range and remit in a new set of interdisciplinary directions'.[4] More recently, Mom stated that the field of transport history was in crisis,[5] and shortly after Massimo Moraglio, the editor-in-chief at the time of writing, argued that we should seek a '(new) ontology' for transport history, that we need to redefine the field and take ourselves out of our comfort zones.[6]

To a large extent, scholars are meeting these calls and we have a progressively diverse field. For instance, one of the original claims was that a 'cultural turn' was required, Divall and Revill arguing for the adoption of 'a conception of culture that does more than merely consider (although this is no simple matter) how and why transport technologies are represented in the arts and popular imagination'.[7] It is undeniable that this shift towards culture – whether that be the cultures that influence travel choices, how cultures shape how people experience travel, and representations in cultural productions – is represented throughout this book. Three chapters consider the relationship between transport and culture. Martin Higginson and Jodie Matthews examine the cultural representations of public road transport and canals, whilst Oliver Betts examines the social and cultural discourse around the permanent way in the nineteenth century (the railway track bed and other permanent equipment). Two studies also consider how policy and practice, and the cultures that govern this, can shape, reconstitute and reconfigure transport and mobility. Through considering the history of Concorde, Peter Lyth examines how powerful narratives can shape transport policy, whilst Susan Major demonstrates the social forces that shaped mobility for leisure via excursion trains in the nineteenth century. Examinations of the relationship between culture and transport are therefore alive and well.

There has also been more collaborative working and discourse with scholars in disciplines beyond history to expand the perspectives, approaches and methodologies used. Reflecting this, transport and mobility historians progressively move in a milieu of historical geographers, sociologists, industrial archaeologists, cultural and literary scholars, ethnographers and anthropologists, these encounters enriching and diversifying our studies. The chapter in this collection by Peter Cox is demonstrative of the positives that can arise from such interactions; he uses an ethnographic methodology originating in his work on the modern use of bicycles to examine films of Germany and Belgium in the 1930s. A further indicator of the field's diversity is the contribution of Megan Doole, a building and historic site historian, who combines contemporary and historic sources to explore transport's impact on the urban built environment. In sum, these and the other studies in the book suggest that plurality is an important part of the field.

Something else that moving the field into pastures new means, is that we encounter new theories, concepts and hypotheses, and this is worth considering in slightly more detail because it is here that there is some cause for reflection. Where rejection of theory in other strands of historical research is now uncommon, and expanding our potential theoretical frames of interpretation and approaches is invariably seen as a positive thing,[8] an idea pervades that many in the transport and mobility history field are unsettled by engagement with abstract concepts. The leaders in the field have therefore stated a desire to infuse it with much more.[9] Mom lamented in his survey of the history of the *JTH* that 'the theory-driven fields of large technical systems or diffusion studies received only scant attention in *JTH*, mostly through book reviews'.[10] Moraglio recently considered that transport history is 'severely under-theorized'.[11] There is evidently therefore much more space and scope for theory to be discussed, deployed and utilised in the field, and indeed Divall has argued that 'an important trend is the greater use – although not without substantial disagreements over which schools of thought are most appropriate – of concepts drawn from cultural theory'.[12]

Yet we perhaps need to be a little cautious, and consider carefully what the relationship between theory and historical research in the transport and mobility history sphere should be. It is not as clear cut or simple as saying that 'we need to develop into a more theory-driven field', as this is arguably somewhat vague and imprecise as a proposition. Rather, historians need to define the terms of engagement with theory, because whilst sharing aims, and supporting interdisciplinary work, historical research is not wholly like sociological, anthropological and geographical study.

It is possible to understand why some scholars of an earlier generation might have proclaimed their rejection of theory. Excessive recourse to theorising and using abstract concepts, some argued, might smooth out the many varied bumps and ripples in the historical continuum, potentially downplay the agency of individuals, or pre-judge what occurs in the complex tapestry of human life. Indeed, theory might, for some, be seen as trying to provide totalising answers for all human behaviour and activity, where this is deemed perceptibly impossible. Alongside this, some might consider that new theories can be advocated simply by picking the evidence to fit them, pushing extrapolation and supposition too far. Consequently, these twin concerns stimulate a broader perspective that by accepting theory, one might blot out rigorous interpretation of the evidence to determine what people actually did in the past in their many and varied times and circumstances, a process which is arguably the bedrock of historical scholarship.[13]

There is no doubt, as Tosh has argued, that 'theory-orientated history is certainly prone' to over theorising and cherry picking. The way forward, he suggests, is not however to throw theory out or reject it. Rather, we should be careful not to theorise to an excessive degree. For him, this is undertaken by higher levels of testing of theories with evidence, perhaps higher than is found in other disciplines. And thus,

> ...the business of historians is to apply theory, to refine it and to develop new theory, always in the light of the evidence most broadly conceived. And they do so not in pursuit of the ultimate theory or 'law' which will

'solve' this or that problem of explanation, but because without theory they cannot come to grips with the really significant questions in history.[14]

With this in mind, and as Tosh considered of all historical scholarship, we as transport and mobility historians should therefore accept the useful role we can play. Whilst of course recognising that theories developed about the world today are not always applicable to the circumstances of the past, if they are engaged with in our field, we should use evidence to test them rigorously, refine them more closely and to give them historicity.

This is something that is already occurring. To take one example, Gunn sought to qualify Urry's proposition that the car system, a multifaceted collection of economic, socio-technical, political, and cultural interdependencies, 'is a way of life, an entire culture' which transformed wholesale the world in which we now inhabit.[15] Gunn provided evidence from Britain between 1955 and 1970 that whilst motor car usage increased rapidly, the spread of the 'car system' was uneven, and by the end of the period only 52% of households owned a car and under one-fifth of women held a driving licence. Moreover, rather than changing people's social habits wholesale, the motor car was adapted into existing patterns of life.[16] Transport historians are also starting to develop their own theories that could help to inform transport policy. Tennent's work in this book is one example; he suggests that despite the existence of rails in transport systems, they actually have the potential to undermine their longevity and effectiveness, as elites can abolish them easily when it suits their interests, casting them as obstructions in the transport landscape.

Something that also must be stressed when considering theory's position in transport and mobility history is that not all historical research and writing needs to explicitly deal with or seek engagement with a noted theory from a particular school or deal with a big idea. Suggesting that historians should act in a certain way and maintain a constant relationship to theoretical considerations denies the fact that refining them, informing them and enhancing them is not historians' sole occupation. Developing our knowledge of historical events, patterns and processes found and discussed in pre-existing published works, as many of the chapters in this book do, is another important strand of research and writing in our field, adding to its richness. As Decker, Kipping and Wadhwani have argued of similar discussions in the field of business history, historical research

> ...is often aimed at uncovering sequences and processes, or at synthesising complex developments related to the phenomenon being studied, rather than verifying specific claims... Often, the events and developments we study in business history are understood as important *in themselves*, rather than as an instance of a testable rule or claim [italics in original].[17]

There is nothing to say that outputs of this nature cannot underpin or inform later broader theoretical considerations (perhaps by the individual in question or another), nor that they cannot be enlightening. Indeed, if we want to promote the idea that we should be a community where there is plurality of ideas, methodologies and approaches, we must also accept that there is freedom to be creative and for individual scholars to forge their own path in varied directions towards different ends, even if they run against the current of what might be the particular vogue in the field.

Herein lies the point of departure for the next section, which offers a critique of the mobilities shift and advocates a continued role for the dedicated and focussed study of transport history, suggesting that following such a course might prevent a fracturing of the field, whilst also enhancing its vibrancy. It is undeniable that a specific path is currently being forged. As noted, a huge, perhaps dominant, influence stems from study concerned with, as Urry has proposed, the 'diverse mobilities of peoples, objects, images, information, and wastes; and of the complex interdependencies between, and social consequences of, these diverse mobilities'. Its focus is elements such as 'networks', 'flows' and 'scapes', and how these things shape what we do and how we live our lives.[18] In the last 10 years, and following the calls for the use of more cultural theory in the field in the early 2000s, many scholars have implied a desire to morph transport history into 'mobility history'. Divall in 2013 asked 'how far it has moved in the direction of a "mobility studies paradigm"'[19] calling the drive towards developing mobilities history a 'project'.[20] Mom made the argument in 2006 that the field must 'formulate a set of common questions that drive mobility historians'.[21] Such arguments were echoed in 2017 with Moraglio's call for a mobility-oriented field where what is desired is a history that explores how people and objects transit between places. In his view, a mobilities turn is required where we approach 'the history of transport in a much more rounded way'.[22]

Whilst it is recognised that such an approach can be very fruitful, and that we should continue to push the boundaries of mobility history, the adoption in the field of a seemingly singular mobilities-oriented path theoretically and conceptually may not be wholly healthy. Could it have the potential to replicate the problems recent shifts initially sought to challenge; narrowness and insularity? Transport history before the recent mobilities shift did not have one theoretical or conceptual consideration, perspective or position. One of its principal features was that it was a community that transcended the borders of *historical* study, encompassing scholars of society, labour, leisure, politics, gender, travel, business and economics, amongst other things. Even if these subject areas were unevenly represented, and there was a problematic narrowness of scope that needed to be challenged, it was a community of scholars whose common focus of study was research on transport, where their different interests and passions overlapped and where the sharing of ideas, information and debate across the boundaries of sub-areas was common, even if two scholars were studying very different subjects.

The shift towards the field becoming dominated by the study of mobility nonetheless has the potential to establish categories of inclusion and exclusion within the established constitution. Merriman echoed this sentiment, arguing that academic pushes to become something new and to transform the character of fields 'inevitably lead to a situation where some voices prevail (and others are lost) in the formulation of common questions or the codification of research agendas'.[23] The potential for loss is apparent if we consider that whilst some pre-existing subjects of study found within the domain of transport history can be easily aligned with the move towards mobility history, others cannot not so easily, if at all. To provide some examples from this book, Esbester's chapter touches on the history of labour relations, employment legislation and, most specifically, the development of understandings about occupational health and safety. Phil Batman's work focusses on the kinship communities of railway workers found in York in the nineteenth century, speaking more to discourses on communities and families of railway workers. Both these chapters draw on long-established strands of research in our field, yet arguably neither fit neatly with the mobility history trajectory, or at very least their authors have not sought to meet it. The potential for us to lose connection with some established parts of our community is also emphasised if we consider that ideas and concepts that were once championed as part of arguments for a 'cultural turn' in the field have received no mention in recent critiques of it. Work identity amongst transport employees, notably worked on by Tim Strangleman, who was cited in *JTH* editorials calling for a new trajectory in the early 2000s, has seemingly not been mentioned of late.[24] Similarly, whilst Margaret Walsh's calls for more research on gender in transport history is being heeded to a great extent where users are concerned, calls for the exploration of women transport workers' lives has seemingly gone by the wayside. As such, as mobility history rises to dominance in the field, we must recognise that such changes may make many dedicated *transport* historians feel their research has no home within it. They will possibly face the dilemma of having to either get in line with mobility history (somehow) or depart for other scholarly communities, diminishing the richness of ours. Indeed, anecdotally, this author can report that this is already happening.

This sense of some of our established community being unable to connect with the mobilities shift is further heightened if we consider the position of independent scholars, some of whom we proudly feature in this volume. Divall correctly pointed to the fact that amateurs and amateur groups are a resource for mobility historians.[25] We must however be wary of making this relationship a one-way street, where the mobility historian is only using what these individuals produce. If these non-academic allies do not move towards mobilities, and perhaps focus on researching the detail of technical systems, transport management or family histories in a more traditional vein and/or without a theoretical bent, through no one's explicit intention they might be disinclined from becoming *contributors* to the field, as they have been in the past, diminishing its richness. Indeed, regrettably, this author must again report anecdotally that the mobility shift has already forced away from our shores established non-academic allies on numerous fronts who do not feel they have common cause with the direction of travel and are feeling alienated. This is worrying, and should give all transport and mobility historians cause for thought about what converging towards one approach might mean.

Of perhaps more significance, there is also scope to critique the rising dominance of 'mobilities' for a narrowness of vision that potentially constrains what can be considered 'new' in the field, consequently limiting the capacity of more traditional, if narrower, strands of transport history to evolve to their full potential. Calls for change in the field over recent decades have focussed on advocating the greater engagement with theories drawn to a greater extent, although not exclusively, from sociology, geography and cultural studies. This is of course welcome, however new approaches, theories and developments found elsewhere within the academic spectrum – for example, in the scholarly domains of labour relations, management, law, organisational studies, business or political science – have been little advocated for inclusion in the new direction, despite offering many opportunities to advance our understanding in new ways. To take one hypothetical example, institutional logics theory, increasingly finding favour in organisational studies, is described by Thornton and Ocasio as 'the socially constructed, historical patterns of material practices, assumptions, values, beliefs, and rules by which individuals produce and reproduce their material subsistence, organize time and space, and provide meaning to their social reality'. We may potentially see how this could apply to the internal organisational dynamics of transport providers to develop a more theoretically driven understanding of how and why transport officials made decisions in the past and the ways that they reacted to changes in external factors?[26]

Recent explorations of transport history also provide good evidence of where theories and concepts emanating from varied disciplines outside mobility scholars' usual domains of enquiry can be applied to transport history to great effect. It might be useful to apply theories, concepts and models found in political science to transport, as Dudley and Richardson did to transport policy in Britain between 1945 and 1999. They explored why there was a 'hollow core' in British railway policy in the 1950s, and how this was filled in the 1960s by Ernest Marples, the Minister of Transport, and Richard Beeching the Chairman of the British Railways Board.[27] As evidenced in the recent work of Hannah Reeves on the 'railway family' between 1900 and 1939, political scientist Benedict Anderson's concept of 'imagined communities' remains a useful way through which to understand railway workers, their families, and their relationship to railway companies, amongst other things.[28] We might use the concept of supply chain governance – which has emerged from operations management and considers the institutions and structures that lead, guide and control supply chains through policy and regulations – to inform our thinking on freight systems, as Thomas Spain has, to explain changes in food distribution in Britain between 1919 and 1975.[29] Ultimately, these cases and others suggest that there is still much scope for more developed, theoretically and conceptually rich versions of long-established strands of transport history scholarship to emerge. Such developments might connect at some points with mobilities history directly, and mobility historians might derive much from such interactions, but it is entirely acceptable for them not to. As such, by advocating a *range* of directions and possibilities for the field, rather than a singular direction and common of enquiry, both transport and mobility historians potentially stand to gain much through greater exchange, debate and discussion. As Merriman has argued, 'Dissensus, plurality, fragmentation, and multiplicity...can be healthy, productive, and creative'.[30]

Moreover, adopting a plural approach to the field's direction might perhaps provide a range of ways to use history to inform current and future policy and practice, so we can better face down the climate emergency and social challenges we face as a world – something Divall has called the 'usable past.'[31] Those who have an influence on the shape and nature of transport and mobility in the modern world are diverse in background and work goals, and so deploying concepts, ideas and research from mobility-orientated studies might not always be the most effective way to connect with and influence them to affect change. What works with the public, might be different from what works, for instance, with politicians, council leaders, environmentalists and businesspeople. Consequently, by developing further all parts of established transport history alongside and intertwined with mobilities history, we might come to possess a suite of different tools to inform policy, practice and public opinion that can be deployed in different ways, in different combinations, at different times, dependent on the understandings and outlooks of the audience. Finally, by advocating that the long-established areas of transport history should continue to develop, we might mitigate or even eradicate the feelings of exclusion from it, that some of our community are progressively having, and encourage those who have already departed for academic places beyond our line of sight to reconnect.

With these considerations in mind, this collection shows how the field's diversity and richness can be maintained without necessarily advocating that it should become one thing. The four chapters of the book's first part, demonstrates through historical cases how policy and practice, and the cultures that govern them, can shape, reconstitute and reconfigure transport and mobility in the modern world. Peter Lyth examines how powerful dominant narratives can shape transport policy; since the 1980s a cultural shift amongst the public and politicians from a 'paradigm of speed' towards a 'paradigm of mobility' was a factor that ultimately spelled the end of Concorde. Susan Major demonstrates how in the mid-nineteenth century powerful, but complex, social forces – 'Saint Monday', Sabbatarianism and Whitsun holiday – influenced individuals' mobility for leisure via excursion trains. Using the case of trams and trolleybuses, in Chapter 3 Kevin Tennent suggests that despite the rails suggesting the permanence of transport systems, they actually have the potential to undermine such systems' longevity and effectiveness, as elites can abolish them easily when it suits their interests. Finally, through using the brewing industry before 1914 as a case study, David Turner argues in Chapter 4 that businesses may affect modal shift in their distribution arrangement for a range of reasons other than cost reduction, although this is a factor. The enthusiastic uptake by some breweries of motor transport was driven in different places to different extents by their financial health, social change, the actions of the railways, and government policy. Section one therefore strongly demonstrates to scholars, practitioners and decision-makers the diverse range of factors that can influence policy and practice.

The second section, "Cultures of Transport", examines how transport and mobility has been represented in culture, how culture has shaped perceptions and understandings of the role and nature of transport and mobility, and also challenges readers to think about areas of study beyond the field's obvious and established targets. Oliver Betts explores away from the established areas of the study of traffic and travel, taking us down to the permanent way of the railways. His chapter discusses who worked on this piece of infrastructure, how it was administered and how this metal road through the landscape created cultural ripples that extended far beyond the track-bed. In the sixth and seventh chapters, Martin Higginson and Jodie Matthews pose the same question about public road transport and canals, respectively; why have these transport modes not had the same degree of cultural representation as the railways? Using film, music, theatre, fiction, non-fiction and journalism, on the one hand, and literature on the other, they set out to demonstrate and deconstruct how these transport forms have been represented and how this sheds light on nineteenth and twentieth century attitudes to, and perceptions of transport and mobility. The second section therefore highlights to scholars old, new and in the future, that many dimensions of the cultural impact and perception of transport and mobility remain unexplored.

Finally, the "Methodologies" section demonstrates the diversity of research approaches that scholars are currently bringing to transport and mobility history. Phil Batman in his chapter on kinship families amongst railway workers in York uses a unique surname index analysis of census decennial returns to track their lives, their migrations, their families and their communities. Following this, Peter Cox explores the sensory experiences of cycle riders in the past using films of 1930s Germany and Belgium, to locate current practices in historical contexts. This chapter will help us to think about how the moving image can be used in cycling history research, but also how it may be deployed in research on other transport forms. Megan Doole then demonstrates how combining contemporary and historic sources can be used to explore transport's impact on the urban built environment over time. Using horse-drawn transport in the nineteenth century as an example, her chapter explores the power and possibilities that arise from using maps to gauge the importance of transport in history. Mike Esbester concludes the section, exploring how crowdsourcing could open up new opportunities for transport and mobility historians, providing an example of how this has been be applied to better understand railway accidents amongst railway workers from the 1890s. He demonstrates the huge value that can come through working with non-academic partners and volunteers in developing new research outputs. Overall, this final section demonstrates the range of research approaches historians of transport and mobility are using in their endeavours, challenging us to think about how we might explore the 'new' in our own research.

As this collection shows, the developing direction of the transport and mobility history field is hugely exciting; we are a diverse church, and recent developments that have been stimulated by an infusion of new ideas and perspectives – once sorely needed – is to be celebrated and welcomed. Nonetheless, as identified above, the shift towards mobility history becoming increasingly dominant has also potentially given rise to problems that should concern us. Should theoretical or conceptual considerations from certain domains of academic study come to dominate the field, the danger is that this may unintentionally restrict the potential development of the more traditional strands of transport history research, or at very most exclude from our community those who wish to pursue it. Indeed, there are already some signs that the field is fracturing through some scholars not being able to align their research so easily with 'mobility history'. The boundaries that could result from this emerging situation significantly concerns this author. Contrary to the views of many of my colleagues, it is my belief that the way to avoid division in the transport and mobility history field should not be for it to try and 'formulate a set of common questions', as Mom suggested.[32] Rather, it should embrace many and varied areas and types of study and research, and look to develop all the strands of its fabric in new ways, even if in many cases 'mobility history' is not the focus and we simply call it 'transport history'. Through doing this, it will continue to truly be a place for collaboration, exchange and fellowship.

Notes

1 Colin Divall, "Mobilities and transport History," in *The Routledge Handbook of Mobilities*, eds. Peter Adey, David Bissell, Kevin Hannam, Peter Merriman, and Mimi Sheller (Abingdon: Routledge, 2014), 36.
2 Margaret Walsh, "Gendering Transport History: Retrospect and Prospect," *Journal of Transport History* 23, no. 1 (2002): 1.
3 Gijs Mom, "What Kind of Transport History Did We Get? Half a Century of *JTH* and the Future of the Field," *Journal of Transport History* 24, no. 2 (2003): 121–138.
4 John Walton, "Transport, Travel, Tourism and Mobility: A Cultural Turn?," *Journal of Transport History* 27, no. 2 (2006): 129.

5 G. Mom, "The Crisis of Transport History. A Critique, and a Vista," *Mobility in History* 6 (2015): 7–19.
6 Massimo Moraglio, "Seeking a (new) Ontology for Transport History," *Journal of Transport History* 38, no. 1 (2017): 4.
7 Colin Divall and George Revill, "Cultures of Transport: Representation, Practice and Technology," *Journal of Transport History* 26, no. 1 (2005): 109.
8 Joyce Appleby, Lynn Hunt, and Margaret Jacob, "The Impact of Postmodernism," in *Historians on History*, ed. John Tosh (London: Routledge, 2017), 305.
9 Colin Divall, "Ideas In Motion. Mobility: Geographies, Histories, Sociologies," ed. Rhys Jones and Peter Merriman *Transfers* 3, no. 1 (Spring, 2013): 153.
10 Mom, "What Kind of Transport History Did We Get," 132.
11 Moraglio, "Seeking a (new) Ontology for Transport History," 3–10.
12 Divall, "Mobilities and Transport History," 38.
13 For a discussion of these debates, see: John Tosh, *In Pursuit of History* (6th edn, London: Routledge, 2015); Joyce Appleby, Lynn Hunt, and Margaret Jacob, *Telling the Truth about History* (London: Norton & Company, 1994), 223–224.
14 Tosh, *In Pursuit of History*, 266.
15 John Urry, *Mobilities* (Cambridge: Cambridge University Press, 2007), 133.
16 Simon Gunn, "People and the Car: The Expansion of Automobility in Urban Britain, c.1955–70," *Social History* 38, no. 2 (2013): 236–237.
17 Stephanie Decker, Matthias Kipping, and R. Daniel Wadhwani, "New Business Histories! Plurality in Business History Research Methods," *Business History* 57, no. 1 (2015): 31.
18 John Urry, "Mobile Sociology," *British Journal of Sociology* 61, no. 1 (2010): 348.
19 Divall, "Ideas In Motion", 152.
20 Divall, "Mobilities and Transport History".
21 Mom, "The Crisis of Transport History".
22 Moraglio, "Seeking a (new) Ontology".
23 P. Merriman, "Mobilities, Crises and Turns: Some Comments on Dissensus, Comparative Studies, and Spatial Histories," *Mobility in History* 6, no. 1 (2017): 22.
24 Mom, "What Kind of Transport History Did We Get", 132. Divall and Revill, "Cultures of Transport: Representation, Practice and Technology," 106.
25 Divall, "Mobilities and Transport History," 41.
26 H. Thornton Patricia and William Ocasio. "Institutional Logics," in *Handbook of Organizational Institutionalism*, eds., Royston Greenwood, Christine Oliver, Kerstin Sahlin, and Roy Suddaby (London: Sage, 2008).
27 Geoffrey Dudley and Jeremy Richardson, *Why Does Policy Change?: Lessons from British Transport Policy 1945–99* (London: Taylor and Francis, 2000).
28 Hannah Reeves, "An Exploration of the 'Railway Family': 1900–1948" (PhD Thesis, Keele University, 2018).
29 Thomas Spain, "'Food Miles': Britain's Transition from Rail to Road-based Food Distribution, 1919–1975" (PhD Thesis, University of York, 2016).
30 Merriman, "Mobilities, Crises and Turns," 20–34.
31 Divall, "Mobilities and Transport History". 41.
32 Gijs Mom, "Editorial," *Journal of Transport History* 27, no. 1 (2006): iii–v.

Bibliography

Appleby, Joyce, Lynn Hunt, and Margaret Jacob. *Telling the Truth about History*. London: Norton & Company, 1994.
———. "The Impact of Postmodernism." In *Historians on History*, edited by John Tosh, 287–314. London: Routledge, 2017.
Decker, Stephanie, Matthias Kipping, and R. Daniel Wadhwani. "New Business Histories! Plurality in Business History Research Methods." *Business History* 57, no. 1 (2015): 30–40.

Divall, Colin, and George Revill. "Cultures of Transport: Representation, Practice and Technology." *Journal of Transport History* 26, no. 1 (2005): 99–111.

———. "Ideas in Motion Mobility: Geographies, Histories, Sociologies." Edited by Rhys Jones and Peter Merriman. *Transfers* 3, no. 1 (Spring, 2013): 147–165.

———. "Mobilities and Transport History." In *The Routledge Handbook of Mobilities*, edited by Peter Adey, David Bissell, Kevin Hannam, Peter Merriman and Mimi Sheller, 36–44. Abingdon: Routledge, 2014.

Dudley, Geoffrey, and Jeremy Richardson, *Why Does Policy Change? : Lessons from British Transport Policy 1945–99*. London: Taylor and Francis, 2000.

Gunn, Simon. "People and the Car: The Expansion of Automobility in Urban Britain, c.1955–70." *Social History* 38, no. 2 (2013): 220–237.

Merriman, P. "Mobilities, Crises and Turns: Some Comments on Dissensus, Comparative Studies, and Spatial Histories." *Mobility in History* 6, no. 1 (2017): 20–34.

Moraglio, Massimo. "Seeking a (New) Ontology for Transport History." *Journal of Transport History* 38, no. 1 (2017): 3–10.

Mom, Gijs. "Editorial." *Journal of Transport History* 27, no. 1 (2006): iii–v.

———. "The Crisis of Transport History. A Critique, and a Vista." *Mobility in History* 6 (2015): 7–19.

———. "What Kind of Transport History Did We Get? Half a Century of *JTH* and the Future of the Field." *Journal of Transport History* 24, no. 2 (2003): 121–138.

Reeves, Hannah. "An Exploration of the 'Railway Family': 1900–1948." PhD thesis, Keele University, 2018.

Spain, Thomas. "'Food Miles': Britain's Transition from Rail to Road-based Food Distribution, 1919–1975." PhD thesis, University of York, 2016.

Thornton, Patricia H., and William Ocasio. "Institutional Logics." In *Handbook of Organizational Institutionalism*, edited by Royston Greenwood, Christine Oliver, Kerstin Sahlin and Roy Suddaby. London: Sage, 2008.

Tosh, John. *In Pursuit of History*. Sixth edition, London: Routledge, 2015.

Walsh, Margaret. "Gendering Transport History: Retrospect and Prospect." *Journal of Transport History* 23, no. 1 (2002): 1–8.

Walton, John. "Transport, Travel, Tourism and Mobility: A Cultural Turn?" *Journal of Transport History* 27, no. 2 (2006): 129–134.

Urry, John. "Mobile Sociology." *British Journal of Sociology* 61, no. 1 (2010): 347–366.

———. *Mobilities*. Cambridge: Cambridge University Press, 2007.

Part 1
Policy and practice

1 Supersonic/gin and tonic

The rise and fall of Concorde, 1950–2000

Peter Lyth

> Concorde was born from dreams, built with vision and operated with pride. Concorde has become a legend today.
>
> *Captain Mike Bannister, on the occasion of the last scheduled Concorde flight from New York to London, 2003*[1]

> What little I did know about Concorde had persuaded me it was a prize technological monstrosity, the latest example of how scientific brilliance could be fatuously mis-applied.
>
> *Michael Foot, British Member of Parliament and sometime leader of the Labour Party, 1971*[2]

On 25 July 2000 an Air France Concorde crashed in flames at Gonesse near Paris, killing all 100 passengers and 9 crew members. It was the first and only crash of the Anglo-French supersonic aircraft, which at the time had been in airline service for nearly 25 years. The crash marked the end of an era, and although Concorde services were revived briefly in 2001, the aircraft was finally retired in 2003. Since then Concorde has become something of a legend. To some extent, this can be attributed to the fact that it has had no successor; no second-generation supersonic passenger aircraft has been built or even developed to the prototype stage, although the United States did undertake a considerable amount of preliminary research on a 'son of Concorde' in the 1990s.[3] Why? Why did the envelope of aviation speed, which had expanded steadily from around 160 km/h in 1920 to 2,100 km/h in the 1970s, expand no further? Why was Concorde not replaced by a bigger aircraft carrying more passengers at an even higher speed? Why did the 'paradigm of speed' appear to end with Concorde? Or, to put it another way, did the doctrine of ever-increasing speed in commercial transport, which we can trace back to the early railways of the 1830s, finally hit the social, economic and political buffers with the Gonesse crash?

The Concorde, jointly built and brought into commercial service in 1976 by Britain and France, was a thing of technical brilliance and outstanding beauty, but it was also a supreme waste of public money. In the appraisal and historiography of the aircraft, there appear to be three schools of thought. In the first, writers are lavish in their praise of Concorde's technological achievement, in particular of the engineers who built it and pilots who flew it. Theirs is a story of far-sighted individuals, striving against the odds at the cutting edge of scientific endeavour.[4] The second school of thought is the opposite of the first and represents an all-encompassing critique of the aircraft's genesis in a muddle of government policy-making, the aircraft's development without proper evaluation of its potential market, its dire impact on the natural environment, in particular its infamous 'sonic boom' and its spiralling cost, resistant to every attempt to control it. The literature from this school has few illustrations of the aircraft, but a great many facts and figures.[5] The third school of thought on Concorde, positioned somewhere between the first and second, sees the aircraft as a noble European attempt to push forward the boundaries of high technology, subverted and destroyed by a conspiracy of forces, mostly in the United States, opposed to its creation.[6]

This chapter, while not siding with any of these approaches, has a different purpose. Concentrating on the British side of the story, it seeks to contextualise Concorde within an historical 'paradigm of speed', for which, it is argued, it represents both a culmination and an epitaph, or to use the terminology of the paradigm's creator, a 'paradigm shift'.[7] It focuses on the first decade of the Concorde's history, i.e. from 1954 to 1964, during which early ideas about supersonic transport aircraft in Britain were developed in government departments, research institutions, aircraft manufacturers and commercial airlines. For over a century, progress in transport technology had been seen in terms of ever-greater speed, but in the 1970s – at precisely the moment when Concorde was launched – enthusiasm for speed was waning in the face of greater concern for two other factors in commercial aviation: the economics of airline operation and air transport's impact on the natural environment. This 'shift' was not so much a diminution in the modern urge to go faster as a sign of greater willingness to balance the advantages of speed against other factors, such as economic and environmental sustainability, which were becoming of paramount importance in the last quarter of the twentieth century. Above all, as this chapter aims to show, the doctrine of national prestige and its long association with ever-greater increments of speed was giving way to more pressing political ideas arising out of the rise of neo-liberal market economies and the rapidly spreading 'Green' movement. Reflecting this political focus, the chapter explores the evidence provided in the records of the 1950s Ministry of Aviation, focusing in particular on the final report of the 'Supersonic Transport Aircraft Committee', which was delivered to the British government in 1959.

Aeronautical Britain in the 1950s

The Concorde's genesis lies in the 1950s at a time when the British, Americans, French and Russians were all thinking about a supersonic transport aircraft, a so-called SST, which would fly faster than the speed of sound. In Britain the Bristol Aeroplane Company was working on preliminary designs for the Type 233, in France Sud Aviation was engaged in a similar direction on the Super Caravelle, and in the United States, with the delta-winged Convair B-58 'Hustler' bomber having made its first flight in 1956, thoughts were turning to the question of how supersonic *military* aircraft could be turned into civilian airliners. British and French planning focused on a transatlantic aircraft for about 100 passengers, the project to be funded largely by government. This was accepted practice; indeed, it is fair to say that unlike any other transport mode, the rapid development of aviation in the twentieth century would have been impossible without the steady and generous hand of government. Aircraft inspired awe, wonder and respect for their creators and had become associated in the minds of both politicians and the public with progress, and the seemingly limitless opportunities offered by new technology. Governments, in particular European governments, grasped and frequently overestimated the prestige value of possessing and deploying technologically advanced aircraft. And for this reason, they willingly applied enormous resources in a sustained effort to support the technology of flight. Concorde must be seen as within this tradition – it was a creation of government, not of airlines and aircraft manufacturers working together according to the laws of supply and demand. Concorde is an extreme example of this tradition and, in the words of American scholar Elliot Feldman, 'unlike other commercial aircraft in development', in that 'it had no airline sponsor, and indeed the airlines were not consulted when the first crucial planning was done'.[8]

The British context of Concorde's genesis was overtly political, with the government seeing it in more or less strategic terms, in much the same way as it saw the acquisition of nuclear weapons in the late 1940s. The approach of the government and the government-funded Royal Aircraft Establishment (RAE) also had what can now be seen as obsessive characteristics. During the Second World War, Britain, in agreement with the United States, had abandoned civil aircraft construction in order to concentrate on military types. This gave a significant head start to American manufacturers like Boeing, Douglas and Lockheed in the post-war years and forced British firms into a game of 'catch-up' as they sought to design and develop new airliners for the 1950s. Great hopes were placed on the de Havilland Comet jet airliner when it entered airline service with British Overseas Airways Corporation (BOAC) in 1952; at last the British had not only 'caught up' with, but seemed to have overtaken the Americans in the field of jet transport aircraft. But the early promise of the Comet was frustrated in 1954 when the aircraft suffered a series of crashes, later attributed to the little-known phenomenon of metal fatigue. The Comet crashes were especially unfortunate for the de Havilland company which in 1946 had built the supersonic DH 108 Swallow with the aim of being the first to break the 'sound barrier'; at an early proving trial the test pilot Geoffrey de Havilland had been killed when the uncontrollable aircraft broke up in mid-air at a speed of Mach 0.9.[9]

By 1955, the 'obsessive' character in British aerospace decision-making was even more striking. The Comet episode had meant not only the loss of Britain's 'lead' in jet airliner technology to the Americans, who within the next five years had successfully launched the Boeing 707 and Douglas DC-8, it also meant the British were running out of arenas in which they could challenge American supremacy in the air. Despite this there remained a widespread notion in British government circles that aerospace was one of the few sectors of high technology manufacturing where Britain could compete with the United States. For the many in the Conservative government in London, experiencing the trauma and insecurity associated with the retreat from Empire towards the more modest dimensions of a European consumer society, 'beating the Yanks' had become an abiding and irrational preoccupation, further exacerbated in 1956 when the crisis over the Suez Canal forced Britain to confront the reality that it was no longer a 'great power'. A new aeronautical project was needed and building a supersonic passenger aircraft appeared to offer the right combination of status, prestige and potential to challenge the Americans. Whether or not the aircraft could be built at a reasonable cost to the nation, or any of them sold to the world's airlines, seemed to be of secondary importance.

Supersonic aircraft were already well established in the military by the mid-1950s. Besides the American B.58 bomber, mentioned above, design development on delta wing fighters in Britain and France had yielded the Fairey Delta 2 and the Dassault Mirage, and Concorde's aerodynamic pedigree undoubtedly embraced ideas from all three aircraft. Building *civilian* airliners capable of flying at supersonic speeds posed much bigger challenges than building fighters or bombers but there seemed nonetheless to be backing in aeronautical engineering circles for the idea that supersonic travel was inevitable; it was only a question of who was to build the aircraft. Writing in 1955 a discussion group at the RAE asked what the world of civil aviation would look like in 1965, suggesting that supersonic airliners were a *natural progression* from subsonic ones:

> In ten years time high subsonic speed (ie. Mach 0.75) civil air transports should be well-established on the longer air routes of the world. These aircraft will reduce journey times to around half of present day times. *In the nature of things, the question must then arise – what is to be the next step; will it be practicable to increase cruising speed to a supersonic value, and, if so, to what value?*[10]

> (Italics added – PL)

It was into this political and scientific landscape that a new 'Supersonic Transport Aircraft Committee' (STAC) was set up in the Ministry of Aviation in November 1956 with the RAE's deputy-director Morien Morgan as chairman. It encompassed representatives from the British aircraft industry, from the airlines and from government departments, and was supported by leading figures in British aviation such as Sir George Edwards, head of Vickers.[11] The STAC committee deliberated for nearly three years before delivering to the government in March 1959 a 198-page confidential document, accompanied by an introductory letter from Morgan to Air Chief Marshall Sir Claude Pelly at the Ministry of Supply. In this letter Morgan, a strong enthusiast for the Concorde programme, combines an astute blend of scientific reasoning and patriotic aero-propaganda:

> ...it seems clear that the earlier supersonic transports will represent the start of whole new generations of very fast long range machines. Over the longer ranges we can certainly look forward with some confidence to speeds rising to four or five times the speed of sound.
>
> ... we must emphasise that a decision not to start detailed work fairly soon on the transatlantic aircraft would be, in effect a decision to opt altogether out of the long range supersonic transport field – since we would never regain a competitive position. *This could have a profound effect on the pattern of our Aircraft Industry and on our position as a leading aeronautical power.*[12]
>
> (Italics added – PL)

The STAC Report itself contains detailed proposals for several alternative designs of supersonic transport aircraft which for the non-scientific layman are largely impenetrable. However, two points are clear to anyone reading it with the benefit of hindsight. First, the cost of the enterprise is suspiciously low, and second, the potential market for the aircraft is subject to only rudimentary research and appears very optimistic:

> The potential market for supersonic aircraft has also been explored and although the forecasts must be treated with caution at this stage, it would appear that in 1970 a total demand for between 150 and 500 supersonic aircraft could arise.[13]

On the question of market research, the Report admits that it had not been possible 'to get very far with this problem':

> Except for our scheduled operators, it is very unlikely that any information of value will be obtained at this stage from an approach to the major world airline operators. Experience has shown that until it is possible to put before prospective purchasers a concrete proposal... any opinions or views obtained will be of little value.

This seems a poor excuse. Admittedly, the two airlines represented on the STAC were state-owned British enterprises (BOAC and British European Airways [BEA]), and likely to follow instructions from the British government regarding aircraft procurement, but provisional discussions could have been held with leading international carriers such as Pan American Airways and TWA. The Report notes that the transatlantic market had not expanded greatly with the introduction of Economy Class in 1958, but had merely taken customers from the earlier Tourism Class (1952). It goes on to say:

> Although no firm conclusion can be drawn at present, *it does raise the question whether the public will pay for high speed when alternative cheaper and slower services are available.* These thoughts indicate that until a clear indication can be given of the economic and operating characteristics of the ultimate aircraft, any research undertaken will have to include variables which are open to considerable debate.[14]

Two forecasts of what world traffic might be in 1970 were made by the Ministry of Transport & Civil Aviation (MTCA) and Vickers-Armstrong. The MTCA forecast estimated the number of aircraft required to carry the total world's scheduled passenger traffic, over stage lengths greater than 500 miles:

> If all the traffic is carried by subsonic aircraft then 2,830 aircraft cruising at Mach 0.85 would be required, and if all by supersonic aircraft, between 2,100 and 1,300 would be required, depending on the cruising Mach number. However, the general feeling ... is that the proportion of traffic carried by supersonic aircraft, in the period under discussion, may be as low as 10 per cent, ie. 210 at a Mach speed of 1.2.[15]

Vickers-Armstrong came to a more optimistic estimate, suggesting

> ... that 50 percent of the medium range and short range aircraft would remain subsonic. A total demand of between 300 and 500 supersonic aircraft could then be expected.[16]

Both estimates of the demand for supersonic aircraft turned out to be wrong; by 1970 the number in service with international airlines was zero and even in 1980 it was only 14 (7 Concordes each for British Airways and Air France). But it would be wrong to view the STAC estimates of 1959 out of their historical context: nobody in 1955 could have accurately guessed the size of demand for subsonic aircraft in 1970, and supersonic jets, as we will see later, were seen as a natural continuation in the line of technological development from subsonic jets.

On the question of Concorde's development cost, the STAC Report's predictions appear even more erroneous than its estimates of market size. Recognising that costs were difficult to estimate, the Report claimed that for a Mach 1.2 aircraft, they 'may be' in the following range, depending on whether new or existing engines were used (in fact, a variant of an existing military engine was used – the Bristol Siddeley Olympus).[17]

Table 1.1 Expenditure on Concorde development

	Variant of existing engines	New engines
Prototype development	£ million	
Airframe	17	17
Engine	6	24
Development of four aircraft to certificate of airworthiness		
Construction	12	12
20,000 hours proving flights	24	25
Total	**59**	**78**

Source: DSIR 23/26696, TNA, 'Supersonic Transport Aircraft Committee' Report, 3, 24.

Thus even choosing the most costly option, a Mach 1.2 aircraft with entirely new engines, the programme would cost no more than £78 million. By way of demonstrating the degree of error in this costing, at the time of its introduction in 1976 the British government's figure for Concorde's development cost, shared equally with the French, was £1,154 million.

Of course, STAC was by no means alone in the twentieth century in under-estimating the cost and over-estimating the potential benefit of a major transport or infrastructure project. There are many historical examples in both Europe and the United States of disastrous cost over-runs. The question here is why, on the basis of such palpably flawed estimates, did the British government decide to go ahead with Concorde? The answer seems to be twofold. First, the STAC Report did contain a powerful scientific ace-in-the-pack which made Concorde not only plausible, but technologically *possible*. Working at the RAE was the brilliant German engineer Dietrich Küchemann, a former Messerschmitt aerodynamicist and an expert on swept wing geometry who was brought to England after the war, along with a number of the Me-262 jet fighters, which he and his German colleagues had designed.[18] Küchemann's contribution to Concorde was critical, both scientifically and *politically*. Thanks to his work at the RAE, with his colleague E. C. Maskell, Küchemann was able to declare in 1957 that using a thin 'ogival' delta wing, a supersonic passenger plane was 'just possible'.[19]

The second reason for Concorde's advancement, despite the clear limitations of the STAC report, lies in the nature of the British Conservative government in the late 1950s: because it was élitist and habitually secretive, it proceeded with the very minimum of engagement with parliament, the press or the British people. For the select group of senior politicians involved with Concorde at this early stage, flying was for the rich and famous, and progress in air transport was measured by incremental increases in speed. For these men, Concorde was an act of faith, unencumbered by the need for reliable estimates of future demand. They acted in secret, with little respect for the democratic process, in the manner of earlier generations of British leaders, governing a 'great power'. But why did the engineers and scientists involved in the project not display more scepticism about the forecasts of Concorde's viability? The obvious explanation lies in the history of the British aircraft industry in the 1950s: the companies they worked for needed aircraft projects – any projects – to be able to retain their skilled labour force. In fact, the scientist Küchemann knew that the STAC cost estimates were more or less dreamed up on the basis of what 'politicians would stand'. He said later 'in the whole STAC report, those estimates are the only thing that are rubbish. I have a very bad conscience about that'.[20]

The momentum behind Concorde's take-off in 1959 was heavily augmented by a sense of urgency, born out of a sense of national insecurity, about the need to act and avoid delay. STAC itself prefaced its Report with the following passage:

> Delays between research work and the design and development of an operational aircraft must be avoided since *any delay would affect seriously the competitive aspects of the aircraft...* A successful supersonic transport aircraft would not only be a commercial venture of high promise but would also be of immense value to this country as an indication of our technical skill.[21]
>
> (Italics PL)

And shortly after the submission of the Report, the Aeronautical Research Council (ARC), a government agency which reported directly to the Ministry of Supply, wrote in a short paper entitled "Comments of the ARC on the Report of the STAC":

> ... The building of such an aircraft must therefore be *regarded as an act of faith*, but in the opinion of the Council (ARC) it is an essential act of faith in the future of the British aircraft industry.[22]
>
> (Italics – PL)

For ARC, a medium-range supersonic aircraft of Concorde's general specifications was a 'natural extension of the present generation of subsonic civil airliners...'.[23] And this reassuring note was echoed in the United States where there is evidence that some Americans also saw supersonic travel as a logical extension of subsonic air travel, the move to speeds over Mach 1.0 not requiring any kind of major technological breakthrough. For example, R. C. Sebold, the Vice-President of Convair and builder of the B.58 bomber, said in 1959 that

> It would be possible to build such a (supersonic) transport by conventional extrapolation and design compromise.[24]

The stage was set and the STAC report had pronounced that supersonic transport was both practical and feasible. But it has also said something else: even the unfeasibly low estimated cost would be beyond the resources of Britain alone, and it would need to find a partner in the project.

No escape clause – 1960–1980

The Concorde was a creation of the 1950s which from the early 1960s became more and more a Frankenstein monster for the British government and taxpayer. In its search for Concorde partners, and after short-lived negotiations with the Americans, Britain decided to share the project with the French.[25] As early as 1960, the costs of prototype development had already become so high that the British government told the chief contractor, British Aircraft Corporation (BAC) to look for an international partner and only France showed any serious interest. Discussions with the French began in 1961 and led to the signing of an agreement to share costs, design, development and production, and the proceeds of the sale of any supersonic aircraft. This was a more than a mere Anglo-French commercial agreement, it was a binding political treaty between the two countries from which there was no provision for escape. On the British side of negotiations towards the treaty the key figures in the Conservative government were two Francophiles. The first was Geoffrey Rippon, parliamentary secretary at the Ministry of Aviation, who wanted Concorde at any cost and who hoped, as a by-product, to get French agreement to British entry into the European Economic Community (EEC).[26] Rippon had chaired the STAC sub-committee within the Ministry of Aviation and was closely acquainted with its secrets, particularly the path-breaking delta-wing design pioneered by Küchemann and his team at RAE. In April 1960, in an extraordinary act of covert government, Rippon handed the French a copy of the STAC Report, closed to the public gaze in Britain at the time and marked "Confidential: UK Eyes Only". Rippon knew the Report was the most tempting bait he could offer the French and that sharing Concorde's aerodynamic secrets with them offered the best chance of getting the French government locked into the project.[27] Thus, it was that for many years to come the French government and aircraft industry would know what only a few select individuals in Britain's aeronautical circles knew; and certainly not the British parliament or the press.[28]

The second key figure, and possibly even more of a 'Concorde warrior' than Rippon, was Julian Amery, who took over as Minister of Aviation in 1962 and who signed the formal Concorde Treaty with the French in November of that year.

> Concorde was an entirely political aeroplane. The plan was to show the French that we were good Europeans.[29]

Thus began what we can call the 'Concorde epoch'; around 20 years of design, development and production of the world's only supersonic airliner, during which time the project was subjected to every kind of controversy and debate, fierce arguments over its cost and environmental impact and an increasing sense of desperation in the British government, both Labour and Conservative alike.

Concorde's production history is straightforward: in the years between 1965 and 1979 a total of 20 aircraft were built, including 2 prototypes and 4 pre-production models, with 14 production aircraft delivered to Air France and British Airways. Construction of the two prototypes began in 1965 simultaneously in Toulouse, France and Bristol, UK, with the BAC sharing responsibility for the airframe with the French company Sud Aviation. Rolls Royce, which had by this stage absorbed the Bristol Siddeley Engine Company, built the Olympus 593 engines, with the French engine maker SNECMA in Bristol. These prototypes made their first flight in March 1969 and attained supersonic speed in October.[30]

But before any construction could begin there was a change of government in Britain. Popular support for Harold Macmillan's Conservative administration had gradually ebbed away in the years since the delivery of the STAC Report and the perception had grown that 'Britain's anachronistic class system had been shored up to the detriment of its stagnating economy. The Conservative Party of the 1960s, it seemed, could only walk backwards into the future'.[31] A new Labour government came to power in the election of October 1964, offering a technological revolution for everyman rather than for a small social élite. And almost the first thing on the agenda of Harold Wilson's government was a review and hopefully a cancellation of the Concorde project. Concorde, for many in the new Labour Cabinet, was not only an appalling waste of money at a time when Britain's economy was in deep trouble and experiencing a serious run on the £ Sterling, it was also deeply symbolic of the kind of 'great power' prestige projects which they wanted to abolish. Labour was advised that the money devoted to Concorde would be much better spent on more democratic infrastructure investment, such as updating Britain's moribund railways, or as the aviation consultant and Harold Wilson confidante, Richard Worcester, suggested, on a large-capacity subsonic airliner, with up to 500 seats, and 'within the state of the art'.[32]

In tune with this sentiment, the new Minister of Aviation, Roy Jenkins, was dispatched immediately to Paris to talk to the French; Britain wanted to abandon the Concorde project, or at least drastically scale back its involvement. This mission proved to be a total failure. The French had no intention of letting the British back out (or at least that is what they claimed), and they were supported in their position by a cast-iron agreement which had no 'escape clause' for either party. It is worth reproducing in some detail what Prime Minister Harold Wilson wrote later:

> The Concorde arrangement was not a commercial agreement which could have allowed the two parties to break off the programme when costs escalated or commercial prospects grew dim. It was the subject of

an international treaty, registered at the United Nations and subject to all the procedures of the International Court at the Hague. Had we unilaterally denounced the treaty, we were told, we could have been taken to the International Court, where there would have been little doubt that it would have found against us. This would have meant that the French could then have gone ahead with the project no matter what the cost, giving us no benefit either from the research or the ultimate product. But the Court would almost certainly have ruled that we should be mulcted for half the cost. At that time half the cost was estimated... at £190 millions. This we should have had to pay, with nothing to show for it, the result of what we considered an improvident treaty on the part of Julian Amery... Faced with this situation, we had little alternative but to go on.[33]

And go on they did. In the years between 1964 and 1970, Concorde was successfully developed to the prototype stage, flew at supersonic speed and garnered a considerable number of purchase 'options' from interested airlines, under a seemingly reluctant Labour government. In fact, Concorde was pursued in the years after the French rebuttal with considerable purpose and determination by the Labour Government. Tony Benn, the new Minister of Technology, justified the expenditure and the élitist nature of the Concorde on the familiar socialist grounds that it protected jobs in the industry and his Bristol political constituency.

If Concorde fails it would be a national disaster and a tragedy for Bristol.[34]

Indeed nothing illustrates the overt political nature of Concorde more than the fact that its construction in Britain took place under the supervision of a Labour government and a left-wing Minister of Technology for whom the prospect of thousands of job losses in the highly skilled aerospace sector outweighed the offence of creating an expensive means of transport which would only be used by a few rich people.[35]

By the end of the 1960s, with two Concorde prototypes built and pre-production models in proving trials, there was some cause for optimism. The manufacturers had received non-binding options for over 90 aircraft from 16 airlines led by Air France, BOAC (shortly to become British Airways) and Pan American.[36] But any optimism was to be short-lived. As Britain entered the 1970s and Harold Wilson's Labour government gave way to Edward Heath's Conservative administration, a new and more troubled economic regime dawned. The oil crisis of October 1973 and the subsequent tenfold rise in fuel prices served as a rude awakening to both the airline and automobile industries. It was not only 'gas-guzzling' American cars but also Concorde's thirsty engines which now looked hopelessly inefficient and unsustainable.[37] Before the Arab oil embargo, Pan American had already judged that Concorde would be uneconomic to operate and cancelled its options for seven aircraft in January 1973. Thereafter, all the remaining orders, except those from Air France and British Airways, melted away like snow in the spring.[38]

Even the state-owned British flag-carrier had little enthusiasm for the plane and wasted little time lobbying the government to get its investment in eight aircraft written off at the tax-payer's expense. British Airways had been cautious from the outset about Concorde's commercial prospects. As early as 1973, its enthusiasm for plane appeared to be distinctly muted and although the beautiful aircraft graced the cover of BA's first annual report, mention of it was low key; the new airline certainly did not give the impression that it was desperate to get its hands on a supersonic airliner:

> The uncertainties that underlie the planning and evaluation of British Airways deployment of Concorde on the routes available to us are numerous. There are undoubted advantages to the customers in terms of speed and time savings, but there are problems created by narrow tolerance in performance, noise characteristics and other features... The range of financial results now expected from our calculations is wide and involves risks beyond the margins of commercial prudence that we are entitled to adopt *without some special arrangement for underwriting.*[39]
>
> (Italics – PL)

By 1976, when it finally entered airline service with Air France and British Airways, Concorde faced a gloomy commercial future. Regardless of its speed, nobody wanted a noisy and polluting aircraft, and the British had to fight hard even to get landing rights at New York, the only destination that offered Concorde the slightest prospect of profitable operation. The 1970s was an unfortunate time to launch a supersonic aircraft; it was the decade when the 'green movement' and environmentalist philosophy began to move from the fringes into the political mainstream, thanks to the activities of organisations like Greenpeace and Friends of the Earth. Concorde's phenomenal cost and its profligate use of fuel, as much as the extreme nuisance of its 'sonic booms', began to galvanise public opinion against the dogma of 'speed-at-any-cost'. For many people, Concorde was not so much a source of national pride in technological achievement as an environmental menace.

In the 1980s and 1990s, Concorde flew on as a supersonic celebrity vehicle, an apt example of a rich man's status symbol in a new age of neo-liberal capitalism. It is a curious irony that, despite all the cost, what failed to be a viable commercial airliner in a new high-speed age had succeeded instead in becoming a much-loved cultural artefact by the time of the Gonesse crash in 2000. And when it was finally withdrawn from service three years later, there was considerable interest from museums around the world in acquiring a copy, much as they might have bought a painting or sculpture to mark the passing of the millennium. Thus, Concorde came to rest, a stationary

Figure 1.1 One of the last remaining Concordes, rotting away with other museum pieces at Brooklands, England in 2017. Photo: Peter Lyth.

exhibit prompting excitement and curiosity, in the same way as a fairground ride. People paid a modest fee to climb the steps to its narrow cabin, people who had been unable to afford the price when it transported passengers supersonically through the air.

Supersonic/gin and tonic – paradigm shift?

Concorde and supersonic air travel vanished from our skies over a decade ago; with the benefit of hindsight, what can we say about the 'Concorde epoch'? Did the end of Concorde mark the end of speed? Or more precisely, did it mark the end of the search for ever-greater increments of speed?

It is the argument here that the fate of Concorde illuminates the democratisation of international travel and the transformation of the market for air transport. At a more fundamental level, however, the 'Concorde epoch' represents a shift from a 'paradigm of speed' towards a 'paradigm of mobility'.[40] According to its creator, within a scientific paradigm, innovation, or scientific progress, is 'defined and controlled by *tradition* … a set of principles or beliefs that have proven their ability to give order to the experience of a social, economic or scientific constituency'.[41] In other words, progress within the paradigm is controlled by paradigmatic assumptions about its nature and direction; it is argued here that within the 'paradigm of speed' – established for well over a century at the time of Concorde's conception in the late 1950s – the assumption, or *tradition*, ruled that modernity calls for the attainment of ever-greater speed. Speed means progress. Or more precisely, it still meant progress for a small group of British politicians, policy-makers and influential aeronautical engineers. For example, in a lecture published in 1964, Sir George Edwards, former head of Vickers-Armstrong and one of the leading figures in British civil aircraft construction, reported on progress with the Concorde and spoke of aviation speed in a manner which illuminates the power of *tradition* to define and control within a paradigm:

> The one thing air travel sells, and has always sold, is speed. There is the great unrelenting pressure of human progress always demanding reduction in journey times. This goes back to the stage coach, and has always gone on through every form of transportation.[42]

Edwards is speaking here from an entrenched position within the tradition of the speed paradigm; he even invokes the idea of human progress going 'back to the stage coach'. We must go ever faster, for not to do so is self-evidently wrong.

And the idea of *tradition* within a paradigm applies equally to British politicians of the time. The American scholar Lewis Mumford proposed the idea that speed is a function of power and the powerful have always used it as a means by which to demonstrate their authority, and more recently the French social critic Paul Virilio has focused on the anti-democratic nature of speed in elaborating his theory of the 'dromological state'.[43] It is the argument here that the circumstances surrounding the production and delivery of the STAC Report, and in particular the manner in which its findings (including highly dubious cost estimates) and recommendations (stressing the importance of immediate action if Britain was to avoid losing its 'position as a leading aeronautical power') were concealed from parliament, press and public alike, reflect the underlying undemocratic power structure in which decisions on Britain's aeronautical future were made. Had the STAC Report been made public at the time of its submission to the government in 1959, and its cost estimates for Concorde's development discussed and debated, it is unlikely the aircraft would ever have been built. As it was, Concorde was never debated *prior* to the signing of the Anglo-French Treaty in 1962 and the Report itself remained closed to public inspection for years after the aircraft was built and brought into airline service.

In retrospect, the actions of key political actors, such as Geoffrey Rippon and Julian Amery, including the extraordinarily early gift of a copy of the STAC Report to the French, may seem high-handed but they should be seen historically, as within the context of the ruling paradigmatic assumption. Britain was engaged in a 'race' with the United States for leadership in aeronautical progress, and that progress was defined in terms of ever-greater speed. Not to seek to go faster was to lose the race. Voices of caution, such as that of the scientist Dietrich Küchemann, were drowned out by strident expressions of anti-American patriotism and political insecurity. Concorde not only could, but *must* be built; to do otherwise meant the demise of one of Britain's few remaining science-based industries and its status as a great power. The notion that progress in aviation might not be manifest in greater speed, but rather in greater aircraft capacity and lower passenger fares, either did not occur to these actors, or was rejected as being outside the paradigm.

Looking back, it is easy to see that when it was launched in the 1970s, Concorde flew at phenomenal speed, but in the wrong direction. This was the decade in which the future of civil aviation switched from speed to economy. The French had already entered the field with the Airbus-forerunner, the Caravelle, and the British were to have some limited success with the BAC 1–11 twin-jet, but the decision-makers in the critical years between the STAC Report and the signing of the Anglo-French Treaty seemed unable to see a future of air transport in terms of low cost airlines and mass tourism. For them air travel remained a matter of prosperous people sipping gin and tonic and flying faster, not the working-classes with their beer and sandwiches on their first flight to a Mediterranean beach.

By way of conclusion it might be asked: who did benefit from Concorde? Not the United States, whose large aircraft industry was distracted through most of the 1960s by proposals to build a rival SST, but whose large aircraft manufacturing companies had the capacity to proceed anyway with widebody subsonic projects like the Boeing 747, Lockheed L-1011 Tristar and McDonnel Douglas DC-10. Not the Russians, whose own Concorde, the Tupolev TU-144, crashed before appalled spectators at the 1973 Paris Air Show. And not the British, whose amalgamated aircraft industry began to lose its way in the 1960s, unable to make up its mind over joining the European Airbus project as a fully fledged partner, or shrinking in size and significance into what was little more than an Airbus parts supplier (British Aerospace, later BAe).[44] Only the French, it seems, benefited from Concorde. In the 1960s, both Britain and France were in a state of technological rivalry with the United States, but whereas the British, after a traumatic experience with the Comet, saw it as their last chance to 'beat the Yanks', the French, with their étatist tradition of long-term economic planning, saw it as the foundation stone of a major new industry within a 'scientific nation state'.[45]

Notes

1 Quoted in Peter R. March, *The Concorde Story* (Stroud: Sutton Publishing, 2005), 1.
2 Foreword to Richard Wiggs, *Concorde: The Case against Supersonic Transport* (London: Ballantine/Friends of the Earth, 1971), vii.
3 See Erik M. Conway, *High-Speed Dreams: NASA and the Technopolitics of Supersonic Transportation, 1945–1999* (Baltimore: The Johns Hopkins University

Press, 2005) esp. Chapters 7 and 8. Periodically plans and even prototypes of passenger-carrying supersonic aircraft appear but none have ever entered airline service. The latest (2018) is an aircraft, with remarkably similar shape to Concorde, carrying 55 passengers at 2,335 km/h, from the American firm Boom Technology; "Raser im Himmel" *Der Spiegel*, January 20, 2018, 105.

4 See, for example, March, *The Concorde Story*, F. G. Clark and Arthur Gibson, *Concorde: The Story of the World's Most Advanced Passenger Aircraft* (London: Phoebus, 1976) and test pilot Brian Trubshaw's *Concorde: The Inside Story* (Stroud: Sutton Publishing, 2000).

5 Early ones in this genre include Wiggs, *Concorde: The Case against Supersonic Transport* and Andrew Wilson, *The Concorde Fiasco* (Harmondsworth: Penguin, 1973).

6 See, for example, Graham M. Simons, *Concorde Conspiracy: The Battle for American Skies, 1962–77* (Stroud: The History Press, 2012) and John Costello and Terry Hughes, *The Concorde Conspiracy* (New York: Charles Scribner's Sons, 1976).

7 For an introduction to the nature of the paradigm and the paradigm shift, see Thomas Kuhn, *The Structure of Scientific Revolutions* (Chicago: University of Chicago Press, 1962).

8 Elliot J. Feldman, *Concorde and Dissent: Explaining High Technology Project Failures in Britain and France* (Cambridge: Cambridge University Press, 1985), 98.

9 The Americans, with greater resources than the British, were undeterred by de Havilland's death and in October 1947 Chuck Yeager broke the sound barrier for the first time at Mach 1.07 in the rocket-powered Bell XS-1. See Charles Yeager and Leo Janos, *Yeager: An Autobiography* (New York: San Val, 1985) for the full account.

10 Royal Aircraft Establishment, Discussion Group, Report Aero 2546, *The Design and Operation of a Supersonic Civil Air Transport for North Atlantic Routes*, April 1955, Ministry of Supply, AVIA 6/18007, The National Archives (TNA), Kew, London.

11 May, *Concorde*, 484–485. At the original meeting on 1 October 1956, which launched STAC, representatives from 13 airframe and engine makers were present (A. V. Roe & Co, Armstrong Whitworth Aircraft, Bristol Aircraft, English Electric Co., Fairey Aviation Co., De Havilland Aircraft Co., Handley Page, Short Brothers, Vickers Armstrong, Armstrong Siddeley Motors, Bristol Aero Engines, De Havilland Engine Co, and Rolls Royce), as well as the two British airlines (British European Airways and British Overseas Airways Corporation) and two government departments (the Ministry of Transport and Civil Aviation, and the Ministry of Supply).

12 Royal Aircraft Establishment, Farnborough, *Report of the Supersonic Transport Aircraft Committee*, March 1959, National Archives, Kew, Ministry of Supply, DSIR 23/26696, TNA (hereafter STAC Report). This document was closed to scholarly examination, under the '30-year rule' of the British archives until 1990.

13 STAC Report, 13.

14 STAC Report, 44.

15 Provisional forecast of World Passenger capacity requirements 1966 and 1970, MTCA TCA.2145N, Economics Division, Text of letter re. size of future air traffic, MTCA HJ 34/729, D.F. Hedges, STAC Report; 35, TNA.

16 A preliminary estimate of the market for supersonic transport aircraft, Vickers Aero/L/Misc.446, C.J. Hamshaw-Thomas, STAC Report, 35.

17 STAC Report, 3, 24.

18 Rob Lewis, *Supersonic Secrets: the Unofficial Biography of Concorde* (London: London Exposé, 2003), 57.

19 Quoted in Peter Gillman, "Supersonic Bust," *The AtlanticOnline*, January 1977, accessed January 20, 2018, www.theatlantic.com/past/docs/issues/77jan/gillman.htm, 4. See also Costello and Hughes, *The Concorde Conspiracy*, 25.
20 Gillman, *Supersonic Bust*, 5–6.
21 STAC Report, 2, repeated page 15.
22 Aeronautical Research Council (ARC), *Comments on STAC report*, 14th April 1959, DSIR 23/26742, TNA, Kew.
23 Ibid.
24 "Commerical Air Transportration Beyond the Subsonic Jets," paper to the *Supersonic Transport Aircraft Proceedings* of the Annual Meeting of the Institute of the Aeronautical Sciences, held in New York, January 1959, ARC, May 1959, Unclassified report, DSIR 23/26863, TNA, Kew.
25 In October 1961, the British Minister of Aviation, Peter Thorneycroft, tried briefly to persuade the United States to join Britain in the project, but the Americans were more interested in a faster and bigger, all-steel Mach 3 SST than in the aluminium Mach 2 Concorde. See Simons, *Concorde Conspiracy*, 57–58.
26 By 1959, the Harold MacMillan's Conservative government had accepted that the EEC was a success and it now wanted Britain to join, see May, *Concorde*, 493. Also Kenneth Owen, *Concorde and the Americans: International Politics of the Supersonic Transport* (Shrewsbury: Airlife, 1997), 35–38.
27 May, *Concorde*, 488.
28 Parliament finally learnt of Concorde's development costs when Tony Benn gave it the details in March 1974. May *Concorde*, 504.
29 *Sir Richard Way, Permanent Secretary, British Ministry of Aviation, 1963–66* Quoted in Annabelle May, "Concorde – Bird of Harmony or Political Albatross: An Examination in the Context of British Foreign Policy," *International Organization* 33, no. 4 (1979): 500.
30 Meeting minutes and Technical Reports, 1959–1976, Ministry of Technology (1964–70) and Department of Trade & Industry, Concorde Division (1971–1974), Concorde project, TNA, Kew, BT.242.
31 Dilwyn Porter, "'Never-Never Land': Britain under the Conservatives, 1951–1964," in *From Blitz to Blair: A New History of Britain since 1939*, ed. Nick Tiratsoo (London: Weidenfeld & Nicolson, 1997), 131.
32 "How Concord Was Saved," *The Sunday Times*, January 10, 1965. See also Costello & Hughes, *Concorde Conspiracy*, 87–88.
33 Harold Wilson, *The Labour Government, 1964–70: A Personal Record* (London: Weidenfeld & Nicolson and Michael Joseph, 1971), 61–62.
34 Anthony Wedgwood Benn to the House of Commons, March 19, 1974, quoted in Feldman, *Concorde and Dissent*, 94.
35 *The Economist*, "The Concorde Caper," May 25, 1974, 95.
36 The full list is Pan American, Air France, BOAC, Continental, American, TWA, Middle East Airlines, Qantas, Air India, Japan Airlines, Sabena, Eastern, United, Braniff, Lufthansa and Air Canada. www.concordesst.com/history/orders.
37 Concorde's engines – Olympus 593s, originally developed by Bristol Siddeley in the 1950s for the Avro Vulcan V-bomber – were straight-through (as opposed to by-pass) military engines which needed afterburners to augment their thrust to supersonic level. They had a fuel consumption of 13.2 kg/km.
38 Kenneth Owen, *Concorde: Story of a Supersonic Pioneer* (London: Science Museum, 2001), 210.
39 British Airways, *Annual Report & Accounts*, 1973/4, 12.
40 For the latter see Kevin Hannam, Mimi Sheller, and John Urry, "Editorial: Mobilities, Immobilities and Moorings," *Mobilities* 1, no. 1 (2006): 1–22.

41 Kuhn, *Structure*, 77.
42 Sir George Edwards, "Progress with the Concord Supersonic Transport," *Institute of Transport Journal* (May 1964): 351–352.
43 Lewis Mumford, *The Myth of the Machine: Technics and Human Development* (London: Harcourt Brace Jovanovich, 1967), 205. Paul Virilio, *Speed and Politics: An Essay on Dromology* (New York: Semiotexte, 1986), 117, 141–142.
44 See Richard Coopey and Peter Lyth, "Back to the Future," in *Business in Britain in the Twentieth Century*, eds. Richard Coopey and Peter Lyth (Oxford: Oxford University Press, 2009), 231–232.
45 See Robert Gilpin, *France in the Age of the Scientific State* (Princeton: Princeton University Press, 1968), esp. Chapter 1.

Bibliography

Secondary sources

Clark, F.G., and Arthur Gibson. *Concorde: The Story of the World's Most Advanced Passenger Aircraft*. London: Phoebus, 1976.

Conway, Erik M. *High-Speed Dreams: NASA and the Technopolitics of Supersonic Transportation, 1945–1999*. Baltimore: The Johns Hopkins University Press, 2005.

Coopey, Richard, and Peter Lyth. "Back to the Future." In *Business in Britain in the Twentieth Century*, edited by Richard Coopey and Peter Lyth, 225–251. Oxford: Oxford University Press, 2009.

Costello, John, and Terry Hughes. *The Concorde Conspiracy*. New York: Charles Scribner's Sons, 1976.

Edwards, Sir George. "Progress with the Concord Supersonic Transport." *Institute of Transport Journal* (May 1964): 351–352.

Elliot, J. Feldman. *Concorde and Dissent: Explaining High Technology Project Failures in Britain and France*. Cambridge: Cambridge University Press, 1985.

Gillman, Peter. "Supersonic Bust." *The AtlanticOnline*. January 1977. www.theatlantic.com/past/docs/issues/77gillman.htm.

Gilpin, Robert. *France in the Age of the Scientific State*. Princeton: Princeton University Press, 1968.

Hannam, Kevin, Mimi Sheller and John Urry. "Editorial: Mobilities, Immobilities and Moorings." *Mobilities* 1, no.1 (2006): 1–22.

Kuhn, Thomas. *The Structure of Scientific Revolutions*. Chicago: University of Chicago Press, 1962.

Lewis, Rob. *Supersonic Secrets: The Unofficial Biography of Concorde*. London: London Exposé, 2003.

March, Peter R. *The Concorde Story*. Stroud: Sutton Publishing, 2005.

Mumford, Lewis. *The Myth of the Machine: Technics and Human Development*. London: Harcourt Brace Jovanovich, 1967.

Owen, Kenneth. *Concorde and the Americans: International Politics of the Supersonic Transport*. Shrewsbury: Airlife, 1997.

———. *Concorde: Story of a Supersonic Pioneer*. London: Science Museum, 2001.

Porter, Dilwyn. "'Never-Never Land': Britain under the Conservatives, 1951–1964." In *From Blitz to Blair: A New History of Britain since 1939*, edited by Nick Tiratsoo. London: Weidenfeld & Nicolson, 1997.

Simons, Graham M. *Concorde Conspiracy: The Battle for American Skies, 1962–77*. Stroud: The History Press, 2012.

Trubshaw, Brian. *Concorde: The Inside Story.* Stroud: Sutton Publishing, 2000.
Virilio, Paul. *Speed and Politics: An Essay on Dromology.* New York: Semiotexte, 1986.
Wiggs, Richard. *Concorde: The Case against Supersonic Transport.* London: Ballantine/Friends of the Earth, 1971.
Wilson, Andrew. *The Concorde Fiasco.* Harmondsworth: Penguin, 1973.
Wilson, Harold. *The Labour Government, 1964–70: A Personal Record.* London: Weidenfeld & Nicolson and Michael Joseph, 1971.
Yeager, Charles and Leo Janos. *Yeager: An Autobiography.* New York: San Val, 1985.

Newspapers and journals

The Economist

2 Observing 'Saint Monday'

Variations in the potential for
leisure mobility for workers in
the north of England in the
mid-nineteenth century

Susan Major

Introduction

In August 1850, a writer in the *Liverpool Times* noted that tens of thousands
of the labouring classes and their families were arriving in Liverpool on
cheap excursion trains that summer, having travelled from places within
a hundred miles of Liverpool: 'Saint Monday is the favourite day for the
arrival of the trains, and every resident of Liverpool must have noticed the
crowding of our streets, on at least a dozen Mondays, during the present
summer, with the mechanics and artisans of Lancashire, Yorkshire, Staffordshire and Shropshire, and their wives and children'.[1] To modern eyes
this might seem a curious phenomenon, the idea that a worker might be free
to take a summer trip on a Monday, a kind of marker for worker power.
The nearest modern equivalent might be 'Mondayitis', a reluctance to attend work, or a reduction in working efficiency, experienced on a Monday
morning.[2] While the idea of celebrating Saint Monday might seem to be an
outmoded and arcane practice for workers, a present day variation might be
the celebration of 'Poets Day' on Fridays, when some workers may be able to
make a unilateral decision to take time off on Fridays, without threatening
their job security. Poets Day ('Piss off early tomorrow's Saturday') is a slang
phrase which has been used for at least 30 years in the UK, Australia and
New Zealand.[3] Thus, because customary days off reflecting worker power
are still present in society today, it is worth exploring how railway companies reacted to these in the past, in this case Saint Monday leisure practices
in the mid-nineteenth century, as there might be similar examples found in
current transport providers' policies.

Explorations of changes in working-class leisure mobility in the nineteenth century have suffered from a lack of archival evidence, as most such
journeys were undertaken on foot or in carts until at least the middle of the
century. Even when the new railway companies began to offer cheap leisure
trips, they failed to record this activity specifically in their statistics, and it
has remained hidden inside general passenger records. Although the middle and upper classes might write accounts of their journeys in memoirs,

diaries and letters, these are far rarer with the vast majority of people in the country, the working classes. Through the use of newspaper sources however, this chapter explores working-class mobility through the railway excursion. Railway excursions were a key activity in expanding leisure mobility for those with little money and are generally defined as a return trip at reduced fares, either organised and promoted by a railway company or by a private organiser working in concert with the railway company, and restricted to a discrete group and/or offered to the general public.[4] Dramatically expanding in number from the 1830s, they caused shock waves, with crowds of thousands of ordinary people forming at stations, on trains and at destinations. Research has shown how such activity might be seen to be threatening, particularly during the 1840s, when Chartist gatherings and mob unrest gave rise to public concern.[5]

One of the few relevant studies on railway excursions for workers was carried out by Reid in 1996, when he re-examined evidence about the Victorian railway excursion, focusing on Birmingham in 1846.[6] He was particularly interested in the changing nature of the English social class system during this period, its relationship to leisure activity and how the new excursions laid the foundations for the future of cheap travel for the masses. This was a period when the excursion was becoming popular, but it was before the year of the Great Exhibition in 1851, seen by many as a watershed in working-class leisure mobility. Workers had only rare opportunities to benefit from fresh air and open space in their home surroundings in Birmingham at this time, as there was no public park or recreation space. The Birmingham Botanical Gardens, which had opened in 1832, was obliged because of Sabbatarian pressures to close on Sundays, but did open on Mondays, at a cost of one penny entrance fee, supporting the practice of celebrating Saint Monday.[7] By September 1849, it was receiving over 2,000 visitors on that day.[8] The issue gave rise to many complaints, including in 1860 an anonymous correspondent in the *Birmingham Daily Post*, who commented that operatives and labourers in Birmingham who were being lectured about not working on Mondays might be compared with Members of Parliament who did not start work in the Commons until Thursdays, and that the workers actually achieved their targets despite taking Mondays off.[9]

Reid concluded that the excursion opened up individuals' opportunities for leisure. His findings were based on local newspaper advertisements and occasional commentary from the *Birmingham Journal,* with 29 excursions recorded in 1846. Some trips lasted several days, but most of the one day excursions took place on Mondays (7), with none on Sundays.[10] He noted that 15 of the trips were organised by friendly societies such as the Ancient Free Gardeners, reflecting his view that most railway excursions arose from 'essentially popular institutions' in the first five years.[11] These results indicate that participants in railway excursions in Birmingham were almost certainly better paid artisans, a subset of the masses. Birmingham's landlocked location away from steamer trips, its many small craft employers, a large number of working men's' clubs and societies and the prevalence of Saint Monday working practices meant that this case was distinctive. His study does not however explore the repressive influence of Sabbatarianism on the organisation of Sunday trips or the failure of the railway companies to organise their own excursions in 1846, as they did in other towns. This may have been a blip in 1846, for example, caused by the restructuring of major railway companies, or may have been consistent across the decade. It raises the issue of how far excursions actually responded to popular demand. Reid uses the predominance of the friendly society component of his excursion profile to support this, arguing that Yeo's claim of the contribution of 'contrivance from above' in capitalist systems might be questioned as a result. At the same time, however, he demonstrates the important role of the excursion agent as a local entrepreneur, supplying trips in response to what might be perceived to be a demand from the masses.[12]

Judging from the above, the railway excursion therefore offers much scope for exploring nineteenth century working-class leisure mobility nationwide. Saint Monday in particular was a key opportunity for leisure and by examining how railway companies responded more widely to its celebration, this study will highlight some geographical variations. Factors such as levels of Sabbatarianism played a key role in shaping working-class leisure at this time, and Saint Monday at times balanced opportunities restricted by Sunday observance.

It was of course the steamer companies who had led the way in the market for working-class leisure mobility in the early part of the century, offering mass excursions which might accommodate as many as 700 people, but their activity focused on coastal areas and rivers.[13] Steamboat practices had varied, but the steamboat did set a context for Sunday outings and it has been argued that the steamboat excursion helped to secularise Sundays in support of popular tourism. There were however differences in the contemporary logic used to debate practices involving Sunday observance between steamboats and railways, with steamboats being allowed practices based on custom, while the railways suffered powerful constraints. While boats were perhaps regarded as older and more traditional vehicles for leisure, it might have been felt that because the railway companies were new, it would be possible to adopt a principle from their opening to prevent Sunday trips from starting.[14]

Celebrating Saint Monday

Since the eighteenth century, the traditional observance of Saint Monday had been practised in many parts of Britain, where some workers, with much-needed specialised craft skills, could choose not to work on that day, without fear of dismissal by their employers.[15] While we might suppose that Saint Monday was a quaint custom relevant only to the British working classes, it was in fact celebrated more widely. In France it was 'Saint Lundi', especially in the better paid industries such as tailoring and construction, lasting until around the 1870s.[16] In 1857 a report of a Paris election held on a June Monday mentioned that despite the poll closing at 4pm, men were able to vote, as they celebrated Saint Monday religiously every week, 'before adjourning to the wine shops outside the barriers'.[17] In Germany it was known as Blaue Montag, where men were still reported as observing it in Bremen and Dusseldorf, for example, into the early twentieth century.[18] In the United States in 1768 Benjamin Franklin noted that 'Saint Monday is as duly kept by our working people as Sunday; the only difference is that instead of employing their time cheaply at church they are wasting it expensively at the ale house', and it was still being celebrated in the United States until the end of the nineteenth century.[19]

In Britain, Thompson described Saint Monday as part of a framework of irregular working patterns, arising from factors such as weather and structural requirements, with the time needed for repairing machinery and giving in completed work.[20] In the mid-nineteenth century, most employed workers in England worked between 6am and 6pm every day, but there was regional variation, because of custom and practice. At the same time, there were some longer holiday periods, such as Whitsun, when workplaces in many areas closed down, especially in smaller towns in the Midlands and North of England. Sometimes holiday patterns were focused around traditional carnivals and feasts, and such holiday periods generated much excursion traffic. The traditional 'Wakes' weeks enabled workers in the Lancashire cotton towns to enjoy time off from their factory work in a staggered timetable during July and August; the whole community was on holiday together.[21]

Saint Monday could only be practised where power relations between the employer and the employee, for example, as exercised by specialised craft workers, allowed an element of strength for the worker. Harrison has noted that for many workers the idea of having both Sunday and Monday away from work was a fixed arrangement.[22] Where men were in control of their working lives, they could choose between intense working over long hours during the day into the evening, and then idleness on other chosen days. Where work was 'task orientated' then a regular timetable might be regarded as inappropriate, unless an element of synchronisation with others was demanded. Saint Monday could be used as a measure of independence for the worker. Although it might be seen as an urban phenomenon, even in rural areas there would have been self-employed artisans, and agricultural workers working irregular hours. Gradually however employers were able to use clocks and fines to impose a discipline on timekeeping, to suit the employers' purposes.[23]

Many historians and commentators have suggested that Saint Monday was disappearing by the mid-nineteenth century, although there is plenty of evidence of its survival throughout the nineteenth century. Writing in 1867, engineer and social commentator Thomas Wright maintained that it was still continuing at that time: 'numerous day trips... are run every Monday during a great portion of the year'.[24] He famously described it as 'the avowed and self-constituted holiday of the pleasure loving portion of "the million"', and playfully segmented the working-class celebration of Saint Monday by the tribal characteristics of their excursions. In 1976 Reid reviewed Saint Monday observance and its decline in Birmingham and revisited it in 1996, looking at wedding days and their prevalence on Mondays in Manchester, Blackburn, Bristol and in Birmingham.[25] He found that in Blackburn it was most frequently celebrated between 1800 and 1830, then declined severely with the emergence of factories. In Birmingham and Bristol with their small workshops, it was operating up to the 1890s and beyond, albeit by a minority of workers. In Manchester although there was an early decline from the 1820s in Monday weddings, there was still a significant number of workers taking Monday off up to the 1890s. Significantly the fateful meeting on St Peter's Field in Manchester in August 1819 (which led to the Peterloo Massacre) was arranged for a Monday, as it was known that hundreds of handloom weavers would be free from work on that day.[26] Saint Monday was particularly prevalent in Birmingham, because of the many specialised manufacturing craft workers there working in small units with good pay. Some of these workers were reported to take Tuesdays and Wednesdays too. The special correspondent on Labour and the Poor in the *Morning Chronicle* in 1850 mentioned that the day was also known as 'shackling day' in Birmingham, and noticed the frequency of social clubs in beer shops and public houses, which encouraged men to drink while serving a worthy purpose such as friendly societies and sick and burial clubs.[27]

Saint Monday did however decline in some places. In Manchester and Lancashire the development of larger manufacturing units, such as factories and mills, made it difficult to accommodate an unpredictable workforce, as machinery had to be operating continuously in lengthy shifts, with appropriate mechanics on hand to keep it running. Walton has highlighted the differences between Lancashire and the Midlands in the observance of holidays, describing the Midlands as much less 'civilised' for a longer time, because of irregular working practices, lower wages and less thrift.[28] He has suggested that Saint Monday practices were disappearing in Lancashire spinning by the 1840s and then similarly in weaving. But there is evidence from the *Preston Chronicle* in 1841 of 'vast numbers of working men lounging about the streets' in Preston on Mondays.[29] As late as the mid-1850s Preston reporters noted 'the debauch of Saint Monday', linking it to the practice of workers being paid very late in the evening on Saturdays, in the public house.[30]

Where observance continued, critical commentators were frequently keen to moralise by associating reports of Saint Monday practices with the perils of drink and other immoral activities, and some painted a picture of 'evil habits' which were taking place on Saint Monday. Typical was a short story about Saint Monday by the Reverend P B Power in the *Home Visitor and*

District Magazine in 1872, a homily about the folly of worshipping the day.[31] In this tragic tale, two men eventually meet a sad end as a result of going out drinking rather than working on Mondays, 'murdered by Saint Monday'. In 1854 commentators aligned reports about bread riots in Aylesbury with the observance of Saint Monday by the troublemakers.[32] Liverpool journalist Hugh Shimmin wrote about 'Saint Monday and its Consequences', concerned about the spread of this Liverpool practice to women going on a 'spree' on Mondays.[33] In 1843 in Hawkshead in the Westmorland Lake District, Saint Monday was rife amongst tailors and cobblers, who were said to devote the day to drinking and hare-coursing.[34] Prize fighting, considered an undesirable sport, was a particular attraction on Mondays.[35] A report in 1851 about Birmingham workers in brass cock founding, a major local industry, discussed the characteristics and earnings of workers who were celebrating Saint Monday 'to a considerable extent'.[36] Taking a moral viewpoint, it was said that quick and able men were able to earn much money in one day, but would drink and idle their way the rest of the time, whereas a slower man might earn less but would not be tempted to drink away his lower wages. It was of great benefit to the public house interest, very strong in Birmingham, thus supported by them.[37]

While Saint Monday had been linked to such immoral practices, the development of the Monday railway excursion offered an opportunity for some workers to participate in a leisure activity which was supported by reformers as an element of 'rational recreation'. These workers had been denied Sunday travel by the views of powerful Sabbatarians, who may have been happy to accept Monday excursions as a legitimate alternative leisure activity.

The impact of Sabbatarianism on leisure opportunities

Sabbatarianism also played a key role in shaping leisure opportunities for the masses. The value of being free of work on Mondays was important for excursion opportunities, as the only other day normally free was Sundays, and the Sabbatarian movement was particularly powerful in limiting Sunday leisure. This reached a peak in the mid-1850s, based on an evangelical movement devoted to the observance of Sundays as a day of rest and worship, after the establishment of the Lord's Day Observance Society in 1831. It played a leading role behind the forces shaping the availability of Sunday railway excursions.[38]

Sunday trips were commonly running on Sundays from the first stages of railway line development, although the Liverpool & Manchester Railway had agreed in 1830 not to run Sunday services between 10am and 4pm ('the church interval').[39] But the Post Office insisted on running mail trains on Sundays and railway companies took the opportunity to carry passengers on these too. In 1847, almost every railway in England carried Sunday services, but only a few in Scotland.[40] The Chairman of the Midland Railway,

John Ellis, confirmed in 1855 however that they never ran Sunday excursion trains, although they did run some other types of train on that day.[41] Until George Hudson took over in 1845, the Hull & Selby line was very much opposed to 'unnecessary' Sunday services, but few entrepreneurs followed Hudson in seeking to derive economic benefit by harnessing the appeal of cheap Sunday excursions for the working class.[42]

Such services were however confronted by the force of Sabbatarianism. Brooke has described an outstanding period of Sabbatarian activity in the North East of England before 1850, with many petitions or memorials to railway boards about Sunday excursion trains, to be debated at railway shareholder meetings.[43] In many areas railway companies were prevented from offering railway excursions on Sundays either because of the Sabbatarian views of their directors or by concerns about the potential opprobrium showered on them by press commentators, incensed by Sunday leisure activity and invoking heavily criticism of railway companies which dared to offer Sunday trips. For example, at a North Union Railway half-yearly general meeting in Preston in July 1845, it was argued that Sunday excursions lowered the 'moral and religious tone of the community', and were an example of 'a desecration of the Sabbath'. There were concerns that Sunday would be seen as a holiday, with associated mental and physical freedoms, leading to 'vicious indulgences' and 'unsettled habits'.[44] In 1856 a Banbury congregational minister, Joseph Parker, referred to excursionists as including the 'dirtiest, silliest, laziest and poorest of the toiling population', shockingly suggesting that women who travelled on Sunday excursions 'with very few exceptions they are accustomed to licentiousness, robbery and drunkenness'. There was understandably much debate about these outrageous comments.[45]

There are examples of lines managing to hold out against pressures. A threatened resignation of a board member was not enough to defeat those planning Sunday trips; for example, the London & Birmingham Railway refused to close their lines on Sundays, despite protests by director Joseph Sturge, a leading Birmingham Quaker and moral radical, who later resigned on this issue. The Manchester & Leeds ran four trains each way on Sundays from 1841 but the chairman and various directors resigned over this issue. The Manchester, Sheffield & Lincolnshire Railway ran Sunday excursions and was criticised by correspondents. The press also played their part in influencing the policies of railway companies on this issue. In 1850 the *Morning Chronicle* leader writer came out in favour of Sunday excursion trains, when reporting a meeting in Bath where Sabbatarians denounced Sunday excursionists who were 'cooped up for seven hours in close carriages, *indulging in trifling conversation*' [italics in original]. In some cases, railway companies adopted public relations strategies to persuade opinion formers of the value of Sunday trips. In 1850, the Great Western Railway started cheap Sunday excursions out of London in the 1850s, and their secretary published a very carefully argued letter defending their policy on Sunday excursions, on the grounds that a reversal of their decision would withhold 'social and moral benefits' from working people.[46] Even where it may appear that Sabbatarian pressure affected change, it may not necessarily have done so. Walton suggests that when the Lancashire & Yorkshire Railway eventually abandoned Sunday excursions in 1856, this was more an economic move.[47] As such, the forces of Sabbatarianism and Saint Monday practices lingering from the past were factors which shaped the activities of the new railway companies, which by this time were seeking leisure passenger business from the masses.

The response of the railway companies

With the advent of a network of railway lines connecting heavily populated towns and cities in the 1840s and 1850s, now ordinary people could use the railway for cheap leisure trips in great numbers, provided there was a suitable day of the week. The railway companies were able to use Saint Monday to their advantage, for example, on the opening of the Shrewsbury & Birmingham railway line in 1849, the company planned excursions every Monday throughout the summer, to the Wrekin and Wales, for artisans and their families.[48] In 1850 the *Manchester Times* used its account about the cheap excursion trains bringing people in from the towns around Liverpool on Mondays as a proxy to assess the economic welfare of the working classes.[49] It was celebrated by the colliers in Bolton and then right across England to the east coast, where 'monster trains' were used for cheap trips to the seaside at Yarmouth and Lowestoft by operatives from Norwich during the summer season of 1856, usually on Mondays, but also Thursdays.[50] Rather than decrying the practice as allied to intemperance, the newspaper recommended it, suggesting it enabled workers to access fresh air and exhilarating sea breezes, 'surpassing the sanitary improvements which have cost the citizens many thousands of pounds'. In 1851 a total of 70,640 people visited the Great Exhibition in London on a hot Monday in July, apparently mainly country people from the agricultural districts, with Saint Monday said to be by the *Examiner* as 'asserting its claims as the great holiday of the people'.[51]

Railway companies could be quick to react to changing employment practices, for example, in 1844 when commercial firms in Manchester allowed their workers Saturday afternoons off, the Manchester & Leeds Railway responded by offering special excursion rates on trains leaving on Saturday afternoons, to return either Sunday evening or early Monday morning, to allow workers the 'opportunity of visiting their friends'.[52] Sadly such opportunities were not available to all workers, as despite intensive campaigning activity by the Early Closing Movement over 60 years, Manchester retail shop workers failed to get their half day and were still working as many as 85 hours weekly, on average, until after the turn of the century.[53]

There were weekly Monday trips to Bottesford and Belvoir Castle in Leicestershire in 1854, with the press highlighting such a day as normally free from work.[54] The Great Northern Railway ran a Monday trip in August

1856 from Retford, Newark and Nottingham to London, returning the same day (4s–7s in closed carriages).[55] Gainsborough in Lincolnshire attracted Sunday and Monday railway trips from Sheffield in 1855, with observers stating that perhaps the Monday trips alone would suffice as they were so busy.[56] In August 1857, the Manchester Art Treasures Exhibition reported another good day for visitors, Monday, with almost 12,000 by train, and suggesting that it was equal to Saturday in being a 'people's day'.[57]

Case study: Leeds, Hull, Preston, Liverpool and Manchester in 1846

When considering the interaction between the railway excursion and local workplace practices, there are problems involved in examining the prevalence of Saint Monday in relation to particular industries, because of a lack of relevant workplace records, as Kirby has demonstrated in the case of the northern coalfields.[58] However using Reid's approach to shine a light on one year, 1846, by examining contemporary newspapers in other towns and cities in northern England illuminates the responses of the railway companies to local workplace practices, which, when allied to other regional characteristics, had a considerable impact on leisure opportunities.[59] Such factors included religion, geography, steamboat competition, employment structure and the differential availability of resources. This study takes a closer look at Leeds, Hull, Preston, Liverpool and Manchester, for comparison with Birmingham. In the north of England, as was the case elsewhere, railway excursions were growing dramatically in the 1840s and 1850s. Short distance migration had been generated by factories attracting labour to rapidly growing towns and cities, concentrated in Lancashire, Cheshire and the Yorkshire West Riding at this time, and employers were offering cotton workers in the industrial north better wages, which enabled them to benefit from the new excursions – generally day trips without associated accommodation costs, arranged by railway companies, voluntary groups and agents such as Henry Marcus, who offered 'cheap trips' for the masses.[60]

Evidence from Leeds in 1846 suggests that it was Sabbatarian pressures led by a powerful middle-class elite which increased the popularity of Saint Monday trips in that city, especially for the better paid artisan. In West Yorkshire, Leeds was famous for its woollen and flax mills and possessed a prosperous merchant class and a successful engineering and machine tool industry in the mid-nineteenth century. Its population grew from 152,000 in 1841 to 172,000 by 1851.[61] While in general in Britain, apart from Sundays, many workers were only free from work during the annual Whitsun holiday, this was not universal, as in 1846 in Leeds there were no Whit excursion trips advertised or reported on in the *Leeds Mercury*.[62] That weekend the weather was hot, with temperatures of 72°–76°, but this was because unlike some other towns and cities, it appears that Leeds people did not wish to take holidays in celebration of Whitsun and there seemed to be no universal shutdown of its industrial base. There were also no Sunday trips in 1846. Some railway companies serving Leeds (the Manchester & Leeds, Midland and York & North Midland) ran a few limited Sunday services around the time, but not excursions.[63] Similarly, the new Leeds & Bradford Railway was operating some Sunday services at limited times, but advertised clearly that no day tickets would be sold on that day.[64]

This was the result of the new middle-class hegemony exerting a powerful influence on working-class leisure in Leeds, with pressures from Methodist Sabbatarian elite members such as journalist Edward Baines. In August 1840, Baines had exhorted the North Midland Railway not to run Sunday trains, and Chairman George Glyn agreed. In June 1846, Baines's *Leeds Mercury* also complained about 'desecrating the Sabbath' in a report on a Temperance Gala, whilst the influence of such sentiments on Sunday excursion activity was indicated by the absence of negative reporting of trips in the paper.[65] Granville, on his tour in 1841, had been disappointed to find the Leeds Zoological Gardens closed on Sundays, the only day when the industrial classes were free from work, as a result of Sabbatarian pressures.[66] This pressure from Sabbatarianism must have been powerful, given that the religious census of 1851 reported that only around 23% of Leeds's population had attended Sunday morning church or chapel services, and significantly few of these were artisans.[67] Ultimately, it meant that Saint Monday was more important as a possible time for leisure. An examination of press advertising generally during 1846 in Leeds reveals a number of day trips on a Monday or Wednesday (7 out of 15 trips), and trips involving an overnight stay (7 out of 15 trips). These times and durations of visit suggest that, as in Birmingham, it was the middle classes or better paid artisans and self-employed tradesmen who had the flexibility of celebrating 'Saint Monday', getting away from the smoke-ridden city.[68]

One cannot however just put the absence of Sunday excursion wholly down to Sabbatarianism, as business considerations also played a role. George Hudson's York & North Midland Railway and Midland Railway did not appear to offer trips on Sundays from Leeds during 1846. This however seems to have been a business decision, as in his evidence to the Select Committee on Railways in 1844, Hudson complained that Leeds people were not willing to travel much from home, and even if he provided free travel 'they would remain stationary'.[69] When the Hull & Bridlington line opened in 1846, Hudson avoided discussing the issue of Sunday railway travelling.[70] One of his close colleagues, Peter Clarke, had been appointed general manager of the newly amalgamated Midland Railway in 1844, but left the following year to join the London & Brighton Railway, where he played an important role in promoting controversial Sunday excursions. Thus, a potential champion of Sunday trips was lost to Leeds by 1846.[71] However, it is not at all certain these would have been successful in the light of the prevailing Sabbatarian pressures and this well have contributed to his departure. The absence of Sunday trips suggests that ordinary working people were not able to participate in many railway excursions, despite their low cost. The availability of Monday excursions however provides evidence for the continuing celebration of Saint Monday in Leeds.

In Hull, it was the competing steamboat trips which seem to have shaped timings for railway excursions, and thus working-class leisure. The seaport of Hull on the east coast of Yorkshire again had a growing population, from 67,000 in 1841 to 85,000 in 1851.[72] While Saint Monday was usually associated with skilled artisans working flexibly in an urban economy featuring small craft units, able to enjoy leisure trips on convenient days, Hull's economy at this time featured import and export shipping, seed crushing, cotton manufacturing, trawlfishing and industries associated with this, such as transport.[73] An 1839 survey described irregular, seasonal employment, with little work for women and children when compared to Lancashire, for example.[74] These did not necessarily reflect the characteristics of workers able to plan their own leisure. There was no 'aristocracy of labour' which drove the observance of Saint Monday in other towns at the time. Hull had a large lower-middle class of small business owners and clerks, but employment was unstable. Primitive Methodism was however particularly strong in Hull, and this may have held sway over company policies, and thus its excursion profile was similar to that of Leeds. The Hull & Selby line had agreed not to run Sunday excursions in the early 1840s. Although Hudson had been in favour of these when he took over in 1845, there were still strong Methodist Sabbatarian pressures against this activity, which appears to have shaped excursion policies in favour of other days.[75] In Hull in 1846 12 out of 19 railway and steamer trips ran on Mondays, of which several offered overnight options, a more expensive undertaking for participants.[76] Five of the railway trips ran as a day trip on Whit Monday, at a time when workers were likely to have been on holiday, for example, to Scarborough, Manchester and Sheffield, with a further trip the Monday before Whitsun. Of the others, four were steamer trips, of which three were day trips. The remaining two railway trips setting off on a Monday were overnight excursions. Steamer day trips were available in June and July on Mondays and Thursdays. It appears that in 1846 in Hull, railway companies mainly accommodated workers by offering Whit Monday day trips, a traditional holiday. Other railway day trips left on a variety of days, apart from Sunday.

The forces of Sabbatarianism were less successful in Preston than some other towns and cities, thus there were a number of cheap Sunday trips. In north west England near the Lancashire coast, Preston's population had grown from 51,000 in 1841 to 70,000 in 1851.[77] Almost 30% of the population there over 20 years of age were working in the cotton industry, and by 1844 Preston boasted the largest power-loom shed in the world.[78] Trips to the nearby coastline would be cheap, short distance day journeys, suitable for workers with little spare time for enjoyment. The Preston & Wyre Railway (PWR) and steamer companies operated on Sundays to Fleetwood and Blackpool. There were 14 railway and steamer trips noted in the press in 1846, many on Sundays, together with the regular PWR Monday trips to Lytham and Sunday trips to Blackpool and Fleetwood throughout the season.[79] This was because organised Protestant religion had never been a strong influence in Lancashire, with only five English counties having a lower proportion of people attending church or chapel in the religious census taken in 1851. For the Church of England Preston 'had the lowest overall attendance figure ... of any English town in 1851'.[80] Powerful Sabbatarian pressure groups attempted to stop Sunday cheap trains from Preston, objections being raised at the May half yearly meeting of the PWR, and suggestions that they were leading to 'scenes of riot' at Fleetwood 'as would not be seen in any other part of the country'. It was suggested that working people might take a trip for a week in summer instead, to encourage 'the proper preservation of order', but a responding minister did not see that this would solve the problem and that 'people would travel, and that they would not be good'. It was also proposed that the train times might allow people to get to Fleetwood in time to attend church services there.[81] Although arguments about behaviour were used by writers to influence views on the timings of trips, there were commentators who suggested that the largely working-class passengers were well-behaved, with examples of 5,000 passengers arriving in a very orderly manner. Later, in 1857, a writer to the *Preston Chronicle* highlighted how 'Preston enjoys facilities for travelling and for recreation on the Sunday, such as few towns possess'.[82]

An important factor in the timing of excursion trips in Preston was the level of Catholicism in western Lancashire around the middle of the nineteenth century. They constituted around a third of worshippers in Preston, supported by Irish migration through Liverpool. It has been noted by Simmons that there were 'two wholly different attitudes towards Sunday recreation: benevolent in Catholic districts, restrictive and grudging wherever Protestantism prevailed'.[83] It was possible for Catholics to attend a vigil mass on Saturday as an alternative to Sunday churchgoing.

In nearby Liverpool the concentration of Catholicism also meant that attitudes to Sunday trips were less restrictive, and thus Saint Monday was observed to a lesser extent. On the west coast, Liverpool had a population of 299,000 in 1841 rising dramatically to 395,000 by 1851.[84] It benefited from its port position, with wealth based on overseas trade and coastal shipping in the nineteenth century, and a strong commercial base.[85] Almost all of the excursion trips from Liverpool in 1846 were cheap steamer trips (10 out of 12 trips) of which 6 were on Sundays, to nearby coastal destinations.[86] Their fares were low, and the timings and destinations reflected the interests of working-class people. The London & North Western Railway (LNWR) had a railway monopoly until the mid-1860s, but by contrast did not offer Sunday trips, and chose not to compete against the steamer or to innovate by offering trips to inland locations, and indeed one of their two trips was on Whit Monday. It may well be that in Liverpool a high proportion of the working classes featured in excursion crowds, because of the availability of

Sunday trips, reducing the need for railway companies to offer Saint Monday trips. By comparison, cities such as Birmingham failed to offer Sunday trips, and while there were Monday trips there, it was only the higher paid skilled artisans who were able to take advantage of these. At the same time, it appears that, as noted before, Liverpool attracted thousands of Monday visitors to the city from the surrounding towns.

Also in Lancashire, in Manchester Sabbatarianism prevailed. However, the combination of a range of competing railway lines around the town and the large-scale shutdown of manufacturing operations for a week at Whitsun meant this became the most important working-class holiday, enabling workers to take advantage of cheap annual trips at that time. Manchester's population grew from 252,000 in 1841 to 338,000 by 1851.[87] It was the regional capital, an important commercial and trading centre, drawing from textile manufacturing operations in factories and mills not only in Manchester itself, but in the surrounding towns.[88] The adoption of steam power forced manufacturers to keep their machinery working continuously, and this meant that they could not allow their workers to take time off on Mondays, thus Saint Monday faded out at an earlier stage in Manchester compared to the Midlands.[89] Moreover, in 1846, there were no Sunday trips advertised from Manchester.[90] This was possibly because it was a centre of non-conformity at this time, with only 39 Church of England churches out of 137 churches and chapels in Manchester in 1844, and non-conformists were particularly opposed to Sunday leisure.[91] Indeed, while some railways were running Sunday services around this time, this did not apply to excursions.[92]

By contrast, Whitsun saw the running of almost all the excursions in 1846 (10 out of 12 trips reported or advertised): 'the one week in the year when, by mutual consent, almost everyone ceases from labour'.[93] Even before the advent of the railway, Manchester people had enjoyed their Whit week trips, either on foot or in vehicles.[94] Strikingly, excursions around Manchester featured two opposing forces in motion – country people visiting the great town and town people enjoying trips into the countryside. In the 1840s, it was surrounded by a web of population centres, each connected by the railway to the centre: Oldham (43,000), Bury, Rochdale and Halifax (24,000–26,000 each), Bolton, Preston and Chorley (totalling 114,000), Stalybridge, Ashton, Dukinfield and Hyde (80,000), Stockport (50,000), Wigan (26,000) and Warrington (21,000).[95] Thus there was much potential for movement. With one of their much loved statistical collations, the *Manchester Guardian* summarised holiday traffic for the week at Whit in 1846, noting those conveyed on lines which terminated in Manchester, including double tickets, day tickets and Sunday scholars, in carriages and in waggons.[96] These included the Manchester & Leeds Railway (103,000 passengers), Liverpool & Manchester Railway (60,000 passengers), the Sheffield & Manchester Railway (101,600 passengers), the Manchester & Birmingham Railway (85,300 passengers) and the Manchester & Bolton Railway (45,800 passengers), totalling 395,700 passengers in all. This indicates that almost 400,000 people were on the move in Whitsun week around Manchester, a huge spectacle of mobility, with a large proportion of the working classes free from work to take holiday over a lengthy period at this time.

Conclusion

In conclusion, this examination of excursion activity in one year serves to demonstrate how leisure mobility opportunities for the masses varied in selected towns and cities in the north of England, shaped by the railway companies and other factors. The complex variation in the profile of trips across these towns demonstrates how the new excursion crowds were socially constructed by factors which were individual to the locality. Railway companies made decisions about Sunday excursions when pressurised by Sabbatarian agitators, but also responded to the needs of Saint Monday travellers. In Liverpool and Preston in 1846 there were cheap day excursions to suit the needs of the working classes, when they were free to take them, mainly on Sundays, in initiatives led by the rail and steamer companies, rather than by the powerful middle-class groups identified by Reid. They were able to do this because of the presence of a Catholic population whose outlook on Sunday observance was fairly relaxed, whereas other towns were prevented from running Sunday excursions by the Sabbatarian influences of Anglican and non-conformist power elites. From Liverpool and Preston, trips to the nearby coastline would be cheap, short distance day journeys, suitable for workers with little spare time for enjoyment.

In an alternative approach, in 1846 railway companies in Manchester offered the working classes cheap trips at one particular time of year, Whitsun, because of an almost universal shutdown by industrial employers in the city. Thus, operatives had a brief opening for a leisure outing away from work, and the railway companies saw the business benefits of high-volume cheap fare trips at this time. This was enhanced by competition between a range of railway companies providing trips in several directions (whereas in Liverpool there was only single railway company, LNWR, operating at that time, which chose not to meet the competition of Sunday steamer trips). The reporting of large crowds on these day trips from Manchester indicates large-scale participation by the masses, in the absence of specific evidence about affordability. In Birmingham and Leeds, there were several trips on Mondays but no Sunday trips, leading to an assumption that in these towns it was the better-paid workers, with the option to be free on Mondays, that benefited from these opportunities. The role of middle-class groups in Leeds and Birmingham in organising these trips adds weight to this argument. In Hull the Monday trips took place mainly at Whitsun, a time when many workers would have been on holiday. However, there were Monday steamer trips from Hull during the summer, a cheap alternative for those free on Mondays.

This study has demonstrated the dangers of making generalisations about the timing and shaping of working-class leisure practices and mobility, using a range of examples in the north of England in the mid-nineteenth century, showing how the railway companies responded to working-class leisure travel needs. It might be helpful to extend the exercise by examining excursions in 1846 in other regions of Britain, for further comparison with this chapter and Reid's study. It is very likely that the development of excursions was shaped later by other factors, a subject which also requires analysis.

Notes

1 *Manchester Times*, August 15, 1850 (originally in *Liverpool Times*).
2 OED.
3 Of unknown derivation, not included in the OED, see Tom Dalzell and Terry Victor, eds., *The New Partridge Dictionary of Slang and Unconventional English: Vol 11 J-Z* (Abingdon: Routledge, 2006), 1511.
4 Jack Simmons and Gordon Biddle, eds., *The Oxford Companion to British Railway History* (Oxford: Oxford University Press, 1997), 150.
5 Susan Major, "The Million Go Forth: Early Railway Excursion Crowds 1840–1860" (unpublished PhD thesis, University of York, 2012).
6 D.A. Reid, "The 'Iron Roads' and 'the Happiness of the Working-Classes': The Early Development and Social Significance of the Railway Excursion," *Journal of Transport History* 17, no. 1 (1996): 57–73.
7 *Morning Chronicle*, October 14, 1850.
8 *Coventry Herald and Observer*, September 7, 1849.
9 *Birmingham Daily Post*, August 20, 1860.
10 Reid, "Iron Roads," 59.
11 Ibid., 66.
12 Ibid., 65–68; Eileen Yeo and Stephen Yeo, *Popular Culture and Class Conflict, 1590–1914: Explorations in the History of Labour and Leisure* (Sussex: Humanities Press, 1981), 137, 299; Restructuring involved the creation of the London & North Western Railway (1846) and the Midland Railway (1844) around this time. Reid highlighted Thomas Cook in his introductory remarks, despite Cook's absence in the list of agents in his Birmingham data from 1846. Recent research takes a fresh look at railway excursion agents, noting that while Cook predominates in narratives about the development of the railway excursion, there is now evidence which conflicts with this in the context of working-class mobility; S. Major, "Railway Excursion Agents in Britain, 1840–1860," *Journal of Transport History* 36, no. 1 (2015): 22–40; John K. Walton, "Thomas Cook: Image and Reality," in *Giants of Tourism*, eds. Richard Butler and Roslyn Russell (Cambridge, MA: CABI, 2010), 81–91.
13 J. Armstrong and D.M. Williams, "The Steamship as an Agent of Modernisation 1812–1840," *International Journal of Maritime History* 19, no. 1 (2007): 154.
14 1831–32 (697) *Report from Select Committee on the Observance of the Sabbath Day*, 205–210.
15 D.A. Reid, "The Decline of Saint Monday 1766–1876," *Past and Present* 71 (1976): 76–101.
16 Gary S. Cross, *A Quest for Time: The Reduction of Work in Britain and France, 1840–1940* (Berkeley: University of California Press, 1989), 84.
17 *Morning Chronicle*, June 23, 1857.
18 Lenard R. Berlanstein, ed., *The Industrial Revolution and Work in Nineteenth Century Europe* (London: Routledge, 1992), 118.
19 Madelon Powers, *Faces Along the Bar: Lore and Order in the Workingman's Saloon, 1870–1920* (Chicago: University of Chicago Press, 1998), 50.

20 E.P. Thompson, "Time, Work-Discipline and Industrial Capitalism," *Past & Present* 38 (December 1967): 56–97.

21 John K. Walton, *The Blackpool Landlady: A Social History* (Manchester: Manchester University Press, 1978), 34–35.

22 Mark Harrison, "The Ordering of the Urban Environment: Time, Work and the Occurrence of Crowds 1790–1835," *Past & Present* 110 (February 1986): 140.

23 Thompson, "Time, Work-Discipline and Industrial Capitalism," 56–97.

24 A.J. Reid, "Wright, Thomas (1839–1909)," *Oxford Dictionary of National Biography*, online edn (Oxford, 2006) accessed 9 January 2018, www.oxforddnb.com/view/10.1093/ref:odnb/9780198614128.001.0001/odnb-9780198614128-e-47426; T. Wright, *Some Habits and Customs of the Working Classes by a Journeyman Engineer* (London: Tinsley Brothers, 1867), 115–130.

25 Reid, "The Decline of Saint Monday," 76–101; D.A. Reid, "Weddings, Weekdays, Work and Leisure in Urban England 1791–1911: The Decline of Saint Monday Revisited," *Past and Present* 153 (November 1996): 135–163.

26 Ronald Quinault, "The Industrial Revolution and Parliamentary Reform," in *The Industrial Revolution and British Society*, eds. Patrick Karl O'Brien and Roland Quinault (Cambridge: Cambridge University Press, 1993), 195.

27 *Morning Chronicle*, October 7 1850, October 14, 1850; Shackling seems to relate to being 'shackled by drink', and indicates a change to a negative view of Saint Monday, see Reid, "The Decline of Saint Monday," 98.

28 Walton, *The Blackpool Landlady*, 34–35.

29 *Preston Chronicle*, October 2, 1841.

30 *Preston Chronicle*, November 10, 1855.

31 Reverend P.B. Power, "Saint Monday," *Home Visitor and District Magazine* 1 (1872).

32 *Manchester Courier*, September 9, 1854.

33 Hugh Shimmin, "Saint Monday and Its Consequences," in *Living in Liverpool: A Collection of Sources for Family, Local and Social Historians*, ed. Alastair Wilcox (Newcastle-upon-Tyne: Cambridge Scholars Publishing, 2011), 215–218.

34 *Westmorland Gazette*, December 2, 1843.

35 Richard Holt, *Sport and the British: A Modern History* (Oxford: Oxford University Press, 1989), 62.

36 *Morning Chronicle*, January 13, 1851.

37 *Morning Chronicle*, October 7, 1850.

38 D.A. Reid, "Playing and Praying," in *Cambridge Urban History of Britain Vol. III 18401950*, ed. M. Daunton, (Cambridge: Cambridge University Press, 2000), 752; E. Royle, *Modern Britain: A Social History 1750–1997* (2nd edn., London: Bloomsbury Academic, 1997), 244.

39 J.S. Wigley, *The Rise and Fall of the Victorian Sunday* (Manchester: Manchester University Press, 1980), 54.

40 1847 (167) *Railways. Copy of all Regulations of Every Railway Company on the Subject of Travelling on Sunday.*

41 *Sheffield & Rotherham Independent*, August 23, 1856.

42 D. Brooke, "The Opposition to Sunday Rail Services in North Eastern England, 1834–1914," *Journal of Transport History* 6, no. 2 (1963): 95–96; Hull and Selby Railway, *Hansard*, HC Deb., 30 March 1836, vol. 322, cols. 843–6.

43 Brooke, "The Opposition to Sunday Rail Services," 95.

44 *Preston Chronicle*, August 2, 1845. In the case of the North Union Railway on this occasion it was decided that the benefits outweighed Sabbatarian concerns and that Sunday excursions should continue on the line.

45 B.S. Trinder, "Joseph Parker, Sabbatarianism and the Parson's Street Infidels," *Cake and Cockhorse* 1 (1960): 25, 27.

46 *Morning Chronicle*, October 10, 1850; J. Wrottesley, *The Great Northern Railway: Vol 1 Origins and Development* (London: Batsford 1979), 96; Wigley, *The Rise and Fall of the Victorian Sunday*, 85; *The Standard*, October 26, 1850.

47 Wigley, *The Rise and Fall of the Victorian Sunday*, 54; J. Marshall, *The Lancashire & Yorkshire Railway: Volume One* (Newton Abbott: David & Charles, 1969), 49–52; Arthur Jordan and Elizabeth Jordan, *Away for the Day: The Railway Excursion in Britain, 1830 to the Present Day* (Kettering: Silver Link Publishing Ltd, 1991), 29; J.K. Walton, *The Blackpool Landlady*, 18–19.
48 *Morning Post*, November 1, 1849.
49 *Manchester Times*, August 17, 1850 (from the *Liverpool Times* and syndicated to other newspapers too).
50 Robert Poole, *Popular Leisure and the Music Hall in Nineteenth-Century Bolton* (Lancaster: Lancaster University Press, 1982), 52; *Bury & Norwich Post*, September 10, 1856.
51 *The Examiner*, July 26, 1851.
52 *Manchester Guardian*, June 19, 1844.
53 *Manchester Times*, October 8, 1870.
54 *Nottinghamshire Guardian*, August 31, 1854. Frustratingly the press report does not indicate the starting point for these trips.
55 *Lincoln, Rutland and Stamford Mercury*, August 1, 1856.
56 *Lincoln, Rutland and Stamford Mercury*, August 1, 1855.
57 *Manchester Courier*, August 29, 1857.
58 Peter Kirby, "Miner Absenteeism and Customary Holidays in the Great Northern Coalfield, 1775–1864," *Manchester Papers in Economic and Social History* 65, no. 31 (July 2009): 65.
59 *Leeds Mercury*, April 18–October 10, 1846; *York Herald*, October 24, 1846; *Bradford Observer*, July 30, 1846; *Hull Packet*, May 22–September 25, 1846; *Liverpool Mercury*, May 8–October 2, 1846; *Manchester Times*, May 30–July 25, 1846; *Manchester Guardian*, May 16–August 5, 1846; *Preston Chronicle*, April 4–September 12, 1846.
60 K. Morgan, *The Birth of Industrial Britain: Social Change, 1750–1850* (Harlow: Pearson, 2004), 10; Royle, *Modern Britain*, 58–59; Susan Major, *Early Victorian Railway Excursions: The Million Go Forth* (Barnsley: Pen & Sword 2015).
61 Asa Briggs, *Victorian Cities* (Harmondsworth: Penguin, 1968), 139–183; B.R. Mitchell, *British Historical Statistics* (Cambridge: Cambridge University Press, 1988), 26–27.
62 *Leeds Mercury*, April 18–October 10, 1846.
63 1847 (167) *Railways. Copy of All Regulations of Every Railway Company on the Subject of Travelling on Sunday.*
64 *Leeds Mercury*, August 1, 1846.
65 *Leeds Mercury*, August 29, 1840, June 6, 1846.
66 Augustus Bozzi Granville, *Spas of England and Principal Sea-Bathing Places* (1841, reprint, Bath, 1971), 411, 415.
67 J.F.C. Harrison, *Early Victorian Britain 1832–51* (London: Fontana, 1988), 124–130.
68 Reid, 'Iron Roads', 57–73.
69 1844 (318) *Fifth Report from the Select Committee on Railways*, para. 4343.
70 *Hull Packet*, October 9, 1846.
71 *The Standard*, June 26, 1845. *Hampshire Advertiser*, May 22, 1852.
72 Mitchell, *British Historical Statistics*, 26–27.
73 Victor Bailey, *'This Rash Act': Suicide across the Life Cycle in the Victorian City* (Stanford: Stanford University Press, 1998), 106–109.
74 Reid, "Weddings, Weekdays, Work and Leisure," 135–163. Bailey, *'This Rash Act'*, 109.
75 Reid, "Playing and Praying," 791
76 *Hull Packet*, May 22–September 25, 1846.
77 Mitchell, *British Historical Statistics*, 26–27.

78 John K. Walton, *Lancashire: A Social History, 1558–1939* (Manchester: Manchester University Press 1987), 111; *Preston Chronicle*, October 12, 1844.
79 *Preston Chronicle*, April 4–September 12, 1846.
80 Walton, *Lancashire*, 184.
81 *Preston Chronicle*, May 2, 1846.
82 *Preston Chronicle*, August 8, 1857.
83 Jack Simmons, *The Express Train and other Railway Studies* (Nairn: Thomas & Lochar, 1994), 182; Royle, *Modern Britain*, 329; Walton, *Lancashire*, 184.
84 Mitchell, *British Historical Statistics*, 26–27.
85 Walton, *Lancashire*, 114–115.
86 *Liverpool Mercury*, May 8–October 2, 1846; John R. Kellett, *Railways and Victorian Cities* (London: Routledge & Kegan Paul, 1979), 18.
87 Mitchell, *British Historical Statistics*, 26–27.
88 Walton, *Lancashire*, 208–209.
89 Walton, *The Blackpool Landlady*, 34; Reid, 'Iron Roads', 84. There were reports however in 1850 that the London & North Western Railway was advertising cheap trips to Alderley Edge on the first Monday of each summer month, despite complaints from workers that this may have suited shopkeepers rather more than industrial workers who would have preferred Saturdays. *Manchester Times*, March 27, 1850.
90 *Manchester Times*, May 30–July 25, 1846; *Manchester Guardian*, May 16–August 5, 1846.
91 L. Faucher, *Manchester in 1844* (London: Simpkin, Marshall, & Co, 1844), 24.
92 House of Commons Papers, 19th Century House of Commons Sessional Papers, 1847 (167) *Railways. Copy of All Regulations of Every Railway Company on the Subject of Travelling on Sunday.*
93 *Manchester Guardian*, June 3, 1846.
94 *Manchester Guardian*, June 10, 1840.
95 Faucher, *Manchester in 1844*, 15; Mitchell, *British Historical Statistics*, 24–26.
96 *Manchester Guardian*, June 10, 1846.

Bibliography

1831–32 (697) *Report from Select Committee on the Observance of the Sabbath Day.*
1844 (318) *Fifth Report from the Select Committee on Railways.*
1847 (167) *Railways. Copy of All Regulations of Every Railway Company on the Subject of Travelling on Sunday.*
Armstrong, John, and D.M. Williams "The Steamship as an Agent of Modernisation 1812–1840." *International Journal of Maritime History* XIX, no. 1 (2007): 145–160.
Bailey, Victor. *'This Rash Act': Suicide across the Life Cycle in the Victorian City.* Stanford: Stanford University Press, 1998.
Berlanstein, Lenard R., ed., *The Industrial Revolution and Work in Nineteenth Century Europe.* London: Routledge, 1992.
Briggs, Asa. *Victorian Cities.* Harmondsworth: Penguin, 1968.
Brooke, D. "The Opposition to Sunday Rail Services in North Eastern England, 1834–1914." *Journal of Transport History* 6, no. 2 (1963): 95–109.
Cross, Gary S. *A Quest for Time: The Reduction of Work in Britain and France, 1840–1940.* Berkeley: University of California Press, 1989.
Dalzell, Tom, and Terry Victor, eds., *The New Partridge Dictionary of Slang and Unconventional English: Vol 11 J-Z.* Abingdon: Routledge, 2006.

Faucher, L. *Manchester in 1844*. London: Cass, 1969. First published 1844 by Simpkin, Marshall and Co.

Granville, Augustus Bozzi. *Spas of England and Principal Sea-Bathing Places*. Bath: Adams and Dart, 1971. First published 1841 by Henry Colburn.

Harrison, J.C. *Early Victorian Britain 1832–51*. London: Fontana, 1988.

Harrison, Mark. "The Ordering of the Urban Environment: Time, Work and the Occurrence of Crowds 1790–1835." *Past & Present* 110 (1986): 134–168.

Holt, Richard. *Sport and the British: A Modern History*. Oxford: Clarendon Press, 1989.

Hull and Selby Railway, *Hansard*, HC Deb., 30 March 1836, vol. 322, cols. 843–6.

Jordan, Arthur, and Elizabeth Jordan. *Away for the Day: The Railway Excursion in Britain, 1830 to the Present Day*. Kettering: Silver Link, 1991.

Kellett, John R. *Railways and Victorian Cities*. London: Routledge & Kegan Paul, 1979.

Kirby, Peter. "Miner Absenteeism and Customary Holidays in the Great Northern Coalfield, 1775–1864." *Manchester Papers in Economic and Social History* 65 (July 2009).

Major, Susan. *Early Victorian Railway Excursions: The Million Go Forth*. Barnsley: Pen & Sword, 2015.

———. "Railway excursion agents in Britain, 1840–1860." *Journal of Transport History* 36, no. 1 (2015): 22–40.

———. "The Million Go Forth: Early Railway Excursion Crowds 1840–1860." PhD thesis, University of York, 2012.

Marshall, John. *The Lancashire & Yorkshire Railway: Volume 1*. Newton Abbot: David and Charles, 1969.

Mitchell, B.R. *British Historical Statistics*. Cambridge: Cambridge University Press, 1988.

Morgan, K. *The Birth of Industrial Britain: Social Change, 1750–1850*. Harlow: Pearson, 2004.

O'Brien, Patrick Karl, and Roland Quinault, eds., *The Industrial Revolution and British Society*. Cambridge: Cambridge University Press, 1993.

Poole, Robert. *Popular Leisure and the Music Hall in Nineteenth-Century Bolton*. Lancaster: University of Lancaster, 1982.

Power, Reverend P.B. "Saint Monday." *Home Visitor and District Magazine* 1 (1872): 53–63, 77–87.

Powers, Madelon. *Faces Along the Bar: Lore and Order in the Workingman's Saloon, 1870–1920*. Chicago: University of Chicago, 1998.

Reid, A.J. "Wright, Thomas (1839–1909)," *Oxford Dictionary of National Biography*, online edn. Oxford, 2006. Accessed January 9, 2018, http://www.oxforddnb.com/view/10.1093/ref:odnb/9780198614128.001.0001/odnb-9780198614128-e-47426

Reid, D.A. "Playing and Praying." In *The Cambridge Urban History of Britain, Vol.3 1840–1950*, edited by M.J. Daunton, 745–807. Cambridge: Cambridge University Press, 2000.

———. "The Decline of Saint Monday 1766–1876." *Past and Present* 71 (1976): 76–101.

———. "The 'Iron Roads' and 'the Happiness of the Working Classes': The Early Development and Social Significance of the Railway Excursion." *Journal of Transport History* 17, no. 1 (1996): 57–73.

———. "Weddings, Weekdays, Work and Leisure in Urban England 1791–1911: The Decline of Saint Monday Revisited." *Past and Present* 153 (1996): 135–163.

Royle, Edward. *Modern Britain: A Social History, 1750–1997*, 2nd edn. London: Arnold, 1997.

Shimmin, Hugh. "Saint Monday and Its Consequences." In *Living in Liverpool: A Collection of Sources for Family, Local and Social Historians*, edited by Alastair Wilcox, 215–218. Newcastle-upon-Tyne: Cambridge Scholars, 2011.

Simmons, Jack. *The Express Train and other Studies*. Nairn: Thomas and Lochar, 1994.

Simmons, Jack, and Gordon Biddle, eds. *The Oxford Companion to British Railway History from 1603 to the 1990s*. Oxford: Oxford University Press, 1991.

Thompson, E.P. "Time, Work-Discipline and Industrial Capitalism." *Past & Present* 38 (1967): 56–97.

Trinder, B.S. "Joseph Parker, Sabbatarianism and the Parson's Street Infidels." *Cake and Cockhorse* 1, no. 3 (1960): 25–30.

Walton, John K. *Lancashire: A Social History, 1558–1939*. Manchester: Manchester University Press, 1987.

———. *The Blackpool Landlady: A Social History*. Manchester: Manchester University Press, 1978.

———. "Thomas Cook: Image and Reality." In *Giants of Tourism*, edited by Richard Butler and Roslyn Russell, 81–91. Cambridge, MA: CABI, 2010.

Wigley, John. *The Rise and Fall of the Victorian Sunday*. Manchester: Manchester University Press, 1980.

Wright, T. *Some Habits and Customs of the Working Classes; by a Journeyman Engineer*. London: Tinsley Bros, 1867.

Wrottesley, Arthur John Francis. *The Great Northern Railway*. London: Batsford, 1979.

Yeo, Eileen, and Stephen Yeo. *Popular Culture and Class Conflict, 1590–1914: Explorations in the History of Labour and Leisure*. Sussex: Harvester Press, 1981.

Newspapers and publications

Birmingham Daily Post
Bradford Observer
Bury & Norwich Post
Coventry Herald and Observer
Hampshire Advertiser
Hull Packet
Leeds Mercury
Lincoln, Rutland and Stamford Mercury
Liverpool Mercury
Manchester Courier
Manchester Guardian
Manchester Times,
Morning Chronicle
Morning Chronicle
Morning Post
Nottinghamshire Guardian
Preston Chronicle
Sheffield & Rotherham Independent
The Examiner
The Standard
Westmorland Gazette
York Herald

3 The vulnerability paradox

The illusion of permanence in the UK public transport industry

Kevin D. Tennent

Introduction

Much early twenty-first century, public transport planning literature argues heavily for investment in public transport systems with forms of fixed infrastructure.[1] This works on the assumption that fixed infrastructure, such as a heavy rail or metro line, guided bus way, tram track or even just an overhead electric wire, will create an impression of permanence in the public mind. This is said to create a 'psychological rail factor', facilitating modal shift to public transport away from the private car, providing reassurance to local stakeholders that vehicles will run reliably, and because of the visibility of the infrastructure, preventing the later abolition of the system. The rail factor theory is based on surveys of passenger preference in high transit provision environments in Central Europe and Scandinavia, and perhaps most surprisingly does not automatically relate to heavy rail's very obvious ability to circumvent road traffic – research by Scherer and Dziekan showed an even stronger preference for tram travel over subway/metro systems for a range of emotional and social reasons, including the presence of daylight.[2]

Yet if this preference is true of central Europe and Scandinavia since perhaps 1980, it may not be a generalisable rule for all geographies and periods. Twenty or so years earlier, psychology was not a factor to be considered in transport planning. The existence of the factor would seem not to be supported by the empirical evidence that almost all first-generation tram systems in the UK were closed by 1960, many having less than 30 years of operational life, a short time span for transport infrastructure. A clue that this may have been a mistake is provided in the fact that many British cities have either proposed or actually built light rail systems since the 1980s,[3] often advised by transit boosting consultants citing the 'psychological rail factor'.[4] It is worth noting that these systems often differ substantially from their early twentieth-century predecessors in that they utilise more off-road running, usually based on former mainline railway trackbeds. On road or street running is often confined to town centres. This contrasts with surviving systems in continental Europe such as Munich, Milan and Prague, which predominantly share with road traffic or run alongside roads.

Yet, as was seen in cities such as London, Glasgow, Sheffield and York,[5] many of these systems generated trading profits even if the cost of capital was not fully repaid; indeed trolleybuses were often introduced where trams had proved inefficient to extend the life of the overhead equipment. Instead, trams and trolley vehicles were gradually obliterated as they did not fit in with the road and planning environments in a Britain slowly motorising after 1918, a process eventually completed by 1970, shortly before the oil crisis of 1973/4 put a pressure on oil prices and started to introduce doubt regarding the merits of mass motorisation.

This chapter will use Star and Ruhleder's definition of infrastructure to look at how tramways and trolleybuses were categorised as an inferior form of transportation for modern Britain,[6] and how elites can exploit characteristics of such infrastructure to gradually weaken and dispose of it. Evidence from central government policy and from local authorities around the UK will be used. Star and Ruhleder interpret infrastructure as a 'relational property',[7] not something which simply supports socio-economic activity and falls seamlessly into the background, but as a target object for its users, who constitute a community of practice who interface meaningfully with the infrastructure property. They build on the classic work of Lave and Wenger on the practice of learning to show that infrastructure has an installed base with a community of practice around it,[8] which participants learn about as a target object, and which participants acquire a naturalised familiarity with as they integrate as members. Tramways clearly possess a physical infrastructure inherited to a large extent from their parent technology of rail and mining infrastructure; they are organisational socio-technical entities which form a sort of closed, context specific system usually operated by a set public or private body within a single urban area or conurbation. They can support heavy traffic within the limits of the infrastructure; unlike heavy rail, traditional tramway vehicles can be operated at low enough speeds to allow for signalling to take place by sight, and the headway between individual vehicles could be as low as one or two minutes or less. Employees of the organisation maintain the track, and tramcars can be operated as target objects by employees of the system who learn the practice of operation within a closed context. Most users experience the system as passengers for whom the physical infrastructure may take on a degree of invisibility, but they still have to engage in the peripheral practices of understanding where the system can transport them to and how to use it, including the purchase of tickets and the safe usage of the system, for instance boarding and disembarkation of vehicles. Table 3.1 illustrates how we apply Star and Ruhleder's taxonomy of infrastructure to the case of transport.

Road traffic, at least as far as private car transport is concerned constitutes more of an open system; users are direct participants in the target object, within which learning the practice of driving and the rule system set down by the highway allows participation. The barriers to entry to participating in road traffic as a driver are initially relatively high given the cost of a car,

Table 3.1 Tramway, trolleybus and motorised road transport as infrastructures

Infrastructure dimension	Electric urban transport equipment	Motorised road traffic
Embeddedness	Rails, stops, masts and wires literally sunk into and above street system. Closed system provided by a dedicated organisation, whether publically or privately owned	Paved roads appropriate the street system and subvert it for their purpose. Open system provided as a public good which embeds it into public policy
Transparency	Permanence supports intensive usage; reassures potential users	Permanence supports intensive usage and journeys can be tailored to individual needs
Reach or scope	Has reach across an entire urban area and potentially several miles; scope limited to route infrastructure	Infrastructure can reach between urban areas as well as within them; vehicles free to move between systems
Learned as part of membership	Users learn to purchase tickets (in a context specific sense) and (dis)embark safely; staff qualify to work according to a system of managerially codified rules and regulations	Entry constrained by access to a vehicle and ability to use the system safely. Must learn system of signs and to negotiate system of traffic. After 1935, subject to passing of exam and vehicles also subject to testing, as well as use system within governmentally identified rules and regulations
Links with conventions of practice	Partly encouraged by the need for a daytime power load (Hannah); fixed nature inherited from mining tram technology, originally intended to overcome rough ground	Routes and infrastructure initially inherited from earlier horse drawn and cycle-based traffic; reliance on street lighting to work at night
Embodiment of standards	Plugs into existing electrical system, derives from standardised railway gauges, rail and mast standards set by manufacturers, dominance of 'Dick, Kerr type' vehicle design	Plugs into existing street and urban system including system of radial roads; derives from second industrial revolution production system

Built on an installed base	Routes contained within the topography of the urban environment and often follow long established street patterns; but inherits limitations of rail infrastructure which may mean it is not backwardly compatible with other road users	Initially built on urban system but speed and volume of vehicles soon exceeds its limitations; pollution and unpredictability of vehicles a further problem. New system of signs, markings and ultimately faster road infrastructure required overcoming non-backward compatibility with pedestrians, cyclists, tram and horse traffic
Becomes visible on breakdown	Power outages stop operation; vehicle failures or accidents visibly obstruct the system and perhaps other traffic	Accidents based on user error are frequent, cause obstruction to other vehicles. Some flexibility to mitigate

Source: Star and Ruhleder (1996).

and learning to use it, but once these potentialities are acquired the relative costs of use fall away, boosted by apparently endless reach and scope, transparency and embeddedness, with an endless range of journeys possible and diversion also a possibility in case of a breakdown of the install base. While his particular interest is in attacking the myth that urban density is requisite to support successful public transport systems, Mees identifies that whilst the difficulty of use and cost of entry of public transport networks is theoretically lower than the car, it is in reality often relatively high because of 'disintegration'.[9] This is particularly problematic in dispersed, suburbanised cities or conurbations where destinations are scattered around, and there are a multitude of different public transport modes with different install bases, as well as different levels of transparency and embodied standards, even before considering the costs of learning to use them and the reach and scope of the systems. An integrated system with a single interface to the user is therefore necessary to encourage ridership – a zonal fares structure as occurs in Germany or Switzerland,[10] perhaps, or a single public operator providing a unified branding, such as Transport for London.[11] This was at odds with the traditional schema in British cities where transport across the tramway, trolleybus and motorbus modes was operated by profit-maximising municipal trading enterprises, often on a hub-and-spoke model radiating from a city centre, with fares charged for a single route rather than on a zonal basis,[12] a differential in practice between Britain and Germany noted as early as 1912.[13] This in itself promoted disintegration and was likely to encourage users towards the greater reach of the car or bicycle as they became more available. However, the co-existence of the two forms of infrastructure in itself can also be problematic. Mees cites the case of Melbourne around the turn of the millennium, a city with one of the world's largest tramway systems, where tram stops were migrated away from road junctions to avoid causing traffic congestion, yet this move in itself reduced integration because the stops for motorbuses remained at the intersections, deterring travellers from changing from bus to tram![14] Infrastructural clash then could have consequences for the integration of public transport more widely and undermine the case for modal shift. The install base can become the enemy creating aspersions of inferiority, even within large apparently permanently installed systems.

Tramways in Britain

The first wave of tramways in Britain developed in the years after 1870, reaching a peak route mileage of 2,569 by 1919,[15] when mass motorisation was not yet envisaged. Developed initially as horse drawn systems typically operated by private companies,[16] municipal ownership and electrification provided the opportunity for larger-scale expansion based on improved access to capital and the longer operating range made possible by electric traction.[17] Municipal ownership, which had first emerged in the naturally monopolistic gas, water and then electrical power industries,[18] also brought the possibility to improve the business case for electrical powerplants at a time when the diffusion of electric power into manufacturing industry and commerce was low as tramways could provide a 'daytime load' when the domestic lights were off.[19] Thus tramways were products of the socio-technical environment in which they evolved and to a large extent were free to create their own information infrastructure[20] for the road environment. This included electrification, which usually required overhead wires with cast iron supports, and which two of the classic studies of the British tramway industry claimed were controversial.[21] While Schatzburg shows that there was some opposition to the expansion of tramway systems in the United States based on the intrusion of overhead wires,[22] Schmucki evidences that in many cases European opposition to electrification was outweighed by the expected benefits of the growth of a tramway system, including the improved urban hygiene created by eliminating horse droppings.[23]

The common acceptance of, and even popular support for urban tramways meant they were built as the dominant feature of the urban environment. While Schmucki also notes that early objectors to horse tramways expressed concern with the disruption to other traffic and to road maintenance, sometimes managing to block construction, municipalisation meant that urban tramways were built as a central feature of the road environment. This meant they tended to be built in the middle of the road, away from the kerb. The busiest routes and those running through city centres tended to be double tracked,[24] though shopping streets and squares could often include complex crossings, turnouts and interlaced track where streets were too narrow to allow clearance for two parallel tracks.[25] Less busy lines in suburbs were often single track with passing loops,[26] while electrical equipment varied, even within the same system; perhaps most common were side poles or brackets on buildings supporting span wires, while on wider roads central standards which could serve both tracks were used.[27] A few exceptions to overhead traction existed, such as the 'conduit' third rail system used by the London County Council (and then only in Central London), or the 'contact stud' system used on the Mexborough and Swinton Traction Company's lines. Terminus points were often single-track sidings, which allowed trams to reverse, sometimes with automatic pole reversing equipment which allowed the trolley pole to be reversed without the conductor doing it manually.

From this position of infrastructural dominance, British tramways represented an early twentieth-century version of modernity that would gradually slip away; from an apex of 2,398 route miles in 1919 only 1,234 would be left by 1937.[28] The 1940s and 1950s would be even less kind with just 137 route miles left in operation by 1959; Sheffield's decision to close its system by 1960, and Glasgow's by 1962 finished off the industry as a serious entity, leaving just Blackpool's seaside line as a sort of curiosity. Economics undeniably played a role in this decline – as Buckley illustrates in his case study of the Dearne District Light Railways, some of the towns or areas in which tramways were built were too small or too rural to generate the passenger flows required to support them.[29] The rise of the motorbus in the 1920s as a commercial competitor, which required fewer infrastructures together with lower barriers to entry meant that public transport could be provided on a very economic if disintegrated basis to the more dispersed industrial districts of northern England.[30] Bus competition and the economics also played a factor in abandonment middle-sized towns and cities such as York and Doncaster, although as Tennent shows the ideology of municipal trading which saw systems being gestated and operated to create a trading profit rather than for public service skewed the decision of councils towards abandonment.[31] The asset cycle which requires infrastructure and rolling stock to be replaced every 30–40 years at a minimum also undoubtedly played a role as local authorities failed to set aside sufficient sinking funds for renewals, or procrastinated in setting up an on-going cycle of renewals – a risk which Knoop warned of as early as 1912, where Salford Corporation had paid £17,000 to rate relief while only placing £264 in the renewal fund.[32] But in at least some of the places where the install base was strongest – in Edinburgh, Glasgow, Dundee, Aberdeen, Liverpool, Leeds, Sheffield and Sunderland, trams continued to be a central feature of the transport scene into the 1950s with modernised cars even being introduced in Liverpool and Glasgow in the 1930s, and extensions installed in Leeds, Glasgow and Sunderland after the war.[33] Trams provided a higher capacity than motorbuses, and in the austerity years after the Second World War carried record levels of passengers per mile;[34] this ensured they remained important, even though materials costs were rising and the procurement of new cars was proving more difficult.[35] Further, Buckley shows that the Sheffield system continued to return gross profits to the local authority through the 1930s, and indeed Munby's statistics show that the UK's tramway systems as a whole earned positive net receipts up until 1937, and again in the 1950s, the remaining systems earning an £819,000 surplus in 1953.[36] These systems were therefore well suited to the densely populated industrial cities of the North and Scotland, and were capable of overcoming the asset cycle – economics, and even the profit making municipal trading ideology were not the only driving factors behind the removal of tramway systems – the infrastructure itself was.

Coping with mass motorisation: the 1929–31 Royal Commission

The UK government started to move towards mass motorisation with the introduction of the numbered primary road system administered by the newly created Ministry of Transport (MoT) from around 1921 onwards,[37] which eroded local control over the road environment, previously the preserve of local authorities. This happened in tandem with a substantial increase in the volume of road traffic after the First World War – entrepreneurs started to provide road passenger and freight services in considerable numbers, while manufacturers such as Austin, Morris, Singer and Ford started to produce smaller cars to appeal to a more middle-class suburban market.[38] Commercial vehicle numbers doubled between March 1919 and August 1921,[39] making an impact such that the London and North Western and Midland Railway companies attempted to use the 1921 Railways Act to be granted road powers; these were not granted until 1928 because the Ministry of Transport felt that rail and road, being technologically different, should have different operating companies.[40] It was around this time that intellectual justification for the re-design of the urban environment to create a pure road traffic environment started to emerge, led by the Swiss architect Le Corbusier who gained sponsorship from a French motor manufacturer, Voisin, to put forward his vision for a re-ordering of central Paris to the needs of the car in 1924.[41]

Despite the government's pursuit of road funding and classification, the 1920s represented a chaotic 'wild west' period on the roads. Anyone able to afford a vehicle could use one without formal training or licensing, and regulation of commercial traffic was scant. Total vehicle numbers expanded from 245,235 in 1912 to 952,432 in 1922, and further doubled to 2,227,099 in 1932; around half of these vehicles were private cars.[42] In the emerging suburbs and in the countryside a motorbus network, both local and long distance emerged out of the enterprise of many thousands of small business owners which gradually consolidated together, making easy acquisition targets for the 'big three' groups, British Electric Traction, Tilling and Crossville, which emerged by avoiding direct competition with each other.[43] Freight haulage by road saw a similar expansion in organisation with the formation of a number of commercial clearing houses which acted as inter-mediaries, matching loads to lorries, acting as a 'front end' for customers but avoiding the risk of owning vehicles themselves.[44] This facilitated the entry of thousands more entrepreneurs, while enabling intense competition between them, keeping shipping costs down – even as late as 1932, more than half of the hauliers in south-east England owned only one vehicle, and 95% fewer than ten.[45]

Yet, this rapid expansion in road use saw relatively little investment in the actual infrastructure by the MoT, except for a programme of improving the road surface on A and B roads together with some bypass building, largely undertaken using labour from unemployment relief schemes on the arterial trunk routes radiating from London, especially the A1, A3 and A4.[46] These schemes were based upon pre-war plans to improve London's traffic flows, at that time largely horse drawn, but the new schemes had the unexpected side-effect of encouraging road use for leisure purposes in the south-east, for instance day-trips to beauty spots and to 'roadhouse' entertainment ven-ues.[47] In terms of specific infrastructure Lord Montagu of Beaulieu had pro-posed to build a privately owned toll motorway from London to Liverpool and Salford in the mid-1920s which would allow through traffic to bypass the streets of Birmingham, but failed to gain parliamentary assent.[48] Large towns such as Doncaster on the A1 and Preston on the A6 would continue to have primary roads running though their town centres, often on streets that were also used by the tramways, leading directly to conflict between different road user groups. Even traffic lights at busy junctions were rare and the police frequently had to employ scouts from the AA or RAC to con-trol the traffic.[49] Despite the relatively low level of road traffic compared to modern day standards, the cost of infrastructural breakdown was high and accidents led to a sense that the condition of the roads constituted a pub-lic health emergency – between 1909 and 1929 the annual number of road accidents involving serious injury or death had more than quintupled from 27,161 to 147,582;[50] government intervention was required to re-establish control of the infrastructure.

The resulting 1929–31 Royal Commission on Transport heard evidence on the structure and form of transport in Britain from a number of inter-ested parties such as transport operators and motoring organisations, with the first report of the commission focusing entirely on road safety.[51] Trams were considered within this report from the perspective of other road users, though the high preponderance of accidents that could be attributed to the lack of rules for motorists in general was an emerging theme. There were as yet no clear rules for priority at junctions, which lead to confusion as traffic built, and the commission found a lack of consensus as to how priority might be dealt with, the AA for instance suggesting that vehicles approaching main roads from the right might be given priority.[52] Similarly, there were also no rules for signing dangers such as sharp bends and steep hills, and private individuals had on occasion taken responsibility and erected their own signs.[53] The report therefore recommended that a 'code of customs' be introduced by the MoT which would allow for motorists to be sanctioned for breaking it,[54] for instance by ignoring roadsigns or traffic lights.

This 'code of conduct' formed the basis for the Highway Code, first published in 1931, but through its instructions to road users crystallised the creation of an alternative information infrastructure to the tramway. This document did not just aspire to set standards of behaviour for motorists, but for all road users, and in addition to drivers of motor vehicles included specific instructions for motor-cyclists, pedal cyclists, drivers of horse drawn vehicles, those in charge of animals and pedestrians.[55] Tram drivers and conductors had long been issued with their own rulebooks that prescribed how they should operate on the road, derived from long-established railway rules books, and were excluded from the Highway Code.[56] The only mention of tramways in the Highway Code was in relation to overtaking:

> Subject to any local provision to the contrary, tramcars may be overtaken on either side. Before you overtake a tramcar which is about to stop or is stationary, **watch carefully** to see if passengers are intending to board or alight. **Go slowly or stop** as the circumstances require.[57]

This provision sat at odds with the rest of the code's rules which allowed for overtaking other motor or horse drawn vehicles only on the right, and potentially put pedestrians at risk. While this could be rationalised from the position that trams could not autonomously 'keep left' as other vehicle types were required to, the published rule represented a watering down of the commission's original proposal, which had allowed motorists only to pass stationary tramcars on the left when traffic conditions allowed, and only after sounding the horn. If passengers were boarding or alighting motorists would have to stop dead.[58] Rather than integrating the tramway into the Highway Code, the Highway Code was imposed around the tramway and in ignorance of it in order to create the expectation of a 'pure' motor traffic environment.

The Royal Commission's third report on the co-ordination and development of transport did accept that tramways had some advantages over motorbus-based transport. It was noted that those tramway systems built under the 1870 Tramways Act, which required operators to provide and maintain the road surface between the rails and on 18 inches each side of the tramway, had played an important role in maintaining 2,500 miles of roads, though private operators that were not also highway authorities were relatively few by this time.[59] Further, tramways retained certain advantages as an infrastructural system – their tractive effort was lower than buses while they relied on electricity often made from British mined coal rather than imported oil, they were comparatively easy to drive and control, and their high speed of acceleration and deceleration meant that a competitive average speed could be maintained.[60] On well-maintained systems tramways could be quieter than bus traffic while as simpler mechanical systems break downs were less frequent, but of course more visible when they did occur as trams were less easily moved. Because average seating and standing capacity remained superior to buses, trams were also considered to be more efficient per passenger mile than buses, though it was felt that this was unlikely to remain the case forever.[61]

Overall, the Royal Commission decided to recommend that tramways be considered an obsolete form of transport and therefore should be gradually abandoned. Part of their rationale for this was financial; while it was conceded that a tramcar had a longer operating life than a motorbus, the capital cost of the systems was greater with annual track maintenance priced at £400–£500 per year, though this included the road maintenance costs mentioned above. The poor levels of capital redemption mentioned above were also cited, with more than £40 m worth of capital still outstanding on municipal tramways.[62] Nevertheless the case against tramways was also operational and safety based. Evidence collected from stakeholders such as the AA was used alongside economic evidence to recommend that tramways should be gradually abandoned.[63] They were portrayed as an unsteerable obstruction to traffic unable to pull up at the kerb, while the rails were characterised as likely to cause motor vehicles to skid in wet weather.[64] The AA Secretary, Mr Stenson Cooke, gave evidence to the committee suggesting that tramway standards placed lines in the centre of the road, something originally done to avoid cluttering pavements, and this was a danger to motorists. Cooke further claimed that the introduction of one way streets to speed up the traffic flow in many towns had caused problems, because trams often continued on their traditional routes, causing confusion.[65] It was further claimed that the inability to steer a tramcar if it left the rails, especially if it was liable to overturn, made them particularly dangerous.[66] The commission summarised its position thus:

> After carefully examining the evidence which we have received from various Witnesses, our considered view is that tramways, if not an obsolete form of transport, are at all events in a state of obsolescence, and cause much unnecessary congestion and considerable unnecessary danger to the public. We recommend, therefore, (a) that no additional tramways should be constructed, and (b) that, though no definite time limit can be laid down, they should gradually disappear and give place to other forms of transport.[67]

The very permanence of the infrastructure and its install base, which still retained many technological advantages over motorised transport, was being used to attack the tramway as a form of public transport.

This was being done not for the benefit of public transport users, but for the motorist, still a relative elite. The Royal Commission recommended the replacement of tramways with trackless trolley vehicles, or trolley-buses, a strategy that would allow some of the capital not yet redeemed to be realised through the continued depreciation of the overhead line and electrical supply equipment, while retaining some of the advantages of re-liability through not requiring a petrol or diesel engine. Trolleybuses were steerable around obstacles, within the limits of the trolley poles at least, and because they could pull into the kerb could fit into the normal over-taking logic of the Highway Code. The Commission had visited Wolver-hampton where conversion from tramway had been conducted with real success.[68] Trolleybuses seemed to offer the infrastructural compromise that could give electrically powered fixed link public transport in Britain a bright future.

Still inflexible: abandoning trolleybuses and
The Buchannan Report

After the 1931 Royal Commission aspirations for the further motorisation of society were slowed by the depression of the early 1930s, which saw the MoT scale back its arterial by-pass construction plans,[69] and then the Sec-ond World War. The motorway age eventually opened in Britain in 1958, with the construction of the M6 Preston Bypass, though the MoT's planned network of motorways, based on the 'tea-room plan' of 1946 was largely inter-city rather than intra city.[70] On the intra-city side creation of a purer road traffic environment in which motor vehicles could travel rapidly and without obstruction on a hierarchy of roads was a major feature of post-1945 urban and regional planning, epitomised by Sir Patrick Abercrombie's 1943 *County of London Plan* and 1944 *Greater London Plan*, which envisaged five concentric ring roads around London, linked together by radial roads.[71] The emphasis was now on a holistic view of urban planning based around the dispersal of population out of congested urban cores into satellite towns held together by arterial road systems, with all land use carefully considered around road access and capacities. This agenda was, as much about slum clearance and improving sanitary and living conditions as much as it was about motorisation, but it was clear that car and motorbus transport would take priority in the new environment.

The 1931 Royal Commission had had no statutory power over local au-thorities, and some that had financially viable tramway systems, such as Glasgow and Sheffield Corporations had done nothing to convert to trol-leybus. It was in the case of Glasgow that density in urban planning had its last stand – in 1946, Robert Bruce, the City Engineer, clashed with Ab-ercrombie and his ally Robert Matthew whose regional plan for the Clyde Valley involved the dispersal of population out of Glasgow. Bruce proposed building high within Glasgow instead, in a sort of 'Le Corbusier lite' vision.

Abercrombie and Matthew's vision won out as it gained central government support, resulting in the creation of East Kilbride as a car and motorbus oriented New Town in 1947,[72] but it appeared that whichever vision of building was adopted the long-term, the direction of travel was clear – any new building, whether low rise or high rise, would be comprehensively supported by access for motor vehicles. New developments, which might now take place on bombed out land as much as on Greenfield sites, would be planned around road access, not retrofitted to it. In Sheffield's case, Buckley demonstrates that the key driver was the Corporation's aspiration to rebuild the city with car traffic in mind, anchored by a new 'civic circle' road and gyratory systems. Trams did not fit because they prevented cars from overtaking and it was also claimed that trams could not negotiate roundabouts, which were thought necessary to regulate the traffic flow. Indeed, so strong was this narrative in Sheffield that the city's transport manager's report, which recommended closing the tramways made very little of the financial case for doing so.[73]

Meanwhile, around 50 local authorities or tramway operators had either converted their tramway systems to trolleybus or even built new networks;[74] 35 systems were in operation by the Second World War.[75] Some, such as Doncaster, had already began the process in the 1920s,[76] but other operators, such as London United Tramways, and their successors the London Passenger Transport Board energetically threw their energies into the conversion process during the 1930s, operating more than 1,800 vehicles by 1939.[77] The war and austerity period through the 1940s would also mean that trolleybuses made financial sense, relying on domestic coal fired electricity rather than imported oil, and totally new systems were opened in Cardiff in 1942, and Glasgow in 1949, extending to streets not served by the existing tram network. Trolleybuses were cheaper to expand than tramways, and in an era when most working-class journeys were still by public transport, new trolleybus routes also served some of the new post-war suburban housing developments.[78] Route miles would never be as extensive as tramways, but in their peak year, 1952, 883 route miles were in operation generating net receipts of £1,447,000.[79]

Yet the trolleybus provided a false renaissance for British electrically powered transport, and only five years after the opening of the Glasgow system London Transport took the decision to gradually replace its trolleybus system with its new Routemaster diesel buses, a process that was completed by 1964.[80] Other corporations followed suit and gradually dismantled their systems through the 1950s and 1960s, the last to close being Teesside in 1971 and Bradford's in 1972. Financial rationales and the nationalisation of electricity supply and generation, which took it out of municipal hands, undoubtedly played a part in undermining the infrastructure, as did expanding costs for maintenance as the install base diminished.[81] Doncaster Corporation, for instance was still expanding its network as late as 1958,[82] yet decided to close its system after it moved out of net profit in the

1960–1961 accounting year, although motorbuses would ironically move out net profit the following year.[83]

Finance and control of the electricity supply were not the only imperatives. Thirty-two years on from the Royal Commission, Newcastle City Council, which had obediently replaced trams with trolleybuses between 1935 and 1950 used the excuse of traffic flow to close its trolleybus system between 1962 and 1966. Newcastle's transport committee attacked the permanence of the trolleybus infrastructure, arguing that the 'buses were too slow across crossings and not manoeuvrable enough to cope with city traffic. Worse, trolleybuses were particularly vulnerable to disruption or a power cut, even citing the city's traffic police in this regard.[84] Trolleybuses were being attacked for the same inflexibilities that tramways had previously been accused of, even though they were able to manoeuvre much more flexibly around the road surface (and on a busy street, arguably just almost as flexibly as a large motor bus). Newcastle Corporation argued that diesel buses were the way forward, although the city planned its own urban motorway system, most of which was never realised, and was ironically cancelled in the early 1970s favour of a rail based metro system.[85] Indeed, many of the 1960s tower blocks developed by charismatic council leader T. Dan Smith were given only five or six parking spaces, suggesting that residents were still expected to use the Corporation's buses![86] Back in Doncaster the town had unveiled a major replanning exercise in 1955 that involved the construction of two new ring roads and widenings of other arterial roads to compliment it;[87] the availability of government money to implement these schemes from the early 1960s perhaps encouraged the town to get rid of 'inflexible' infrastructure for good.[88]

The local authorities hoped and perhaps expected that many of those who had relied upon trams and then trolleybuses would continue to use their motorbus services, which often continued to run on the same routes as their predecessors, but the publication of the Buchannan Report in 1963, commissioned by Transport Minister Ernest Marples, showed that central government policy had shifted towards the expectation that the car would be the default mode of urban transport in the future.[89] Parking space may have been limited but households were keen to gain access to the freedom of car ownership, with four million additional private cars coming onto the roads between 1952 and 1962.[90] Ironically the report reflected a rising unease at the social, environmental and visual effects of motorisation, showing that the incursion of the motor vehicle into the traditional street environment had created problems of noise, pollution and encroachment, with cars and motorcycles parked on any available spare land. There was further social concern at the high accident rate and traffic speed as low as 11 mph on many congested urban roads, which negated any gain from the ubiquity of motor vehicles.[91] The report used a detailed study of the passenger and freight traffic flows found in small, large and historic cities as well as in London's West End to support a Le Corbusian hypothesis that short and long distance car traffic ought to be separated as much as possible, as well as the notion that pedestrian traffic ought to be separated from car traffic, on separate levels and pathways. Systems of distributor roads would route traffic around 'environmental areas', though the report conceded that such schemes to create a pure road traffic infrastructure and separated pedestrian infrastructure would not come cheap. Marples responded to this by aiming to almost triple annual road spending from £50 million in 1963 to £140 million in 1970.[92] The period 1965–1975 would turn out to be the most intensive periods of city centre re-development and road building in the post-war era, supporting further motorisation, although many of these schemes reflected the realisation of earlier ambitions.[93] Local authorities such as Doncaster put this into practice by concentrating commercial and shopping facilities into pedestrian streets and purpose built shopping centres fed by multi-story car parks and purpose built bus stations, planning for pedestrians to circulate through the town centre without coming into contact with motor vehicles.[94] But as Gunn identifies, in its quest for purity Buchannan saw pedestrian circulation as only an adjunct to car use, not a replacement for it,[95] while the advantage of road based public transport, that it can deliver people close to their destination without a significant land take, was overlooked. It was perhaps realised too late that a pure motor traffic environment was not going to solve the mobility or environmental problems of Britain's cities.

Conclusion

The twentieth century had opened with British towns and cities ploughing capital and resources into a tramway infrastructure, but this would increasingly find its existence contested as the century wore on. This process progressed through a sort of elite motorisation in the 1920s and 1930s, together with a shift in freight transport away from the railways, and then a rush for mass motorisation from 1950 onwards, even as contemporaries such as Buchannan realised that Britain had failed to develop the installed base required to support it. Motor transport had initially seemed able to piggyback on the broader (and perhaps invisible) infrastructural characteristics of urban areas; paved roads were embedded, were transparent and permanent, and had apparently infinite reach or scope to the individual user, and it cosmetically appeared that the appropriation of earlier roads allowed it to inherit the door to door universal pathing characteristics of foot, horse and cycle. In practice membership was more easily gained and learned than for horse drawn traffic, creating congestion, and Le Corbusier soon argued that it was necessary to move beyond what he called the 'pack donkey's way'.[96] Le Corbusier, in his quest for purity based around the right angle believed that railed transport should only be used where convoys of vehicles were carrying large loads. The tramway did not do this in Le Corbusier's view, and the fixed rails meant that it could be construed as an obstructive enemy of the rationalising process.[97] Once the infrastructural war against the tramway was won, Buchannan would advise that Britain should not be frightened of radically restructuring its cities, including historic Norwich and London's West End to fully take advantage of the rationalising potential of the car.[98]

Yet by the early 1960s a sense was growing that something had been lost. British planners did not go quite to the extremes of those in the United States, but as early as 1962 Jane Jacobs was arguing that the move away from the corridor street, in which buildings had frontages onto roads also used for through traffic, was discouraging pedestrian circulation and social interaction, this encouraging alienation and crime.[99] One of the reasons that Mees was such a passionate advocate of public transport in the automobile age was that using it also encouraged people to walk more,[100] and its integration into the urban fabric, attacked by the motorisers, was an important element in this. Le Corbusier, however, had not in fact argued for all public transport to be migrated to the motorbus, thus rendering it a secondary safety net for those unable to afford motorisation, but rather argued that rail transport should be moved onto a separate level of its own with each city having looped systems of tube and outer suburban railways.[101] Few British cities outside of London attempted this as a parallel to motorisation in any substantial way, with the possible exception of the Tyne and Wear area, though the turn to rail there came only after the collapse of road plans. Buchanan had also speculated that alternative forms of transport such as monorail, the hovercraft, the jetpack and short take-off and landing aircraft might play a role in future,[102] and almost certainly the 1960s obsession with the potential of the monorail, as much as it may have been driven by manufacturers,[103] stemmed from the fact that it could deliver permanence and potentially a local reach and scope without interfering with road traffic. The original local authority planners of the new city that would become Milton Keynes envisaged, for instance, that while every house would have a garage, a municipal monorail system funded from the rates would provide free at the point of entry public transport within the city. This idea was discarded as soon as Whitehall planners took over the project that would become the ultimate in British car-oriented planning,[104] but it demonstrated a belief that the car should not be the solution for all journeys. Proposals to bring back trams in some form also started appearing in the 1960s; as early as 1966 *The Guardian* featured a proposal for a new 'duorail system' for Manchester featuring 'a light form of electric railway vehicle' able to run along the central reservation of dual carriageways, and promoted as more flexible than rival monorail proposals.[105]

Ultimately while permanence may be important in encouraging public transport use as it creates a feeling of accessibility, reliability and ultimately transparency, rather than making public transport systems harder to abolish it can actually be used as the basis of their undermining. The relative elites who started to own cars from the early twentieth century onwards, and the entrepreneurs who entered the freight haulage and motorbus industries, did not interface with these transport systems as users of them, but rather as users of the immature motor traffic infrastructure. These elites, and to some extent the entrepreneurs, were able to form and use representative organisations such as the AA and RAC to influence the policy process through reviews such as the 1931 Royal Commission, and were also able to create the financial imperative that to exist public transport systems must create a positive return on the rates. Dominant architects such as Le Corbusier, and planners such as Sir Patrick Abercrombie also took the narrative of motorisation on board, giving intellectual justification to the undermining of the notion of permanence. It was therefore possible to create the impression that infrastructure that was in some cases less than 30 years old was already 'old-fashioned' and obstructive not just to traffic, but to progress, and that it should be dismantled. Thus, infrastructure can be used to undermine and abolish transport systems if their opponents feel that it is in their interests to do so. The history of Britain's tramway and trolleybus systems should serve as a warning to the public transport planners, projectors and managers of today.

Notes

1 Gabrieal Beirão and Sarsfield Cabral, "Understanding Attitudes towards Public Transport and Private Car: A Qualitative Study," *Transport Policy* 14, no. 6 (2007): 478–489; Milena Scherer and Katrin Dziekan, "Bus or Rail: An Approach to Explain the Psychological Rail Factor," *Journal of Public Transportation* 15, no. 1 (2012); Vukan R. Vuchic, *Urban Transit: Operations, Planning and Economics* (Hoboken: John Wiley & Sons Inc, 2005); Vukan R. Vuchic, *Urban Transit Systems and Technology* (Hoboken: John Wiley & Sons Inc, 2007).
2 Scherer and Dziekan, "Bus or Rail: An Approach to Explain the Psychological Rail Factor".
3 Manchester Metrolink opened in 1992, Sheffield Supertram in 1994, the Midlands Metro between Birmingham and Wolverhampton in 1999, Croydon Tramlink in 2000, Nottingham Express Transit in 2004, and Trams for Edinburgh in 2014. The systems in Manchester, Nottingham and Birmingham/Wolverhampton have seen considerable expansion since opening.
4 Steer Davies Gleave, *Leeds New Generation Transport: Permanence in Public Transport Systems*. Vol. C-1-12, 2014; TransForm Scotland, *Trams for Edinburgh* (Edinburgh: TransformScotland, 2006).
5 David A. Turner and Kevin D. Tennent, "Progressive Strategies of Municipal Trading: The Policies of the London County Council Tramways c. 1891–1914", *Business History*, online first, 2019; Richard John Buckley, "A Study in the Decline of the British Street Tramway Industry in the Twentieth Century With Special Reference to South Yorkshire" (unpublished PhD Thesis, University of Hull, 1987); John P. McKay, *Tramways and Trolleys: The Rise of Urban Mass Transport in Europe* (Princeton: Princeton University Press, 1976); Kevin D. Tennent, "Management and Competitive Advantage in the Public Transport Industry," *British Academy of Management*, Conference Proceedings, Liverpool, 2013; Kevin D. Tennent, "Profit or Utility Maximizing? Strategy, Tactics and the Municipal Tramways of York, C. 1918–1935", *Journal of Management History* 23, no. 4 (2017): 401–422.

6 S.L. Star and K. Ruhleder, "Steps Toward an Ecology of Infrastructure: Design and Access for Large Information Spaces," *Information Systems Research* (1996).

7 Ibid., 5.

8 Jean Lave and Etienne Wenger, *Situated Learning: Legitimate Peripheral Participation* (Cambridge: Cambridge University Press, 1991).

9 Paul Mees, *Transport for Suburbia: Beyond the Automobile Age* (London: Earthscan, 2010).

10 Ibid., 129–143.

11 Ibid., 157–158.

12 Tennent, "Profit or Utility Maximizing?

13 Douglas Knoop, *Principles and Methods of Municipal Trading* (London: Macmillan, 1912), 258.

14 Mees, *Transport for Suburbia*, 173.

15 D.L. Munby and A.H. Watson, *Inland Transport Statistics: Great Britain, 1900-1970* (Oxford: Clarendon Press, 1978).

16 Charles Klapper, *The Golden Age of Tramways* (2nd ed., Newton Abbot: David and Charles, 1974); McKay, *Tramways and Trolleys*; Oliver Green, *Rails in the Road: A History of Tramways in Britain and Ireland* (Barnsley: Pen & Sword Transport, 2016).

17 McKay, *Tramways and Trolleys*, 51–83.

18 Malcolm Falkus, "The Development of Municipal Trading in the Nineteenth Century," *Business History* 19, no. 2 (July 1977): 134–161; Hugh Coombs and J.R. Edwards, *Accounting Innovation: Municipal Corporations 1835-1935* (Abingdon: Routledge, 1996); Derek Matthews, "Laissez-Faire and the London Gas Industry in the Nineteenth Century: Another Look," *The Economic History Review* 39, no. 2 (May 1986): 244–263; Kellett, "Municipal Socialism, Enterprise and Trading in the Victorian City," *Urban History* 5 (1978): 36–45; James Foreman-Peck and Robert Millward, *Public and Private Ownership of British Industry: 1820-1990* (Oxford: Oxford University Press, 1994); Robert Millward and Robert Ward, "From Private to Public Ownership of Gas Undertakings in England and Wales, 1851–1947: Chronology, Incidence and Causes," *Business History* 35, no. 3 (July 1993): 1–21; Robert Millward, *Private and Public Enterprise in Europe* (Cambridge: Cambridge University Press, 2005); Robert Millward, *The State and Business in the Major Powers: An Economic History 1815-1939* (Abingdon: Routledge, 2014); Richard Roberts, "Business, Politics and Municipal Socialism," in *Businessmen and Politics: Studies of Business Activity in British Politics, 1900-1945*, ed. John Turner (London: Heinemann Educational, 1984).

19 Leslie Hannah, *Electricity before Nationalisation: A Study of the Development of the Electricity Supply Industry in Britain to 1948* (London: Macmillan, 1979), 19; Foreman-Peck and Millward, *Public and Private Ownership*, 163–165.

20 'Information infrastructure' is defined by Hanseth as "a shared, evolving, open, standardized, and heterogeneous installed base".

21 McKay, *Tramways and Trolleys*, 95; Buckley, "A Study in the Decline of the British Street Tramway Industry in the Twentieth Century," 19.

22 Eric Schatzberg, "Culture and Technology in the City: Opposition to Mechanized Street Transportation in Late-Nineteenth Century America," in *Technologies of Power: Essays in Honor of Thomas Parke Hughes and Agatha Chipley Hughes*, eds. Michael Thad Allen and Gabrielle Hecht (Cambridge, MA: MIT Press, 2001); Eric Schatzberg "'Technik' Comes to America: Changing Meanings of 'Technology' before 1930," *Technology and Culture* 47, no. 3 (2006): 486–512.

23 Barbara Schmucki, "The Machine in the City: Public Appropriation of the Tramway in Britain and Germany, 1870–1915," *Journal of Urban History* 38, no. 6 (2012): 1060–1093.

24 Such as those running along Argyle Street, Trongate and Gallowgate in Glasgow. Ordinance Survey Map 25 Inch Series, 'Lanarkshire VI.11' (Glasgow; Govan), 1913.

25 For instance, Piccadilly Gardens in Manchester was the epicentre of the Manchester Corporation system, also with cars running in from Salford and other towns in the area. A complex system of lines ran round the square and radiated in various directions. Ordinance Survey Map 25 Inch Series, Lancashire CIV.6 (Manchester; Salford), 1922; Lancashire CIV.11 (Manchester), 1922; Lancashire CIV.10 (Manchester; Salford; Stretford), 1922.

26 The York Corporation system relied heavily on single lines, for instance on its outer branches to the villages of Fulford, Acomb and Dringhouses. Ordinance Survey Maps 25 Inch Series, 'Yorkshire CLXXIV.15 (Fulford; Heslington; York)', 1929; 'Yorkshire CLXXIV.10 (York)', 1929; Yorkshire CLXXIV.9 (Askham Bryan; Knapton; Rufforth; York), 1929.

27 McKay, *Tramways and Trolleys*, 182.

28 Munby and Watson, *Inland Transport Statistics*, 338–341.

29 Buckley, "A Study in the Decline of the British Street Tramway Industry in the Twentieth Century with Special Reference to South Yorkshire," 77–177.

30 Buckley, "A Study in the Decline of the British Street Tramway Industry in the Twentieth Century with Special Reference to South Yorkshire"; David Holding, *A History of British Bus Services: North East* (Newton Abbot: David and Charles, 1979).

31 Tennent, "Profit or Utility Maximizing? Strategy."

32 Knoop, *Principles and Methods of Municipal Trading*, 142.

33 Green, *Rails in the Road*, 181–182, 200.

34 Munby and Watson, *Inland Transport Statistics*.

35 Green, *Rails in the Road*, 198–200.

36 Buckley, "A Study in the Decline of the British Street Tramway Industry in the Twentieth Century with Special Reference to South Yorkshire," 295–300; Munby and Watson, *Inland Transport Statistics*, 242.

37 Chris Marshall, "Road Numbers: How It Happened," CBRD.co.uk, 2017. www.cbrd.co.uk/articles/road-numbers/how-it-happened.

38 Michael John Law, "'The Car Indispensable': The Hidden Influence of the Car in Inter-War Suburban London," *Journal of Historical Geography* 38, no. 4 (2012): 427.

39 Peter Scott, "British Railways and the Challenge from Road: 1919–39," *Twentieth Century British History* 13, no. 2 (2002): 103.

40 Roy Edwards, "Shaping British Freight Transport in the Interwar Period: Failure of Foresight or Administration, 1919–34?" in *From Rail to Road and Back Again? A Century of Transport Competition and Interdependency*, eds. Ralf Roth and Colin Divall (Farnham: Ashgate, 2015), 77–90.

41 Le Corbusier, *The City of To-Morrow and Its Planning* (1987 repri. New York: Dover Publications, 1929), 277–288.

42 Colin Buchanan, G.H.C. Cooper, Ann MacEwen, D.H. Crompton, Geoffrey Crow, G. Michell, D. Dallimore, P.J. Hills, and Derry Burton, *Traffic in Towns: A Study of the Long Term Problems of Traffic in Urban Areas* (London: H.M. Stationery Off., 1963), 11.

43 Hibbs, *The History of British Bus Services*.

44 Peter Scott and Chris Reid. "'The White Slavery of the Motor World': Opportunism in the Interwar Road Haulage Industry," *Social History* 25, no. 3 (2000): 300–314.

45 Ibid., 302–303.
46 Michael John Law, "'Stopping to Dream': The Beautification and Vandalism of London's Interwar Arterial Roads," *The London Journal* 35, no. 1 (2010): 58–84.
47 Michael John Law, "Turning Night into Day: Transgression and Americanization at the English Inter-War Roadhouse," *Journal of Historical Geography* 35, no. 3 (2009): 473–494.
48 Peter Merriman, "Motorways and the Modernisation of Britain's Road Network, 1937–70," in *From Rail to Road and Back Again? A Century of Transport Competition and Interdependency*, eds. Ralf Roth and Colin Divall (Farnham: Ashgate, 2015), 316–317.
49 Royal Commission on Transport, *First Report of the Royal Commission on Transport: "The Control of Traffic on Roads"* (London: HMSO, 1929), 24.
50 Ibid., 5.
51 Ibid.
52 Ibid., 19.
53 Ibid., 13.
54 Ibid., 39–42.
55 Ministry of Transport, *The Highway Code* (London: HMSO, 1931), 2.
56 See for instance: London County Council Tramways, *Rules and Regulations for Motormen* (London: London County Council, 1927).
57 Ministry of Transport, *The Highway Code*, 6.
58 Royal Commission on Transport, *First Report of the Royal Commission on Transport: "The Control of Traffic on Roads,"* 41.
59 Royal Commission on Transport, *The Co-ordination and Development of Transport* (London: HMSO, 1931).
60 Ibid., 102.
61 Ibid., 103.
62 Ibid., 104.
63 Ibid.
64 Ibid., 104.
65 Royal Commission on Transport, *Minutes of Evidence Taken Before the Royal Commission on Transport, 14 November 1928–25 June 1930* (London: HMSO, 1929), 201–203.
66 Royal Commission on Transport, *The Co-ordination and Development of Transport*, 104.
67 Ibid., 104–105.
68 Ibid., 105–106.
69 Merriman, "Motorways and the Modernisation of Britain's Road Network, 1937–70," 317.
70 Ibid., 320–322, 325.
71 J.H. Forshaw and Patrick Abercrombie, *County of London Plan* (London: Macmillan, 1943). Patrick Abercrombie, *Greater London Plan* (London: HMSO, 1944).
72 John Grindrod, *Concretopia: A Journey around the Rebuilding of Postwar Britain* (Brecon: Old Street, 2013), 148–150.
73 Buckley, "A Study in the Decline of the British Street Tramway Industry in the Twentieth Century with Special Reference to South Yorkshire," 372–377.
74 British Trolleybus Society, "Former UK Systems," 2015. Available online: accessed April 1, 2020, https://www.britishtrolley.org.uk/former-uk-systems.
75 L. Brunton, "The Trolleybus Story," *IEE Review* 2, no. 3 (1992): 59.
76 Buckley, "A Study in the Decline of the British Street Tramway Industry in the Twentieth Century with Special Reference to South Yorkshire," 267–282.
77 Brunton, "The Trolleybus Story," 59.
78 Ibid.
79 Munby and Watson, *Inland Transport Statistics*, 244–245, 340–341.

80 Brunton, "The Trolleybus Story," 59.
81 Ibid., 59–60.
82 Doncaster Corporation Transport Committee 1957–1974 minutes, 10 June 1958, 9; 9 December 1958, 15, AB/2/6/66/3, Doncaster Archives & Local Studies, Doncaster, United Kingdom.
83 Doncaster Corporation Transport Committee 1957–1974 minutes, /2/6/66/3, 4 September 1961, 43 and 10 October 1961, 45; Doncaster Transport Summary Accounts – AB/Trans/1/30–32, 1960–62, Doncaster Archives & Local Studies, Doncaster, United Kingdom.
84 Newcastle Corporation, "City and Council of Newcastle Upon Tyne: Council Minutes."
85 Steven Jukes, "Tyne Side Story Part 2 – The Death of a Plan," *Pathetic Motorways*, 2014. www.pathetic.org.uk/features/tyneside/1970s/.
86 Grindrod, *Concretopia*, 217.
87 The Doncaster Plan, March 1955, 7, DX WAR/G10, Doncaster Archives & Local Studies, Doncaster, United Kingdom,
88 Highways and Public Works Committee Minutes, 18 July 1961, 47; 19 March 1963, 114, AB2/6/29/1, Doncaster Archives & Local Studies, Doncaster, United Kingdom.
89 Buchanan et al., *Traffic in Towns*; Simon Gunn, "The Buchanan Report, Environment and the Problem of Traffic in 1960s Britain," *Twentieth Century British History* 22, no. 4 (2011): 521–542.
90 Buchanan et al., *Traffic in Towns*, 11.
91 Ibid., 14–23.
92 Gunn, "The Buchanan Report," 532.
93 Gunn, "People and the Car: The Expansion of Automobility in Urban Britain, c.1955-70," *Social History* 38, no. 2 (2013): 233–234.
94 'County Borough of Doncaster: Proposed Pedestrian and Vehicular Segregation', n.d. DD/WHIT/38, Doncaster Archives & Local Studies, Doncaster, United Kingdom.
95 Gunn, "The Buchanan Report," 534–535.
96 Corbusier, *The City of To-Morrow and Its Planning*, 12.
97 Ibid., 165.
98 Buchanan et al., *Traffic in Towns*, 112-123-163-201.
99 Jane Jacobs, *The Death and Life of Great American Cities* (London: Jonathon Cape, 1962).
100 Mees, *Transport for Suburbia*.
101 Corbusier, *The City of To-Morrow and Its Planning*, 166.
102 Buchanan et al., *Traffic in Towns*, 28–29.
103 Lawrence D. Taylor, "The Monorail 'Revolution' of the 1950s and 1960s and Its Legacy," *Journal of Transport History* 37, no. 2 (2016): 236–257.
104 Guy Ortolano, "Planning the Urban Future in 1960s Britain," *Historical Journal* 54, no. 2 (2011): 477–507.
105 Baden Hickman, "Manchester is Told Duorail Better and Less Expensive," *The Guardian*, January 31, 1966, 7.

Bibliography

Abercrombie, Patrick. *Greater London Plan*. London: HMSO, 1944.
Beirão, Gabriela, and J.A. Sarsfield Cabral. "Understanding Attitudes towards Public Transport and Private Car: A Qualitative Study." *Transport Policy* 14, no. 6 (November 2007): 478–489. doi:10.1016/j.tranpol.2007.04.009.
British Trolleybus Society. "Former UK Systems." 2015. Available online: accessed April 01, 2020, https://www.britishtrolley.org.uk/former-uk-systems.

Brunton, L. "The Trolleybus Story." *IEE Review* 2, no. The trolleybus story (1992): 57–61. doi:10.1049/ir:19920024.

Buchanan, Colin, G.H.C. Cooper, Ann MacEwen, D.H. Crompton, Geoffrey Crow, G. Michell, D. Dallimore, P.J. Hills, and Derry Burton. *Traffic in Towns: A Study of the Long Term Problems of Traffic in Urban Areas*. London: H.M. Stationery Off., 1963.

Buckley, Richard John. "A Study in the Decline of the British Street Tramway Industry in the Twentieth Century with Special Reference to South Yorkshire." Unpublished PhD thesis. University of Hull, 1987.

Coombs, Hugh, and J.R. Edwards. *Accounting Innovation: Municipal Corporations 1835–1935*. Abingdon: Routledge, 1996.

Corbusier, Le. *The City of To-Morrow and Its Planning*. 1987 repri. New York: Dover Publications, 1929.

Edwards, Roy. "Shaping British Freight Transport in the Interwar Period: Failure of Foresight or Administration, 1919–34?" In *From Rail to Road and Back Again? A Century of Transport Competition and Interdependency*, edited by Ralf Roth and Colin Divall, 77–90. Farnham: Ashgate, 2015.

Falkus, Malcolm. "The Development of Municipal Trading in the Nineteenth Century." *Business History* 19, no. 2 (July 1977): 134–161. doi:10.1080/00076797700000023.

Foreman-Peck, James, and Robert Millward. *Public and Private Ownership of British Industry: 1820–1990*. Oxford: Oxford University Press, 1994.

Forshaw, J.H., and Patrick Abercrombie. *County of London Plan*. London: Macmillan, 1943.

Green, Oliver. *Rails in the Road: A History of Tramways in Britian and Ireland*. Barnsley: Pen & Sword Transport, 2016.

Grindrod, John. *Concretopia: A Journey around the Rebuilding of Postwar Britain*. Brecon: Old Street, 2013.

Gunn, Simon. "People and the Car: The Expansion of Automobility in Urban Britain, c.1955–70." *Social History* 38, no. 2 (2013): 220–237. doi:10.1080/0307102 2.2013.790139.

———. "The Buchanan Report, Environment and the Problem of Traffic in 1960s Britain." *Twentieth Century British History* 22, no. 4 (2011): 521–542. doi:10.1093/tcbh/hwq063.

Hannah, Leslie. *Electricity before Nationalisation: A Study of the Development of the Electricity Supply Industry in Britain to 1948*. London: Macmillan, 1979.

Hibbs, John. *The History of British Bus Services*. Newton Abbot: David and Charles, 1968.

Holding, David. *A History of British Bus Services: North East*. Newton Abbot: David and Charles, 1979.

Jacobs, Jane. *The Death and Life of Great American Cities*. London: Jonathon Cape, 1962.

Jukes, Steven. "Tyne Side Story Part 2 – The Death of a Plan." *Pathetic Motorways*, 2014. www.pathetic.org.uk/features/tyneside/1970s/.

Kellett, J.R. "Municipal Socialism, Enterprise and Trading in the Victorian City." *Urban History* 5 (1978): 36–45. doi:10.1017/S0963926800003199.

Klapper, Charles. *The Golden Age of Tramways*. 2nd ed. Newton Abbot: David and Charles, 1974.

Knoop, Douglas. *Principles and Methods of Municipal Trading*. London: Macmillan, 1912.

Lave, Jean, and Etienne Wenger. *Situated Learning: Legitimate Peripheral Participation.* Cambridge: Cambridge University Press, 1991.

Law, Michael John. "'Stopping to Dream': The Beautification and Vandalism of London's Interwar Arterial Roads." *The London Journal* 35, no. 1 (2010): 58–84. doi:10.1179/174963210X12598738033459.

———. "'The Car Indispensable': The Hidden Influence of the Car in Inter-War Suburban London." *Journal of Historical Geography* 38, no. 4 (2012): 424–433. doi:10.1016/j.jhg.2012.04.005.

———. "Turning Night into Day: Transgression and Americanization at the English Inter-War Roadhouse." *Journal of Historical Geography* 35, no. 3 (2009): 473–494. doi:10.1016/j.jhg.2008.09.002.

London County Council Tramways. *Rules and Regulations for Motormen.* London: London County Council, 1927.

Marshall, Chris. "Road Numbers: How It Happened." *Roads.org.uk*, 2017. www.roads.org.uk/articles/road-numbers/how-it-happened.

Matthews, Derek. "Laissez-Faire and the London Gas Industry in the Nineteenth Century: Another Look." *The Economic History Review* 39, no. 2 (May 1986): 244–263. doi:10.1111/j.1468-0289.1986.tb00405.x.

McKay, John P. *Tramways and Trolleys: The Rise of Urban Mass Transport in Europe.* Princeton: Princeton University Press, 1976.

Mees, Paul. *Transport for Suburbia: Beyond the Automobile Age.* London: Earthscan, 2010.

Merriman, Peter. "Motorways and the Modernisation of Britain's Road Network, 1937–70." In *From Rail to Road and Back Again? A Century of Transport Competition and Interdependency*, edited by Ralf Roth and Colin Divall, 315–338. Farnham: Ashgate, 2015.

Millward, Robert. *Private and Public Enterprise in Europe.* Cambridge: Cambridge University Press, 2005.

———. *The State and Business in the Major Powers: An Economic History 1815–1939.* Abingdon: Routledge, 2014.

Millward, Robert, and Robert Ward. "From Private to Public Ownership of Gas Undertakings in England and Wales, 1851–1947: Chronology, Incidence and Causes." *Business History* 35, no. 3 (July 1993): 1–21. doi:10.1080/00076799300000084.

Ministry of Transport. *The Highway Code.* London: HMSO, 1931.

Munby, D.L., and A.H. Watson. *Inland Transport Statistics: Great Britian 1900–1970.* Oxford: Clarendon Press, 1978.

Newcastle Corporation. *City and Council of Newcastle Upon Tyne: Council Minutes.* Newcastle-Upon-Tyne: Newcastle Corporation, 1962.

Ortolano, Guy. "Planning the Urban Future in 1960s Britain." *Historical Journal* 54, no. 2 (2011): 477–507. doi:10.1017/S0018246X11000100.

Roberts, Richard. "Business, Politics and Municipal Socialism." In *Businessmen and Politics: Studies of Business Activity in British Politics, 1900–1945* edited by John Turner. London: Heinemann Educational Books, 1984.

Royal Commission on Transport. *First Report of the Royal Commission on Transport: "The Control of Traffic on Roads."* London: HMSO, 1929.

———. *Minutes of Evidence Taken Before the Royal Commission on Transport, 14 November 1928–25 June 1930.* London: HMSO, 1929.

———. *The Co-ordination and Development of Transport.* London: HMSO, 1931.

Schatzberg, Eric. "Culture and Technology in the City: Opposition to Mechanized Street Transportation in Late-Nineteenth Century America." In *Technologies of Power: Essays in Honor of Thomas Parke Hughes and Agatha Chipley Hughes*, edited by Michael Thad Allen and Gabrielle Hecht. Cambridge, MA: MIT Press, 2001.

———. "'Technik' Comes to America : Changing Meanings of 'Technology' before 1930." *Technology and Culture* 47, no. 3 (2006): 486–512.

Scherer, Milena, and Katrin Dziekan. "Bus or Rail: An Approach to Explain the Psychological Rail Factor." *Journal of Public Transportation* 15, no. 1 (2012): 75–93. doi:10.5038/2375-0901.15.1.5.

Schmucki, Barbara. "The Machine in the City: Public Appropriation of the Tramway in Britain and Germany, 1870–1915." *Journal of Urban History* 38 (2012): 1060–1093. doi:10.1177/0096144211435121.

Scott, Peter. "British Railways and the Challenge from Road: 1919–39." *Twentieth Century British History* 13, no. 2 (2002): 101–120. doi:10.1093/tcbh/13.2.101.

Scott, Peter, and Chris Reid. "'The White Slavery of the Motor World': Opportunism in the Interwar Road Haulage Industry." *Social History* 25, no. 3 (2000): 300–314. doi:10.1080/03071020050143338.

Star, S.L., and K. Ruhleder. "Steps toward an Ecology of Infrastructure: Design and Access for Large Information Spaces." *Information Systems Research* 7, no. 3 (1996): 111–134.

Steer Davies Gleave. *Leeds New Generation Transport: Permanence in Public Transport Systems*. Vol. C-1–12. London: Steer, Davies, Gleave, 2014.

Taylor, Lawrence D. "The Monorail 'Revolution' of the 1950s and 1960s and Its Legacy." *Journal of Transport History* 37, no. 2 (2016): 236–257. doi:10.1177/0022526616667955.

Tennent, Kevin D. "Management and Competitive Advantage in the Public Transport Industry." *British Academy of Management Conference Proceedings*. London: British Academy of Management, 2013.

———. "Profit or Utility Maximizing? Strategy, Tactics and the Municipal Tramways of York, C. 1918–1935." *Journal of Management History* 23, no. 4 (2017): 401–422. doi:10.1108/JMH-05-2017-0026.

TransForm Scotland. *Trams for Edinburgh*. Edinburgh: TransformScotland, 2006.

Turner, David A., and Tennent, Kevin D., "Progressive Strategies of Municipal Trading: The policies of the London County Council Tramways c. 1891–1914." *Business History* (2019), online first. doi:10.1080/00076791.2019.1577823.

Vuchic, Vukan R. *Urban Transit: Operations, Planning and Economics*. Hoboken: John Wiley & Sons, 2005.

———. *Urban Transit Systems and Technology*. Hoboken: John Wiley & Sons, 2007.

4 Barrels rolling free

Modal shift in the brewing industry, 1897–1914

David A. Turner

In 1913 George Watson, the Commercial Motor Users Association's inspecting engineer, stated that "From the earliest days of the motor industry the brewery and allied trades realised the possibilities of mechanical transport".[1] Brewers were some of the earliest adopters of steam and petrol motor vehicles, and by 1905 about 60 nationwide were known to be using them, with uptake increasing rapidly thereafter.[2] In a period when motor technology was in its formative stages, this chapter considers why brewers were such fervent adopters, where other sectors were not. It argues that this was the result of a combination of financial, technological, social, competitive and legislative factors combining to create favourable conditions for motor usage, thus emphasising how complex factors shape transport choices by organisations who control the governance over all or part of the supply chain. Significantly, it demonstrates that, rather than the adoption of motor vehicles across economies being an inevitability, as some authors have intimated,[3] in different sectors or businesses it was contingent on their unique circumstances, and their strategic and operating concerns. Significantly, the chapter demonstrates the importance of examining the pre-1914 period for identifying trends in road motor goods haulage that become more starkly apparent after 1918, it being the first dedicated study of a sector's employment of this emergent technology in the period.

Examining transport from the user's perspective has increasingly been on the agenda amongst transport and mobility historians. As De Graef argued "the broader tendency in transport history was to give the supply side of transport infrastructure centre stage, whereas the specific demand for transport remained largely overlooked".[4] Yet whilst increasingly passenger perspectives are being understood, freight transport's use within supply chains has remained underexplored. This is possibly because supply chains and networks through which materials and goods pass are made up of many actors and organisations.[5] For instance, in the British brewing industry of 1900 the chain included farmers (hops/barley), importers (hops/barley/sugar), maltsters, intermediaries (factors, wholesalers and merchants), retailers (publicans and agents) and brewers. All these players needed goods and produce moved between them, and thus transport choice and innovation within this and other supply chains like it, was determined by the complex interrelations between them, the actions of transport providers, who had governance and decision-making authority within the supply chain, the regulatory and competitive environment in which all operated, and ultimately the need to match supply with demand at each stage.

Any assessment of supply chains is therefore not straightforward, and currently where many industries are concerned only a fragmented picture exists. The transport history literature has largely focussed on providers' operations and their regulation, rather than their changing relationships with and between their users. By contrast, histories of corporate transport users frequently only touch on choices and provision briefly, usually then only to discuss cost, and in a manner isolated from the influence on business performance of other actors along the supply chain. Indeed, this is so where brewery histories are concerned, where supply chain and transport matters are rarely considered at length, the focus being on companies' production functions.[6] Similarly, histories of consumption have focussed on the cultural dimensions of demand at the retail outlet and have not considered how it was shaped by decisions and transport within the supply chain that lay behind.[7] Spain argued that this "approach to distribution history risks overlooking basic factors such as technology, geography and economy."[8] Reflecting this, in the case of beer (and alcohol generally) the social and cultural influences on consumption have been discussed frequently, but considerations of how changes to the beer trade influenced what happened along the supply chain behind the bar are absent.[9]

A joined-up approach to how transport is impacted by and impacts the nature and development of supply chains and the demands of the different users – shaped by various broader factors for instance government and competition – is required. Some studies have provided such analysis, particularly highlighting the consumer society's emergence and how downstream demand was served by the development of motor vehicles. Hamilton, examining this in the United States from the 1920s, argued that this was dependent on the rise of independent road haulage, emphasising the centrality of transport in economic change; "[a]gribusiness relied upon independent truckers to shift U.S. capitalism into overdrive, introducing lean and mean business strategies and cultivating a culture of economic conservatism welcomed by both rural producers and urban consumers".[10] Vahrenkamp found similar when examining the development of logistics in Germany between 1880 and 2012, arguing that "complex logistical services…evolved in parallel with the consumer society". Change in transport choices and supply chain management by companies was the result of direct stimulation by the consumer society driving searches for improvements in costs, flexibility and management. These factors were nevertheless dependent on stable political and social externalities.[11] In both cases, therefore, transport innovation was driven largely by external factors.

Similarly, studies of food distribution in Britain from 1919 until the 1970s have emphasised how changes in consumption habits drove shifts in who governed supply chains, and how this shaped transport requirements. Where retailing was concerned, Spain argued that between 1919 and 1975 "responses to influences such as the cost of living, inter-firm competition and the demands of the final consumer" led to a shift in supply chain governance towards the store, "which heightened the need for cheap, flexible and reliable distribution that the railways could or would not provide, but that road transport could.[12] Wilcox argued that in the white fish industry the move to road-based distribution was the result of post-war, consumer preference for processed and frozen fish, rising incomes, and larger retailers pushing out smaller ones. Thus, "large processors and retailers could operate their own lorry fleets, which enabled them simply to bypass the established [fragmented, rail-based] supply chain".[13] Again, therefore, in the UK experience, downstream demand and competition significantly influenced transport choices in the supply chain, as this chapter echoes in the case of brewing before 1914.

Nonetheless, other factors also influenced shifts from rail to road in the UK food supply. Before 1945 the railways appeared reluctant to invest in new technologies or systems on their own account to keep traffic from various food sectors, relying on the trader to invest, whilst after the war they could not meet companies' changing demands for flexible delivery, found in road transport.[14] In the fish industry, the small-load traffic that dominated before 1945 was increasingly unviable for British Railways, yet it held onto this and let bulk hauls that were more viable go to road, the result of antagonism between it and the industry.[15] These situations were compounded by user complaints "about the quality of service provided by Britain's railways", the railways being a source of immobility and challenge for them. Moreover, railway strikes in 1919 and 1955 proved the viability of road transport, demonstrating to traders they did not need the railways for their transport needs.[16] The sum result is that British railways were frequently not providing the flexible, reliable and secure service transport users needed between 1919 and the 1970s, something this chapter emphasises was also the case before 1914.

Finally, Spain emphasised the importance of the regulatory and legislative influences on transport choice after 1919. For instance, the creation of the Milk Marketing Board in 1934 – designed to provide a fixed and fair price to producers – shifted governance of the supply chain away from established wholesalers, and after 1945 its commitment to reducing long-distance delivery of milk and increasing localised delivery, led to a diminishment of rail usage after 1945.[17] Livestock hygiene, wartime rationing, and the adopting of qualitative licensing – where licencing was based on driver aptitude rather than lorry size – in 1968, all influenced the availability, structure and adoption of road haulage,[18] whilst steady increases in railway rates, sometimes imposed by government and sometimes requested by the railway industry, raised transport costs for food producers and hence the appeal of motor haulage.[19]

These studies therefore evidence the complex influences on transport choices in a supply chain, as this chapter also demonstrates. Whilst it does not consider transport in the whole beer supply chain – there broadly being stasis where raw material supply was concerned – it develops this emergent literature in the case of brewers' distribution arrangements. Transport innovation between 1897 and 1914 was driven by various factors, most of which were external to individual brewers. Government action played a role, through increasing taxation on brewers and allowing railways to raise rates in 1913, compelling searches for cost reductions, whilst government also relaxed restrictions on motor vehicle usage and thus stimulated development. Moreover, in a period when brewers were under financial pressures, they initially looked for cost reductions in existing operations, motors meeting this desire. Motors also provided more reliable, quicker and flexible delivery to public houses and agencies than the railways could provide. Indeed, in a period of intense competition, they enabled brewers to remain and enhance their competitive advantage; extending their range of direct delivery into the territory of competitors at minimal cost, opening up new markets and growing their market share. Significantly, such developments were precursors to the development of the merger and acquisition movements amongst brewers between the wars, demonstrating how the application of transport can be an indicator of corporate strategy and structural shift in industry.

A more theoretical point will however be made in this chapter about the relationship between new transport technologies, users and usage. The discourse outlined above has largely focused on the actual capabilities of the motor goods vehicle, and how this could be beneficial for firms. The statements of brewers' and their allies demonstrated here, nonetheless, will suggest that once a new transport technology arrives, individuals will start conceptualising its possible uses and changes in transport structures, even if the technical capabilities are not present to realise them immediately. This chapter therefore examines the factors that influence the creation and articulation of such future transport possibilities.

Brewery distribution before the motor

Around 1900 the character of brewery distribution – which naturally varied dependent on the brewery size and their operations – constituted several important goods flows. Beer took various possible directions on leaving the production site. Most breweries supplied casks of beer locally to public houses, private customers and to stores or agents (near and far from the brewery), who supplied it to the free trade. Additionally, from the 1870s bottling developed rapidly, spurred on in the 1890s and 1900s by improvements in filtering, carbonation and pasteurisation. Beer was shipped in cask to bottling plants owned by the company or contractors, which was then supplied direct to retailers, public houses or wholesalers. In the opposite direction came empty casks and cases for holding bottles. Breweries were very eager to have casks returned as quickly as possible; they were their largest element of working capital and the more in transit at any one time meant more investment to maintain output. As was commented in 1907, the returning of empty casks to the brewer was "a matter of no slight importance", especially in the busy season of the summer months when demand for beer was higher.[20]

The transport used to facilitate these flows was dependent on the specific characteristics of a brewery's trade. The majority of breweries in 1900 were concerned with supplying dense networks of public houses (mostly tied) and customers using their own horses and drays; rail transport was unsuitable given the stop-start nature of the operation. A typical example were Whitbread's dray teams in 1891, which undertook daily deliveries of up to 12 delivery stops as far as Richmond, some 12 miles away from the brewer's Chiswell Street Brewery, the delivery schedule taking 10 hours and 40 minutes.[21] Using horse and dray teams nonetheless had certain limitations.[22] First, horse stocks absorbed a considerable amount of working capital. One horse could cost between £70 and £90;[23] consequently, the 223 horses possessed by Truman & Co's of London in 1901 had an estimated total value of £20,970. Thus, any investment in new horses had to be carefully weighed against the likely benefits of operation, especially as they required continuous care.[24] Most significantly, the biological limitations of horses constrained the scale and scope of distribution. Two or three horse pairs could only carry approximately 4 tons of barrels and bottles[25] 12 miles from the brewery. Biology also rendered horses inflexible; Taylor and Burdass suggested that a "serious drawback" was that "animals cannot be worked overtime, or at a higher pressure than normal to cope with rushes of extra work that frequently occur".[26] The result was that range and size of delivery, and thus the markets servable, were limited. However, a benefit of the industry having these constraints was that breweries could be shielded from external competition in remoter areas.

Many breweries did however expand their trade beyond this range, and were relying upon the railways to transport between 75% and 86% of their output by 1900.[27] Firms based in Burton-upon-Trent and Guinness in Dublin used the railways almost exclusively from their inception to create extensive nationwide networks of agencies to supply the free trade.[28] The dominant users of the railways were however breweries with local trades seeking to develop specific markets or regional networks of agencies and stores. Greene King of Bury St Edmunds supplied stores in local towns, which in turn supplied 180 of its public houses.[29] Eldridge Pope of Dorchester built a large new brewery next to the railway in 1881 and negotiated a siding agreement with the London & South Western Railway (LSWR),[30] and subsequently remarked upon the continuous development of its trade across western England.[31] From the 1890s, Whitbread also used the railways extensively to build up a nationwide network of bottling depots and stores.[32] Railways were therefore a frequent facilitator of trade development – and competition – beyond the range of the horse and dray. Railway rates and charges, whilst complained about, were in many cases not a hindrance to the growth of brewery's trade over long distances, their own strategic considerations being the cause. For instance, Gourvish and Wilson argued that "larger London breweries failure to attack the country trade vigorously was almost certainly their preoccupation with servicing their complex loan business involving hundreds of publicans apiece".[33]

Exercising governance over long distance distribution nonetheless allowed brewers to assess the merits and demerits of modes of transport. Coastal shipping was used frequently, possibly in response to changing circumstances, although in some cases it was the means of generating trade beyond the local area. Gourvish and Wilson argued that "lower costs of transport by water had to be balanced against the much faster turn-round of valuable casks by rail. The advantages of the latter were, in general, ones of convenience, not cost".[34] Nonetheless, in instances where journeys by boat were short or the flows regular, delivery and return of empties could be relied upon. To offer popular pale ales – popularised in London by Burton brewers – Courage of Shad Thames switched its supply from Flowers & Son of Stratford-upon-Avon, which had to cart deliveries across the city from stations, to Fremlin's of Maidstone, which could supply more directly and cheaply by river.[35] Of Truman's outbound carriage costs in January 1910, 20% was being paid to coastal shippers.[36] Before motors, many brewers were therefore experienced in using a range of transport options to establish flexible, quicker and cheaper delivery and returns and to access new markets, thus allowing some breweries to recognise the opportunities motors presented.

Government intervention – changing laws

Before the advantages of motors could be realised, laws had to change, demonstrating the importance of external legislative factors on transport choices. Legislation from the 1860s and 1870s restricted the speed of self-propelled vehicles – largely heavy traction engines – to 4 miles per hour (mph) in the countryside and 2 mph in the built-up areas, with three employees required to supervise.[37] By 1890s, developing motor technology and increasing calls for liberalisation led to the Locomotives on Highways Act of 1896. The speed of motor vehicles under 1.5 tons increased to 12 mph, those up to 2 tons had a limit of 8 mph, above that the limit was 5 mph. A category of light mechanically powered vehicle of 3 tons unladen weight was also created, and these could pull one trailer, had no supervisory restrictions and a maximum speed of 14 mph.[38] The Act thus created the conditions for the technical development of such vehicles.

The 3-ton limitation remained a frustration, despite trials of heavier vehicles in Liverpool in 1898 and 1899 showing that there was great potential for their development.[39] Fred M. Maynard, when lecturing the Yorkshire and North Eastern Institute of Brewing, called it an "unnecessary, harmful and vexatious restriction", that limited the possibility of loads of 4–10 tons, even if the technology at that stage was not available to haul this.[40] This situation did not however remain unchanged. Again, the result of pressures, the Motor Car Act of 1903 allowed the Local Government Board to increase lorries' maximum tare weight and subject them to further conditions in construction. The 1904 Heavy Motor Car order (active from 1 March 1905) created two new classes of motors; light motors under 2 tons unladen weight and heavy motors, between 2 and 5 tons unladen – the latter being a new maximum – with a limit of 8 tons on each axel.[41]

Across this period, brewers explored the opportunities motors provided. Stressing that unique conditions prevailed in different industries that determined their uptake, even after the First World War some industries did not adopt them in large numbers because of 'dead running', i.e. uneconomic operation of the vehicle when it was unloaded on return legs of delivery, which raised operating costs prohibitively. By contrast, the need to transport beer outward and return empty bottles and barrels meant that brewers were always ensured full or good loads, and thus motors despite their high purchase and operating cost were fully economically employed.[42] Brewers' first forays into using light motors had begun between 1897 and 1898.[43] Brewers initially exercised caution, preferring to hire lorries from external contractors and companies. For instance, Noakes & Co. of Whites Grounds, Bermondsey, hired a vehicle from the Germain Motor Car Co in 1903.[44] At this point, the 3-ton limit was not of concern given that breweries usually used vehicles below 3-tons that never exceeded the 5 mph.[45] After the 1904 order, they took full advantage of the new upper limit by employing heavier vehicles; for instance, in 1913 Whitbread was using a 4-ton Thornycroft, Hodgson's of Kingston-upon-Thames were using a 4-ton Daimler and Fremlin's had three 5-tonners. The result was, Watson argued, that breweries were "amongst the most important buyers of heavy motor vehicles" by 1913.[46]

Pressure on brewers

It is tempting to reduce this progressive adoption of motor vehicles in the brewing industry to a monocausal explanation – operational convenience – when the picture was far more complex. Their adoption was significantly boosted by various external pressures. First, brewers' operational costs increased, one element being rising taxation. In 1880 the government removed malt and sugar duties, whilst re-imposing the beer duty, abolished in 1830, at a rate of 6s 3d per 36-gallon barrel. This steadily rose to 7s 9d per barrel by 1900, which was initially levied to pay for the Boer War, but became permanent.[47] However, a more significant influence on brewers' cost position was the scramble for property. Around 1870 a very large proportion of beer was sold through retail outlets that were 'free', i.e. agents and public houses, although some might have been tied to a brewery by loan or agreement.[48] From the 1880s, the trading environment became challenging. The public house trade was under threat, as new attractions such as railway excursions and the music-hall vied for the working-class pound. Moreover, temperance campaigners with the ear of high-profile members of the Liberal Party pressured the government to reduce the number of on-licenses.[49]

To secure their routes to market, the brewers moved to purchase on-licenses, shrinking the available supply and inflating prices, meaning they ended up "grossly overpaying for public houses".[50] To fund this activity – in addition to the modernisation of brewing equipment – they required increased amounts of capital; traditional family-owned breweries took to incorporation to enable them to turn to the capital market to raise finance. Whilst highlighting that company performance depended upon governance models and management quality after 1900, Acheson, Coyle and Turner argued that breweries had become overextended, putting pressure on profits through excessive debt obligations.[51] Such cost increases would not have been problematic had it not been for the brewers' inability to offset them by raising prices for fear of discouraging patronage – another influence of competition.[52] The *Brewing Trade Review* reported in 1913 that "The retailer is practically compelled to sell a pint of beer for 2*d*, he cannot charge 2¼*d* for it, nor will the law allow him to sell for 2*d* a quantity less than a pint".[53] Collectively, therefore, these pressures amounted to profit margins being squeezed, forcing brewers to expand market share and find operating cost reductions.

Maynard – on the subject of motors in 1900 – argued that breweries possessed "a keen eye for anything conducive to a reduction of working expenses".[54] Indeed, whilst initially unsuitable for the stop-start nature of local delivery as idling time represented a significant cost, initial savings were effected by motors on some deliveries traditionally sent by rail.[55] For instance, Bellamy Brothers's of Grimsby's motor drove in 1905 30–60 miles daily, whilst Ord, Battiscombe & Elwes of Somerton was delivering by steam dray 22 miles away, a 44 mile round trip. The actual cost savings effected are unclear given the sparse information in company accounts; nonetheless, they were considered significant. Vaux & Sons of Sunderland from 1902 delivered bottles to Annfield Plain – a 30-mile round trip – and this effected "a considerable saving on the cost of carriage by rail".[56] One anonymous brewer in 1908 was reported to have switched its deliveries over intermediate distances from rail to road, saving £600 per annum in the process.[57]

The direct replacement of motors for horses on distribution routes closer to the brewery followed.[58] Gourvish and Wilson argued that the cost of running motors could only be compared with horse operation, but that this was problematic given they performed different tasks.[59] However, closer investigation shows that as motor technology improved, fewer motors could perform the task of several horses and drays. For instance, Brakspear of Henley in 1905 stated that their motor replaced five horses,[60] whilst in 1909 Messrs

Hammerton of Stockwell reported the replacement of eight.[61] The cost reductions effected depended upon the motor vehicle type and use, yet consensus emerged that they were potentially significant. In 1907 it was stated that the prime cost of a three-horse and dray was £645 when a steam dray cost only £530. The running costs, including interest, depreciation, fodder, staff, maintenance and all other operating costs per annum for the former was £811 4s 0d, whilst for the steam dray it was £408 10s 0d. Per ton mile, the steam dray also had an advantage, costing 2.3d per ton mile compared with 4.88d for horse and dray.[62] One "authentic case", cited by Watson in 1913, showed a different pattern of costs, but still increased efficiency. A firm operating around Bristol and Bath spent for each 3-horse wagon £5 8s 7d per week, taking loads between the towns. Carrying 3 tons 5 days a week, this cost per ton mile 7s 3d. By contrast, whilst the steam dray cost more to run per week – £6 11s 8½d – it did 32 miles five days a week, carrying 6 tons each time, the equivalent of 4s 10d per ton mile, a reduction of 2s 10d.[63] Therefore, consistently improving operational cost savings played into brewers' thinking when adopting motors.

Service quality

Cost was not the only advantage motors provided, especially over rail, and here the broader context of downstream demand was important in creating favourable conditions for motor vehicle use. From the 1880s lighter and weaker 'running' ales became popular amongst consumers.[64] The *Brewers' Almanack* stated in 1895 that the "public…has come to insist more and more strongly upon extreme freshness of palate with a degree of brilliancy and sparkle that our fathers never dreamt of".[65] Changing tastes in turn changed the hardiness of the product. The beers popular previously – the sweet milds and porters – were more resilient beers that could withstand changes in temperature and storage condition, making some delay in transit of no great concern.[66] Yet running ales, intended for speedy consumption and which remained in condition for as little as a fortnight were far more susceptible to variations in temperature conditions.[67] In an industry where beer reputation was all-important to preserve market share,[68] this put brewers under pressure to maintain stable conditions for the beer during transit, and to ensure the delivery was expedited as quickly as possible.

Brewers did not feel confident that the railways were meeting these demands, as the mode necessitated various transhipments, the *Brewing Trade Review* claiming that "sending beer to a store from one side of a country to another" meant items went "from brewery to station, station to junction, junction to wayside station, wayside station to store", the result being "four to eight handlings, four haulages".[69] This carried many risk factors. Delay in transit, which increased the chance of beer spoilage, was a frequent and persistent complaint both whilst on the rail and over the 'last mile' from station to customer.[70] For instance, Vaux & Sons of Newcastle recorded in 1905 that it frequently experienced delays to its bottled beer at "busy times", even when sending beer a relatively short distance.[71] Others experienced delay in the speed of empties being returned, a matter of no small concern at "busy times".[72] These issues were compounded by other sources of financial loss through rail distribution; "Brewers know", Maynard argued, "only too well that with railway-carried orders complaints of leakages and so forth are of frequent occurrence".[73] For instance, Whitbread's ledger from 1900 to 1912 shows 40 individual claims for loss or damage of barrels, spread between eight different railway companies serving London.[74] Pilferage, especially of bottled beer was also commonplace, and court cases involving railway employees caught in the act bear this out.[75]

The railways' response to these complaints was lacklustre, suggesting a lack of concern for brewers' need for namely expeditious, economical, secure and flexible delivery services. They actively fostered an approach that perhaps alienated or set their customers against them. Where accountability for any damage lay was hazy, the onus being on brewers to prove railway companies were at fault. Railways therefore attempted to transfer the upmost responsibility for damage to the brewers or the publican, rather than provide more secure transit; the Midland Railway – probably the largest conveyer of beer in Britain – in 1914 directed that staff should ensure that all empty brewers' barrels were checked for damage *before* they were received for consignment, so as to avoid the possibility of paying out compensation as far as possible.[76] Indeed, whilst various railways implored staff to reduce damage in handling,[77] only the Great Eastern Railway is known to have provided bespoke wagon facilities for brewers,[78] other companies simply preferring standard wagons, which frequently left barrels open to the elements.

Further vertical integration of distribution arrangements through motors therefore offered brewers the opportunity to diminish the negative impact of rail transit.[79] Damage and pilferage and thus financial loss was reduced, and, for instance, Greenall, Whitley and Co. Ltd., of Warrington reported in 1910 that by sending beer by motor led to "much less damage to the barrels" compared with rail.[80] Moreover, when it did occur they could accurately establish attribution, extract the correct compensation, rather than rely on the incomplete information provided by a third party.[81] Most significantly, in what was a precursor to post-war developments, motors began changing the nature of distribution in ways that maintained breweries' competitiveness. By bypassing the railway, last mile issues were eliminated over longer distances, and combined with the greater flexibility motors afforded, enabled supply to be better and more quickly matched against demand. Instructive was the *Commercial Motor's* following of Canterbury brewer Ash & Co's Tasker steam wagon, which was travelling daily to Folkestone, 15 miles. On the delivery round one publican involuntarily voiced his praise for the motor; "[w]e used, when the beer came by rail, frequently to get it just when we were very busy at 6, 7, or 8 o'clock at night; we were never sure. Now it's here just after breakfast punctual as a clock".[82] Increased delivery speed and reliability also ensured that the quality of the product was maintained in transit, ensuring better that punters were satisfied. The *Brewers' Journal* in 1907 commented that compared with the poor service provided by the railways, "if goods are delivered [by motor] direct from brewery or agency into the customers' cellars" the brewer was "able to exercise more perfect control over the beer, its subsequent condition on tapping being influenced by fewer contingencies".

Later stages, c.1910–1914

By 1910 the motor vehicle had proven itself to brewers both as a replacement for the horse and dray and for rail transport on some delivery rounds, hence their rapid uptake. In the face of challenging trading circumstances, they lowered distribution costs, whilst facilitating the maintenance or even enhancement of breweries' competitiveness in ways that the railways and coastal shippers could not or would not do. Just before the First World War, there were however further developments in these directions. Again, shaped and driven by external competition and political factors, brewers turned to motors to ensure further cost reductions and reliability of delivery. They could be used to cost-effectively expand brewers' market share in ways that challenged the existing structure of the brewing industry. Indicative of this, in this period imaginings about motor vehicles' future capacity and usage came to the fore, with commentators suggesting that it was not a case of *if* they would take over from railways, but *when*.

External events further emphasised the attractiveness of the motor vehicle after 1910.[83] First, instances of labour unrest and the first national railway strike in 1911 raised further concerns amongst brewers over the reliability of the railways for delivery. In the brewing centre of Burton, where 300–400 of the 1000 railway workers were on strike, the dispatch of beer and inflows of supplies ground to a halt, ceasing production at various breweries.[84] The result was, Watson argued, a "feeling of unrest in the haulage and transport departments" and suggested the use of an increasingly viable alternative for distribution; the strike could "only be of advantage to the commercial motor industry".[85] Thus, where various commentators have discussed how road haulage was given a boost by the 1919 strike, where the brewing industry was concerned similar can be observed eight years earlier, thus highlighting its pioneering role in the emergence of motorised goods transport by road in Britain.[86]

Government action was perhaps one of the most significant influences upon motor vehicle uptake, demonstrating again how regulation created favourable conditions for the shift from rail to road. With the possibility of war emerging, the nation's transport requirements came to the fore in 1912, this being the year the Railway Executive Committee was created to run Britain's railways during the conflict.[87] Building upon an earlier arrangement, the War Office launched a scheme that year that subsidised any firm buying motors £50 of the purchase cost and £20 in the three years thereafter, in anticipation that these would be maintained in good order and could be requisitioned if needed.[88] The War Office also ran trials to determine makes and models of motor that would receive subsidies[89] and two classes of vehicle were established – 3 ton or 30 cwts – which were to be able to cover 80 miles satisfactorily. The trials therefore helped to advance road vehicle development, improving design, robustness and reliability, which, as Coates points out, reduced the need for cover from alternative transport in instances breakdown.[90] To what extent brewers took up this scheme and benefitted from the improved machines turned out subsequently is unclear; however it is known that numerous breweries purchased War Office approved types.[91] For instance, Watney Combe Reid owned 11 motors by the outbreak of war, eight of which were requisitioned by the government in August 1914.[92]

Government action also indirectly stimulated a motor-friendly environment by increasing the cost advantage of motors over rail transit. Whilst, as noted, most brewers tolerated railway rates, where brewers relied on rail their margins became susceptible to increases, as demonstrated by the 1913 Railway & Canal Traffic Act.[93] This allowed railway companies to offset increased wage costs, as a result of agreements with the unions, by increasing the maximum rates by 4% from 1st January 1914.[94] This was compounded by increased demurrage charges (a charge payable to wagon owners by failure to load or unload it within the time agreed). At a time when brewers' other operational costs were rising, this constituted another financial pressure, not just through increasing distribution costs, but through increasing costs along the supply chain. "Those...who deliver to distant agencies or bottling stores by rail", the *Brewing Trade Review* wrote, "will be directly affected by the increased rates, and all brewers will have to bear indirectly some part of the increased cost of delivery to them of the materials they use, consequent upon the increased rate..."[95] The result was that excessive transport costs were considered a matter of ongoing anxiety. The chairman of Marston, Thompson and Evershed (of Burton) argued that "increased railway rates had proved, and would continue to prove, a serious item [of cost]."[96] Barclay Perkins's chairman similarly mentioned the increase in carriage costs due to rates increases, stressing the implications for future profits.[97] The response was logical for many. In an industry where motors were already accepted and understood as being of value, and given many brewers' distribution arrangements accommodated them easily, increasing their use was seen as an increasingly attractive option for reducing distribution costs. The *Brewing Trade Review* thus argued that the rates increase would thus deliver a "serious situation" for the railways.[98]

Consequently, due to external pressures and factors, the period 1910–1914 becomes an important tipping point in the relationship between many brewers and the railways. Before 1910, motor vehicles were simply added extras in distribution arrangements; thereafter for many concerns they became seen as a important part of them. This shift is exemplified by the imaginings of the brewing press after 1910 about the possibilities of motor vehicles to fundamentally alter breweries' transport arrangements. In direct response to the 1913 Railway and Canal Traffic Act, the *Brewing Trade Review* commented that:

> ...the question of how far, or how much further, these vehicles can be utilised, not only for the delivery of beer to public-houses, stores and other customers, but for carrying such materials as are required and can be purchased within reasonable distance of the brewery, is one that is certain to receive the careful consideration of all brewing concerns.... we confidently look to great development in the immediate future in the use of motor vehicles in the brewing trade.[99]

Similarly, in 1916 an article entitled "The Construction of Brewery" argued that "motor service will to a very great extent supersede the use of horses"[100] As such, whilst there were still technological and operational limits to brewers' motor operations before 1914, there was a high degree of certainty that they would supplant all other forms of transport.

Yet the future was not only imagined. A key suggestion in the introduction was that motor lorries had a key role in facilitating the rise of the consumer society; a fundamental structural shift in both the buying habits of consumers and the structure and activities of retailers and producers. It has already been seen that the brewing industry was an early exemplar of such developments; the greater uptake and the extension of the use of motors began to disrupt established industry structures before 1914 and set out a pattern of brewery behaviour that would accelerate after 1919. Until the 1900s, local brewers had to varying extents been protected from outside competition by the limited range of horse and drays. As the range and reliability of motors developed this situation was disrupted, as larger brewers could weaken such barriers by buying up public houses in their territories and supply them easily and cheaply by motor, thus expanding their market share and increasing their direct hegemony over districts. Bennison therefore argued of North Eastern brewers that

> it was not the brewing process so much as the distribution of the product that gave the bigger firms the competitive edge, allowing them to extend their markets and enjoying savings which served to weaken the competitive position of the already small brewer.[101]

Motors therefore transitioned from being solely cost reducers and providing more effective distribution to delivering competitive advantage. Indeed, when talking of the pre-war period in 1921, *The Engineer* stated that the "well-to-do" brewer owed a "certain measure of their prosperity" to their foresight in buying motors, "placing themselves in an advantageous position compared to many of their competitors."[102]

Conclusion

It is important to not to overstate the role of the motor vehicle in brewing by 1914; most breweries by this point were still beholden to the horse and dray, and it would take until the 1940s and 1950s before they were almost completely displaced. Yet the brewers were some of the most important users of motor vehicles in the pre-First World War period, and this chapter has asked why this was so. It is firstly important to acknowledge that motor vehicles were fully employed by brewers wherever possible. Use on outward and inward flows of beer and empties meant there was no empty running, and so this primed them for acceptance into breweries' existing distribution operations. Nonetheless, their uptake was also influenced, driven and stimulated by a variety of factors; for instance government legislation, and breweries' squeezed profits caused by tax, debt, railway rates – the result of further government intervention – and competition. The favourable conditions for their adoption was also bolstered by the inflexibility of railway delivery, which motor lorries could improve upon, providing breweries with competitive advantage, as well as the limitations of the horse and dray, and the changing transport needs of brewers.

This chapter has therefore identified that varied factors combined to influence motor adoption, even if in a heterogeneous industry with breweries of varied size and operation, these factors would have played out differently in different places. Through this, it has demonstrated important points that relate to histories of transport innovation, supply chains and distribution. First, brewers' move to motor distribution was to a very large extent the result of external factors of various kinds creating favourable conditions for it, which dovetailed well with their strategic and operational objectives, which in turn were the result of their adverse financial and competitive position. This aligns well with the conclusions Spain has made regarding the influences on the shift from rail to road in various food sectors after 1919.[103]

Where this chapter has departed from the conclusions of previous authors writing about modal shift in Britain, is that it has emphasised that the ascendency of the motor lorry cannot simply be generalised as a post-First World War phenomenon. It does, nonetheless, reinforce the contention that when it did occur, it depended on the unique circumstances and conditions prevailing in specific industries or sectors. The ascendency of the motor lorry was not uniform; however, this chapter has emphasised how Edwardian transport specialists developed ideas that presaged the future trajectory of motor haulage by road. Further investigation into the extent to which post-war thinking was influenced by these pioneers might therefore prove rewarding.

Notes

1 George W. Watson, "The Commercial Motor Exhibition," *The Brewing Trade Review*, August 1, 1913, 394. Also see: "Motor Transport for Breweries," *The Engineer* cited in *The Brewers' Journal*, December 15, 1921, 528.
2 Anon, "Motors for Brewers," *Commercial Motor*, April 13, 1905, 103. "News of the Week," *Commercial Motor*, March 16, 1905, 3.
3 Thomas Gibson, *Road Haulage by Motor: The First Forty Years* (Aldershot: Ashgate, 2001).
4 Pieter De Graef, "The Fruits of Better Roads and Waterways: Facilitating Fertiliser Improvement through Transport Innovations in 18th-Century Flemish Husbandry," *Journal of Transport History* 39, no. 2 (2018): 171.
5 Thomas Spain, "'Food Miles': Britain's Transition from Rail to Road-based Food Distribution, 1919–1975" (unpublished PhD Thesis, University of York, 2016), see introduction.
6 Terry Gourvish, *Norfolk Beers from English Barley: A History of Steward & Patteson, 1793–1963* (Norwich: Centre of East Anglian Studies, 1987); Colin C. Owen, *'The Greatest Brewery in the World': A History of Bass, Ratcliff & Gretton* (Chesterfield: Derbyshire Record Society, 1992); John Pudney, *A Draught of Contentment* (London: New English Library, 1971); Nicholas Barritt Redman, *The Story of Whitbread, 1742–1990* (unknown location: unknown publisher, c.1990–2000); Ian Webster, *Ind Coope & Samuel Allsopp Breweries: A History of the Hand* (Stroud: Amberley, 2015); Richard Wilson, *Greene King: A Business and Family History* (London: The Bodley Head & Jonathan Cape, 1983).
7 Richard Vahrenkamp, *The Logistics Revolution: The Rise of Logistics in the Mass Consumption Society*, (Cologne: Josef Eul Verlag, 2012), 1, 29–45.
8 Spain, "Food Miles," 29.
9 Paul Jennings, *The Local: A History of the English Pub* (Stroud: The History Press, 2011). David W. Gutzke, *Protecting the Pub: Brewers and Publicans Against Temperance* (London: Royal Historical Society, 1989).
10 Shane Hamilton, *Trucking Country: The Road to America's Wal-Mart Economy* (Princeton: Princeton University Press, 2008), 4–5, 12.
11 Vahrenkamp, *The Logistics Revolution*, 1, 29–45.
12 Spain, "Food Miles," 281.
13 Martin Wilcox, "Railways, Roads and the British White Fish Industry, 1920–70," *Business History* 54, no. 5 (2012): 759.
14 Spain, "Food Miles," 282.
15 Wilcox, "Railways, Roads and the British White Fish Industry," 758.
16 Spain, "Food Miles," 282–284. Peter Scott, "British Railways and the Challenge from Road Haulage: 1919–39," *Twentieth Century British History* 13, no. 2 (2002): 103.
17 Spain, "Food Miles," 148.
18 Ibid., 285.
19 Ibid., 200, 252; Scott, "British Railways," 103.
20 Anon, "Motor Vehicles for Brewers," *The Brewers' Journal*, June 15, 1907, 357.
21 Letters, bonds, receipts and notes Individual unrelated items regarding production, 1801–1893. Table showing Loads, Times of Carmen's departure and arrival, and farthest distance travelled each day, for the week ending Friday January 30, 1891. Whitbread & Co. Archive. LMA/4453/A/15/031, London Metropolitan Archive [LMA], London, United Kingdom.
22 Anon, "Motor Vehicles for Brewers," 358.
23 "Motor Traction." Truman's Monthly Report, 1902–08, May 1902, LMA/B/THB/A/121, LMA; Fred M. Maynard, "Motor Traction for Brewers"; Paper given at the Yorkshire and North Eastern Institute of Brewing, 23 February

1900, at the Queen's Hotel Leeds, *Journal of the Federated Institute of Brewing* 6, no. 3 (1900): 202.

24 This is based on Truman's own costing of £90 a horse. Truman's Monthly Report, 1902–08, April 1908 report on Horses, LMA, B/THB/A/121, LMA.

25 T.R. Gourvish and R.G. Wilson, *The British Brewing Industry, 1830–1980* (Cambridge: Cambridge University Press, 1994), 142.

26 R.V. Taylor and G.R. Burdass, "Relative Cost of Transport," Meeting of the Midland Counties section held at the Grand Hotel, Birmingham, on Thursday May 6, 1920, *Journal of the Institute of Brewing* 26, no. 8 (1920): 449.

27 Untitled, *The Brewers' Journal*, January 1920, 8.

28 Gourvish and Wilson, *The British Brewing Industry*, 147–150.

29 Wilson, *Greene King*, 136.

30 London & South Western Railway Traffic Committee Minute Book, Minute 884, 1879, RAIL 411/274. The National Archives [TNA], Kew, London, United Kingdom.

31 "Money Market and City News," *The Morning Post*, May 08, 1897, 4.

32 N.B. Redman, "Whitbread and Bottled Beer, 1869–1930," *The Brewer* (March, 1991): 108–109.

33 Gourvish and Wilson, *The British Brewing Industry*, 97, 144.

34 Ibid., 144.

35 Pudney, *A Draught of Contentment*, 25.

36 Truman, Hanbury & Buxton & Co., Carriage Ledger, January 1910, 1, LMA/B/THB/B/503, LMA.

37 Theo Barker and Dorian Gerhold, *The Rise and Rise of Road Transport, 1700–1900* (London: Macmillan, 1993), 74.

38 Gibson, *Road Haulage by Motor*, 28–29.

39 Ibid., 32–34.

40 Maynard, "Motor Traction for Brewers," 201.

41 The actual arrangements were far more complex, and determined by wheel diameter, tyre type and if a trailer was attached. Gibson, *Road Haulage by Motor*, 38–41.

42 "Motor Transport for Breweries," *The Engineer* cited in *The Brewers' Journal*, December 15, 1921, 528.

43 Watson, "The Commercial Motor Exhibition," 394.

44 Noakes & Co. Ltd Minute book, 18 June and 30 September 1903, 67 and 70, LMA, ACC 2305/12/3, LMA; For Truman: Monthly Report, 1902–08, May 1902, report on Motor Traction, LMA, B/THB/A/121, LMA.

45 Maynard, "Motor Traction for Brewers," 201.

46 Watson, "The Commercial Motor Exhibition".

47 Gourvish and Wilson, *The British Brewing Industry*, 195

48 Ibid., 133.

49 Graeme G. Acheson, Christopher Coyle and John D. Turner, "Happy Hour Followed by Hangover: Financing the UK Brewery Industry, 1880–1913," *Business History* 58, no. 5 (2016): 727.

50 Ibid., 727.

51 Ibid., 727–728.

52 House of Commons Papers, Report from the Select Committee on the Hop Industry, together with the proceedings of the committee, minutes of evidence, and appendix, 1908, iv; Gourvish and Wilson, *The British Brewing Industry*, 283–285.

53 "Railway Rates and Road Transport," *The Brewing Trade Review*, June 1, 1913, 250.

54 Maynard, "Motor Traction for Brewers," 201.

55 "The Commercial Use of Highways," *Commercial Motor*, February 13, 1908, 565.

56 Anon, "Motors for Brewers".

57 "The Commercial Use of Highways," 565.
58 Anon, "Motors for Brewers," 105.
59 Gourvish and Wilson, *The British Brewing Industry*, 302–303.
60 Anon, "Motors for Brewers," 100.
61 "News and Comment," *Commercial Motor*, July 8, 1909, 372.
62 Anon, "Motor Vehicles for Brewers," 357–358.
63 Watson, "The Commercial Motor Exhibition," 397.
64 Gourvish and Wilson, *The British Brewing Industry*, 130.
65 *Brewers' Almanack*, 1895, cited in R.G. Wilson, "Changing Tastes in Victorian Britain," in *The Dynamics of the International Brewing Industry Since 1800*, eds. R.G. Wilson and T.R. Gourvish (London: Routledge, 1998), 101–102.
66 Wilson, "Changing Tastes," 96. House of Commons Papers, Departmental Committee on Beer Materials: Report, Minutes of Evidence, Appendices, Evidence of Dr G.H. Morris, October 15, 1896, 488 and 489; Evidence of Mr J.B. Kibble, October 22, 96, 772 and 773.
67 House of Commons Papers, Report from the Select Committee on the Hop Industry, together with the proceedings of the committee, minutes of evidence, and appendix, 1908, iv, 240; House of Commons Papers, Department Committee on Beer Materials: Report, Minutes of Evidence, Appendices, Evidence of Dr G.H. Morris, October 15, 1896, 368; evidence of Mr P Schidrowitz, February 17, 1898, 3906.
68 Gourvish and Wilson, *The British Brewing Industry*, Chapter 4.
69 "Railway Rates and Road Transport," 250.
70 Maynard, "Motor Traction for Brewers," 201. Anon, "Motor Vehicles for Brewers," 357.
71 Anon, "Motors for Brewers," 103.
72 Anon, "Motor Vehicles for Brewers," 357.
73 Maynard, "Motor Traction for Brewers," 201.
74 Whitbread General Ledgers 4, 5 and 6, Cooper accounts, LMA/4453/B/08/011-013, LMA.
75 Anon, "Motors for Brewers," 103; "An Expensive Drink," editorial, *Sheffield Daily Telegraph*, May 3, 1901; "Stealing a Barrel of Beer," *Manchester Courier and Lancashire General Advertiser*, July 17, 1908.
76 Midland Railway District Goods Managers Unnumbered Circulars, May 12, 1914, Ref: 503/05/05, Midland Railway Centre [MRC], Derby, United Kingdom.
77 Superintendent of the Line Circulars, April 14, 1902, Ref: 502/03/03, MRC,
78 Brian McCarthy, "Wagon Link, 1: Ale Truck," *Great Eastern Railway Journal* 69 (January 1992): 20.
79 "Railway Rates and Road Transport," 250.
80 "Big Savings over Railway Transport," *Commercial Motor*, February 24, 1910, 545.
81 Maynard, "Motor Traction for Brewers," 201.
82 "Runs on Brewers' Petrol and Steam Wagons," *Commercial Motor*, May 29, 1913, 287.
83 "Railway Rates and Road Transport," 250.
84 "Drayman Pulled from his Seat," *Derby Daily Telegraph*, August 19, 1911, 2.
85 Watson, "Motor Transport and the Brewing Industry," 190–191. Also see "Edinburgh United Breweries," *Dundee Courier*, December 29, 1914, 6.
86 Spain, "Food Miles," 282–284; Redman, "Whitbread and Bottled Beer," 111
87 Philip Bagwell and Peter Lyth, *Transport in Britain: From Canal Lock to Gridlock* (London: Hambledon and London, 2002), 69.
88 Michael Seth-Smith, *The Long Haul* (London: Hutchinson, 1975), 80.
89 "The Death-Knell of British Railways," *The Review of Reviews*, September 1912, 280.
90 Robert Coates, *Pulling Pints – Brewery Vehicles Past, Present, Future* (London: Fitzjames Press, 1993), 37.

91 "Thornycroft's Order Book," *The Commercial Motor,* July 25, 1912, 471.
92 Walter Pearce Sercold, *The Story of Watneys* (London: Watney Combe Reid & Co, 1949), 44.
93 P.J. Cain, "Traders versus Railways the Genesis of the Railway and Canal Traffic Act of 1894," *The Journal of Transport History,* New Series, 2, no. 2 (September 1973).
94 The class rate – laid down by the companies' Provisional Orders – remained unchanged, yet the special rate usually charged for sending beer increased. "The Increase in Railway Rates," *The Brewers' Journal,* January 15, 1914, 12.
95 "Railway Rates and Road Transport," 250.
96 "Marston, Thompson and Evershed," *Birmingham Daily Post,* May 28, 1914, 10.
97 LMA, ACC/2305/01/0135, Barclay Perkins Board Minute Books, June 6, 1913, 3.
98 "Railway Rates and Road Transport," 250.
99 Ibid., 250.
100 J. Beardmore, "The Construction of a Brewery," *The Journal of the Society of Architects* 9, no. 107 (September 1916): 227.
101 Bennison, "The Brewing Trade," 153–154.
102 Motor Transport for Breweries," *The Engineer* cited in *The Brewers' Journal,* December 15, 1921, 528.
103 Spain, "Food Miles."

Bibliography

Primary sources

House of Commons Papers, Departmental Committee on Beer Materials: Report, Minutes of Evidence. London: HMSO, 1899.
House of Commons Papers, Report from the Select Committee on the Hop Industry, together with the proceedings of the committee, minutes of evidence, and appendix. London: HMSO, 1908.

Secondary sources

Acheson, Graeme G., Christopher Coyle, and John D. Turner. "Happy Hour Followed by Hangover: Financing the UK Brewery Industry, 1880–1913." *Business History* 58, no. 5 (2016): 725–751.
Barker, Theo, and Dorian Gerhold. *The Rise and Rise of Road Transport, 1700–1900.* London: Macmillan, 1993.
Bagwell, Philip, and Peter Lyth. *Transport in Britain: From Canal Lock to Gridlock.* London: Hambledon and London, 2002.
Cain, P.J. "Traders versus Railways the Genesis of the Railway and Canal Traffic Act of 1894." *The Journal of Transport History,* New Series, 2, no. 2 (September 1973): 65–84.
Coates, Robert. *Pulling Pints – Brewery Vehicles Past, Present, Future.* London: Fitzjames Press, 1993.
De Graef, Pieter. "The Fruits of Better Roads and Waterways: Facilitating Fertiliser Improvement through Transport Innovations in 18th-Century Flemish Husbandry." *Journal of Transport History* 39, no. 2 (2018): 170–192.
Hamilton, Shane. *Trucking Country: The Road to America's Wal-Mart Economy.* Princeton: Princeton University Press, 2008.
Gibson, Thomas. *Road Haulage by Motor: The First Forty Years.* Aldershot: Ashgate, 2001.

Gourvish, Terry. *Norfolk Beers from English Barley: A History of Steward & Patteson, 1793–1963.* Norwich: Centre of East Anglian Studies, 1987.

Gourvish, T.R., and R.G. Wilson, *The British Brewing Industry, 1830–1980.* Cambridge: Cambridge University Press, 1994.

Gutzke, David W. *Protecting the Pub: Brewers and Publicans Against Temperance.* London: Royal Historical Society, 1989.

Jennings, Paul. *The Local: A History of the English Pub.* Stroud: The History Press, 2011.

McCarthy, Brian. "Wagon Link, 1: Ale Truck." *Great Eastern Railway Journal* 69 (January 1992): 20.

Owen, Colin C. *'The Greatest Brewery in the World': A History of Bass, Ratcliff & Gretton.* Chesterfield: Derbyshire Record Society, 1992.

Pudney, John. *A Draught of Contentment.* London: New English Library, 1971.

Redman, Nicholas Barritt. *The Story of Whitbread, 1742–1990.* Unknown Publisher: Unknown Location, c.1990–2000.

———. "Whitbread and Bottled Beer, 1869–1930." *The Brewer* (March, 1991): 106–113.

Scott, Peter. "British Railways and the Challenge from Road Haulage: 1919–39." *Twentieth Century British History* 13, no. 2 (2002): 101–120.

Sercold, Walter Pearce. *The Story of Watneys.* London: Watney Combe Reid & Co, 1949.

Seth-Smith, Michael. *The Long Haul.* London: Hutchinson, 1975.

Spain, Thomas. "'Food Miles': Britain's Transition from Rail to Road-based Food Distribution, 1919–1975." Unpublished PhD thesis, University of York, 2016.

Vahrenkamp, Richard. *The Logistics Revolution: The Rise of Logistics in the Mass Consumption Society.* Cologne: Josef Eul Verlag, 2012.

Webster, Ian. *Ind Coope & Samuel Allsopp Breweries: A History of the Hand.* Stroud: Amberley, 2015.

Wilcox, Martin. "Railways, Roads and the British White Fish Industry, 1920–70." *Business History* 54, no. 5 (2012): 741–764.

Wilson, Richard G. "Changing Tastes in Victorian Britain." In *The Dynamics of the International Brewing Industry Since 1800*, edited by R.G. Wilson and T.R. Gourvish, 93–104. London: Routledge, 1998.

———. *Greene King: A Business and Family History.* London: The Bodley Head & Jonathan Cape, 1983.

Contemporary Newspapers and Periodicals

Birmingham Daily Post
The Brewers' Journal
The Brewing Trade Review
Commercial Motor
Derby Daily Telegraph
Dundee Courier
Journal of the Institute of Brewing
Journal of the Federated Institute of Brewing
The Journal of the Society of Architects
Sheffield Daily Telegraph
The Review of Reviews

Part 2
Cultures of transport

5 Maintaining the connections

A social and cultural history of the permanent way

Oliver Betts

"If social reformers desire to see how slums are created I will show them one created in what was a few years ago a pretty suburban district, the creator being the railway company uncontrolled by a sanitary authority" thundered one bitter letter writer to the Editor of *The Times* in October 1890. It had not been the first written by the author who went by the pen-name Deux Etoiles – she or he had repeatedly lambasted the Lambeth health authority and the railway companies in the letters page prior to this latest outburst. The ill-condition of the Loughborough Junction railway arches in the district, "which were used as depots for filth", thoroughly unsettled Deux Etoiles, and she/he was not alone.[1] Throughout the roughly 80 years between the explosion of the railway mania in the 1840s and the high-point of Railway Grouping in the early 1920s that saw corporate responsibilities and government involvements shift, letters, pamphlets, reports, articles, petitions, investigations, and debates all cited the contagious, dangerous, and dirty condition of the railways in the growing metropolitan hubs of the British mainland. Deux Etoiles, whoever he or she was, was in no way exceptional in his or her indignant rage and its subject was not the rushing engines of the railway but the tracks and viaducts, the bridges and cuttings, the depots and sidings.

Strictly speaking the permanent way refers to the track itself, the 'finished roadbed of a railway' the Oxford English Dictionary maintains, 'distinguished from a contractor's temporary work'.[2] The term seems to have originated with the coming of the railways in the 1820s and 1830s, but was rapidly absorbed into a common parlance by the Victorians to refer to the infrastructure of the railways more generally. Depending on who one asked, by the middle of the nineteenth century the term permanent way could refer to the landscape of the railways that was growing rapidly across Britain in the period, that tangle of places and spaces that Deux Etoiles found intolerably dirty.

Much like the officials of the nascent Permanent Way Institution observed, when holding their first Annual General Meeting in London in 1887, the landscape of the railways, always vital to the effective running of a safe and profitable system, has been often over-looked and under-valued.[3] It has always been a peripheral focus in historical studies of the railways in Britain, particularly from a cultural perspective. Yet there has been little in the way of social or cultural study of the track, despite its long and significant presence in British culture of the time. Chapters in dedicated histories of the Victorian railways, such as Jack Simmons's *The Victorian Railway* or the more recent and popular *The Railways: Nation, Network and People* by Simon Bradley, address the landscape of the railways in primarily infrastructural terms.[4] Andrew Dow's thoroughly researched *The Railway: British Track since 1804* offers a detailed technological history of the permanent way.[5] The work of those who created the landscapes at the dawn of the railway age, both the navvy labourers and the major engineers, has been explored before, as has the wider social-cultural impact of the "Railway Mania" of construction.[6] Michael Freeman argues that the work of early artists recording this burst of construction, and especially the watercolours and line drawings of J.C. Bourne, constituted 'a distinctive iconography of the railway' from the 1840s 'centred on the railway's static structures as distinct from the trains that ran on it'.[7] 'The years 1831–1850 form the brief classical moment in British railway art' Simmons concurs, where images of sweeping bridges and cuttings in-progress formed a popular genre of artistic reflection on railway construction.[8] But the railway infrastructure of the second half of the nineteenth century, a time where it has been argued British people became increasingly accustomed to this new technological innovation, has received far less attention.

The permanent way did, however, continue to elicit social commentary and cultural influence in the later half of the Victorian period. Indeed, as this chapter will show, a concentration on the landscape of the railways and how it filtered into social and cultural discourse provides an interesting contrast to the focus on the speed, light, and mobility of this new technological age. Focusing instead on the permanent way, a landscape often neglected and filled with more troubling associations and emotions, raises questions about who experienced the railways and how in the late nineteenth century.

Thinking about the permanent way

It is perhaps ironic that the permanent way should be so critically absent from studies of the railways place in culture and society in Victorian Britain considering that the most accessible and publicly celebrated book on the railways invoked the track itself in its title. Frederick Smeeton Williams, a Congregational minister, first published *Our Iron Roads: Their History, Construction, and Social Influences* in 1852.[9] *The Morning Post* enthused over the first edition – which it felt contained 'much…matter well worthy of quotation' and dedicated many column inches to – and subsequent editions drew excited comment from reviewers in many British periodicals and newspapers.[10] *The Sheffield Independent,* reviewing the fifth edition (1884), reflected it had only recently finished a previous edition and 'the demand for it justifies all we said about it at the time'.[11] By the end of the century Williams was acknowledged as a leading expert on British railways and *Our Iron Roads* was still being held up as a key text for understanding the railway system that dominated everyday transport for his contemporaries.[12]

Although the permanent way appeared throughout *Our Iron Roads* it received most direct treatment in a dedicated chapter. Here, Williams set it within a context of pre-steam tramways in the North East, told the reader in great detail about the difference between gauges and the competition over them that dominated the early railway scene, and illustrated tentative ways in which sleepers might be arranged to best effect. Yet inevitably the text gave way to a journey – the culmination of the effort of the thousands of gangers who had to walk each length of track 'every morning and evening' as Williams noted – as Williams depicted a trial journey on a new Midland Railway line about to be opened to the public.[13] As Wolfgang Schivelbusch has emphasised, the railway was about time and space in the nineteenth-century and for Williams and his readers the natural progression was from the static landscape to one of movement – from the track to the train.[14]

Following this logical progression too quickly, however, neglects the fact that the track over which the train rumbled was a significant mediated space in the period. Nowhere is this more evident than in the increasing focus paid to fencing-in and securing the railway track against trespass. From at least the 1860s onwards, and quite possibly earlier on some lines, railways went to great efforts to isolate the track from the public. In many cases this was a mixture of pragmatism, government insistence and property safe-guarding. Even before the proliferation of steam engines, the plate-ways of the horse-drawn railways had been a place of dreadful danger. Humans and, far more often, animals were run down with frightening regularity and this continued apace from the 1830s onwards. The 1830s *Wallis's Locomotive Game of Railroad Adventures* included a number of startling incidents featuring the player's train hitting a variety of livestock that had wandered onto the track. Safety, and to a lesser extent the threat of having to pay the compensation resulting from accidents, helped encourage companies to safeguard their track with embankments and fencing and by mid-century large sections of the permanent way were out-of-bounds to the public.

This prohibition against trespass, however, did not stop the Victorian public interacting with the permanent way in many different forms. Companies had to regularly take those found wandering or intruding on the track to court, seeking fines and, in cases of re-offense, custodial sentences. James Milray, found walking along the track by the Station Master at Thelkeld, Cumbria, in 1865 was fined 10 shillings and further court costs, and a few years later an 1868 Act enshrined fines of up to 40 shillings levied on those who 'shall be or pass upon any Railway...after having received Warning by the Company which works such Railway'.[15] Yet perusing the railway-related cases brought to the Old Bailey in the second half of the nineteenth century reveals that a steady stream of people, particularly children, continued to violate these rules. Each year a couple of cases were brought before the Old Bailey of children caught placing objects, often bricks, wood, stones or other debris, on the track or otherwise pelting passing trains with them. Notices posted, it seems, had little effect on preventing this. During the trial of two teenaged stone-throwers there was dispute between the accused and a third friend-turned-witness. 'I told them not to throw stones, or they would be fined 40s' swore 14-year-old Walter Harvey. '...you never mentioned about 40s' shot back one of the accused, 15 year old George Gray, adding 'it was you who began to throw'.[16] Some children had no idea of the severity of what they were doing, and others were repeat offenders, but all of those brought in by police or railway watchmen had been caught red-handed, more-or-less, in the vicinity of the permanent way. In an attempt to dissuade trespass, some London railways took to posting records of those caught and the resultant whippings, fines and hard labour they received.[17] Whether deliberate subversions of adult authority – echoing Howard Chudacoff's work on children seeking out their own play spaces in the nineteenth-century city – or not, this small but persistent infringement on the permanent way indicates just how its presence in a city made it a space that people felt drawn to.[18]

For some visiting the permanent way was an act of artistic or cultural discovery – an act of illicit intrusion into a world increasingly sectioned-off from public access. Nesbit walked the track of the railway near Chesfield in South East London, stepping on the sleepers as the *Railway Children* later did.[19] Reverend Edward Munro, who in 1857 urged fellow clergymen to minister to railway labourers in a pamphlet, described his first meeting with them as he walked down to the line under construction running through his parish and saw their camp fires.[20] Stepping into the landscape of railway work, it seemed, was how to encounter those men who held the key to understanding the network and its secrets. Perhaps the best example of this is Charles Dickens's *The Signal-Man*. Published first in 1866, as part of *Mugby Junction, The Signal-Man* has been oft-included in ghostly anthologies.[21] Norris Pope has pointed out that it evoked for Dickens's mid-Victorian readers a vision of the network they travelled on as high-speed and complex, demanding more and more oversight from skilled workers.[22] It was also a short story profoundly influenced by the railway accidents he both read about and experienced.[23] More than anything else, it depicted one worker caught up in what Munro earlier referred to as the 'large and rough-scale' world of public works.[24]

The landscape of the permanent way intrudes into *The Signal-Man* from the outset, unnerving and alien yet at the same time familiar to the anonymous narrator. Slippering down the slope, down a path of 'clammy stone' that became 'oozier and wetter' as he descended, the narrator moves from the public space above down into the cutting itself. It is an industrial landscape from the start – one where he needs to call out to the Signalman below for help to even enter safely. What he discovers though, pondering on whether the Signalman ever receives visitors or not, is a world beyond what he expected. The man has taught himself a language down here 'if only to know it by sight' and 'worked at fractions and decimals and tried a little algebra'. Amid the iron handles and changing lights that comprised the mechanical portion of his job, the Signalman was at home in his box in a way that Dickens's narrator could observe but not entirely understand.[25]

Yet the narrator is not wholly uninitiated in the ways of the railway. After the Signalman reveals the supernatural apparitions that have been haunting him, the narrator agonizes over whether to report him to his superiors.

> I had proved the man to be intelligent, vigilant, painstaking, and exact; but how long might he remain so, in his state of mind? Though in a subordinate position, still he held a most important trust, and would I (for instance) like to stake my own life on the chances of his continuing to execute it with precision?[26]

The dilemma faced by the narrator, whether to report this otherwise seemingly stable railway worker or allow him to continue and risk terrible calamity, offers an insight into the wider public understanding of the network at the time. Dickens, as noted, had personal experience of the terrible nature of railway accidents – workers replacing rails working from an erroneous timetable had caused the derailment at Staplehurst the year before publication.

His Victorian readers would have been just as familiar. They might have seen accidents depicted, often graphically, on the stage, or read about them in newspapers with detailed illustrations to accompany the textual descriptions of carnage.[27] Newspapers carried the records of inquests and investigations, attempting to convey the reason behind these new mechanical forms of devastation, and the public in turn wrote in to offer their opinions. The railway accident at Thirsk in 1892, for example, drew thick column inches from regional and national newspapers as the relative responsibility of a signalman who had fallen asleep at his station was debated against that of the company that employed him.[28] Letters to Editors repeatedly invoked perceived causes of blame – one anonymous member of the public wrote to *The Times* in 1878 to complain about 'the most reprehensible practice of not slackening speed on trains passing stations' which they felt had been the root cause of a recent accident at Chester.[29] Although few would have understood the nature of the mechanical process of signalling in more detail than Dickens's narrator did, many would have sympathised with the informed horror that came from realising that this man plagued by visions and lack of sleep, who feared ghostly premonitions of death from the black mouth of the tunnel he guarded with his signal lamp, held the potential for calamitous accident in his trembling hands.

Working knowledge and the Victorian railway

The signalman was a figure both known and, at the same time, unknowable for his Victorian contemporaries. Williams dedicated several pages to him, mixed in amongst accounts of other workers one might encounter at a Station, but largely restricted his description to explaining the duties of the signalman and not *how* he performed them.[30] Stories, fictional or real, in periodicals of the period repeatedly emphasised the vital role of the signalman but rarely went into the mechanical detail of his profession. Amid 'the levers and the usual complicated electric and mechanical contrivances' of the signal box they were frequently depicted as living conduits of information.[31] Although uniformed like many railway workers, they were probably the least visible of those who worked on or near the permanent way given the relative seclusion those signal boxes not in immediate proximity to stations, and their roles less understood.[32] The outpouring of interest in the operation of the railways, and accidents in particular, proved that the reading and travelling public were interested in the overall function of figures such as the signalman, though, and imbued him with the technical significance of his work.

Signalmen were, moreover, active in promulgating this view of themselves as skilled, mechanical, workers. It was a role that had developed by mid-century, shifting away from a broader function as trackside point operators and policemen into the more specialised work of operating mechanical signals from a box often elevated above the permanent way. Working in a changing atmosphere of labour, where the definition of skilled work was shifting in response to patterns in technology and working practices, signalmen were keen to portray their industry as a skilled one in a fight for better conditions.[33] At a large meeting of signalmen near Waterloo in 1865, reported in the local press, those present defined themselves as 'a body of men upon whom so much responsibility rested, and in whose hands were entrusted the lives of an immense number of the community day after day, and enormous masses of property'; by 1880 a more formal, dedicated, union, the United Pointsmen's and Signalmen's Society, had been established to represent this new professional identity.[34] Encumbered by long hours of work, often with no excess or overtime pay and terribly thin relief arrangements, signallers struggled to get the railway companies to remunerate their vital work to the level they saw fit.[35] Cases such as the Thirsk accident, mentioned above, however, did ensure that both their claims to skill and the vital significance of their work kept signallers in the public discourse on railways.

What this meant, in practice, was that the public understanding of the role of the signalman and the railway signal network were intertwined as a man-machine ensemble. Part of a wider cultural motif that associated the railway with the telegraph network that ran alongside it, this blended worker and task into an embodiment of vital connectivity. It was also emphasised as a place of rugged masculinity, despite the not insignificant number of women who worked with signals and level-crossings on mainly rural rail lines.[36] Fuelled by the awareness of the long hours and tough trackside conditions faced by signallers, depictions of signallers in Victorian fiction increasingly emphasised their heroic sacrifice in the harsh physical environment of the railway's permanent way. Young Job, the youthful hero of a short story in children's magazine *Young Folks*, for example, is caught between the necessity of reviving his father (passed out from a faulty stove in the signalbox) and performing his duties at the levers and preventing an accident on the line. Choosing the greater good, young Job seizes a lever at random and pulls, somehow replicating the skill of his unconscious father and changing the points at the last minute. Although a typical brave-boy-saves-the-day narrative common across periodicals like *Young Folks,* the story does dwell repeatedly, and at the end especially, on the potential calamity this brief lapse in oversight from the unconscious father threatened.[37] Even darker stories, such as *Saved by a Ghost: A Mystery of the Iron Road* that appeared in *Illustrated Chips* in 1898, were fixated upon the signalman as the figure who knew the ins-and-outs of the permanent way. John Pym, a signaller haunted by his accidental murder of a colleague and love-rival, has been contracted by a criminal gang to wreck the night mail-train near his box by altering the points at the crucial moment. Yet, before this can happen, a ghostly apparition appears to stalk the rails outside and shocks a guilt-ridden Pym so severely that he collapses dead in the box. The lever clicks back, whether improperly set by Pym or, perhaps, released by the ghostly hand of his fellow murdered signalman and the mail train sails by unscathed.[38] In both cases the connection between the signalman's experience, the levers and points of his trade, and the potential of impending mechanical catastrophe were tied together as a natural whole. He was the system of railway signals – it was his skill that prevented calamity on the permanent way. Stories like these repeatedly emphasised the permanent way as a place where only skilled workers, schooled in the industrial secrets of the railway, could safely tread.

New perspectives

If the track bed itself was a place the public were increasingly distanced from, an otherworld created by the rules and regulations of the railway companies and reinforced in the thrilling encounters, ghostly or otherwise, of the periodical press, this was not the case for the entirety of the permanent way. The varied nature of railway construction, as companies sought out potential routes and wrestled with the political, technical, and economic challenges of building them, afforded a range of views and experiences for the railway passenger. In 1876 the literary pages of British newspapers and journals trilled in delight over the latest edition of Gustave Doré and Blanchard Jerrold's *London: A Pilgrimage* or, more specifically, the included image 'Over London by Rail'. The memorable vista of repetitive smoky chimneys, backyards with limp washing lines, and endless terraced housing curving away towards a railway viaduct with a steaming locomotive captured the imagination of reviewers. 'A wonderful picture of that part of London which country visitors don't always see, but which they ought to see' mused

The Western Times, whilst *The Glasgow Herald* deemed it 'full of the weird power' of Doré's 'unrivalled mastery of light and shade'.[39] Yet the *Worcestershire Chronicle's* review was perhaps most interesting. 'Over London by Rail...[is]...full of suggestive exhibitions of *Low* Lifery, as viewed from the high lifery of the predominant railway, showing to the half of the world above how the other half is living below', it surmised.[40] All seen through the arch of a second viaduct from a viewpoint positioned on a possible third, it was an image that emphasised the powerful visuals of society that the railways revealed.

It was not the first appreciation of the elevated vision of society afforded by the new structures of the railway landscape. As early as 1844 Frederick Engels, in his searing indictment of *The Condition of the Working Class in England,* described the 'repulsive' cottages and cellar-dwellings of Stockport viewed from the vantage point of the viaduct. It was 'renowned as one of the duskiest, smokiest holes' in the area, he noted, and 'when viewed from the viaduct, excessively repellent'.[41] Stimulating his imagination, the viaduct afforded Engels an almost x-ray like vision into the crowded cellars given over to housing in this industrial slum that would not, in reality, have been visible from the track. Part of a broader appreciation and examination of the modern city, Engels's text should be understood in a wider genre of exploratory and reforming "overviews" such as Hector Gavin's celebrated *Sanitary Ramblings* around Bethnal Green in 1848, but is also indicative of the new ways of seeing and thinking encouraged by the super-structures of the railway.[42] The suicide of Ferdinand Lopez, in Anthony Trollope's 1876 *The Prime Minister,* offers a darker example of where these new lines of sight might take one. Fictional Tenway Junction is a place of criss-crossing lines, 'pandemoniac noises', and 'doubtful, uneasy and bewildered' men and women having to place their safety in the hands of railway officialdom.[43] One of these officials almost prevents Lopez from killing himself, warning him off and then finally rushing at him when he recognises his purpose, but Lopez is too quick.

> Lopez turned round and looked at it, and again walked towards the edge of the platform. But now it was not exactly the edge that he neared, but a descent to a pathway, —an inclined plane leading down to the level of the rails, and made there for certain purposes of traffic...With quick, but still with gentle and apparently unhurried steps, he walked down before the flying engine—and in a moment had been knocked into bloody atoms.[44]

The vantage point of the platform, here, allows Lopez to consider his approach and time his moment before descending onto the tracks to his certain oblivion. 'The more the land is covered in railroads' argued Émile Durkheim, the father of the modern study of suicide, 'the more general becomes the habit of seeking death by throwing oneself under a train'.[45]

Railway suicides were never more than a small minority of cases of self-destruction in the Victorian age; as Olive Anderson observes despite rising in number and as percentage of overall means of suicide, by 1909 they comprised only 5.8% of male and 3% of female suicides.[46] They remained, however, culturally significant in the Victorian zeitgeist. Covered in colourful detail by a press already interested in the sensational depiction of suicide they presented the permanent way as a place of terrible destruction, a landscape into which it was easy to enter seeking death. For nineteenth-century writers and artists, and their audiences, the structures of the permanent way afforded thrilling and terrifying new viewpoints from which to consider the condition of others or of one's self.

Day-to-day experiences

This was, of course, the work of writers and contemplators – what of the regular traveller – those thousands of season-ticket holders, for instance, that Charles Booth recorded flocking into the capital from South London by rail in silk-hatted shoals?[47] They certainly appreciated the fixed landscape of the railway they travelled over when it intruded into their journey. In the late 1850s Rotherhithe's Vestry was swamped, or at least it claimed, by complaints from travellers. The viaduct smelt – noxious fumes and vapours percolating up into the carriages as trains rumbled slowly over it. The railway company, perhaps typically, demurred – they had rented out the spaces but it was not their responsibility to ensure their occupants were not a nuisance. So it fell to Medical Officer of Health William Murdoch to investigate. Over several years he visited the railway arches and discovered the sources of the smells.

> During the past month they have been frequently visited by the Inspector of Nuisances and myself. All sorts of filthy substances are accumulated under them, bones, horns, hoofs, pigeon's dung, fish and hair with the animal matter adhering to it, just as it is scraped off the hides by the tanners, and the heaps of these substances smell very disagreeably, and when in the process of manufacture of manure, sulphuric acid is poured upon them and powdered coprolite, an indescribably suffocative stench arises.[48]

It took him several months of action and reporting back, including having to take the entire vestry on a tour of the offensive premises, before he was able to effect change by summoning the proprietors of these businesses to court and threatening prosecution.

The steady corruption of the railway arches was not an inevitable part of the Victorian urban landscape. There had been hopes, in the early period of the railway mania, of purposing them in much more "useful" directions. In the 1840s, there had been an experimental scheme to place houses into the arches of the Greenwich viaduct, covered by the *Illustrated London News,* which had ultimately failed to impress investors because of the pervasive trickle-down damp from the ballast above. The idea continued on, however, that these spaces could be rendered useful in the high-pressure urban landscape. In 1866 Mr Barrow Emmanuel, Civil Engineer, presented a paper at the National Association for the Promotion of Social Science conference in which he called for the utilisation of railway arches for private dwellings. The housing crisis in Britain's big cities had inspired him to make the suggestion, he noted, and he cited the growing number of philanthropic building projects as his inspiration. The paper itself is a curious mixture of reassurance (the experience of those few already living in railway arches, he reassured listeners, was that the constant rumble of trains overhead became little more than background noise after a while) and specific detail (the best way to ensure chimney smoke did not blow into carriages above would be combination chimneys raised up high above the line of traffic itself), but ends with a clear vision of who exactly would be occupying these dwellings.[49] This was a Labourer's Dwellings scheme, Emmanuel insisted, and the *Railway News* agreed.[50] The sheer number of working people needed in the capital, those who could not afford the suburban cottages and workmen's fares of the expanding network, would find homes here, the paper reported, while the better-off rumbled overhead on their own way to the city. In building these homes, moreover, the undesirable businesses and workshops would be swept aside and the spaces rendered, at least in the eyes of urban reformers, more objectively useful.

Such suggestions remained, however, suggestions. Railway arches continued to be used for primarily industrial storage purposes. The goods cargo of the Victorian railway, which well into the twentieth century was the staple earner of the British network with passenger ticket sales a distant second-place, required warehousing and storage, led to spills and run-offs, generated waste, and, perhaps most importantly in a pest-sense, smells and trails. All of which drew in rats. Whereas noxious fumes in viaduct arches could be farmed out to another, the railway companies took the financial threat of rats seriously. Rat-catchers, animal and human, were in constant employ across the network. Night-time was key, part of that larger nocturnal toilette that Joachim Schlor has seen dominate the night-time city in the late nineteenth and early twentieth centuries, but the relentless rhythm of the railway demanded this battle continue around the clock.[51] Station cats were vital, even being placed on the company payrolls during the Second World War when the preservation of foodstocks became an issue of national importance, but human rat-catchers were employed throughout the day and night as well. Ike Matthews, looking back on a 25 year career in rat-catching, recalled the social shock of producing his cage of live rats when travelling third class but also remembered hunting the animals out from the very track itself as engines thundered by.[52] Rats could represent a danger not only to freight profits but also to the very operation of the railways, chewing threw signal cables and vacuum tubing and rendering the network unsafe. Yet while there was an obvious awareness of the unsanitary nature of rats, for the companies themselves it was the financial and logistical implications that compelled the fight against them, the very same subordination of health concerns that led them to neglect the conditions of the railway arches that proved such fertile breeding grounds for the animals.

The neglect of the railway arch stood in sharp contrast to the attention companies paid, or rather were forced to pay, to stations. The front of their business operations, the stations of the Victorian railway companies were by far the most commonly mentioned feature of the railway landscape when it came to the letters pages of newspapers. Commenters were rarely complementary. 'Ludgate Hill Station is dark and exceedingly dirty throughout' grumbled one letter from 1871 signed "a daily traveller".[53] Like railway carriages, stations were not barred off from public access and, in contrast to the rest of the permanent way, they were an important space of mediation where the public was sold, as Schivelbusch argues, on the idea of rushing modernity represented by the railway.[54] Unlike the arches and viaducts, track bed and signal boxes of the railway landscape, stations were designed to intrude on the public consciousness.

Conclusion

In his recent history of the railways, Simon Bradley began his chapter on the permanent way by reflecting that the typical 'clickety-clack' rhythm still regularly used in depictions of railways on screen and radio is actually an archaism.[55] Since the advent of continuously welded track the soundscape of wheel-on-rail has changed, yet the well-known rhythm of regularly passing over the joined rail sections that preceded the new system retains a remarkable cultural staying-power. The reality of the permanent way is ignored by those unaware of the technological shift.

This story of general ignorance and neglect is, essentially, the story of the permanent way in British society and culture. As this chapter has shown the permanent way intruded, like the noxious smells of the Rotherhithe arches, into Victorian life in varying forms and intensities. Yet the growing fencing off, both physically and legally, by the railway companies and the corresponding belief that this was, more and more, a space only safely traversed by a knowledgeable few, compartmentalised the permanent way. Whilst the sheer size of the network was a cultural motif, represented in everything from maps to boardgames, when it came to the symbol of the railways in the popular imagination it was always the train and, most likely, the locomotive especially. The permanent way was a marginal space both in terms of public access and public imagination but, as this chapter has attempted to show, this does not mean it was an unimportant one. Increasingly demarcated as an industrial landscape, the study of it sheds light on some of the darker and more troubling relationships between railway, culture, and society in the nineteenth century.

Notes

1 Deux Etoiles, "Offensive Smells in London – To the Editor of the Times," *The Times*, October 22, 1890, 13.
2 "permanent way, n.". OED Online. December 2018. Oxford University Press. www.oed.com/view/Entry/240547?redirectedFrom=permanent+way (accessed January 16, 2019).
3 *Journal of the Permanent Way Institution* 1 (1887): 14–15.
4 Jack Simmons, *The Victorian Railway* (London: Thames and Hudson, 1991), 19–48. Simon Bradley, *The Railways: Nation, Network, and People* (London: Profile Books, 2015), 257–290.
5 Andrew Dow, *The Railway: British Track since 1804* (Barnsley: Pen and Sword), 2014; Simmons, *The Victorian Railway.*
6 Especially of note here is Terry Coleman's seminal text. Terry Coleman, *The Railway Navvies* (London: Pelican, 1972).
7 Michael Freeman, *Railways and the Victorian Imagination* (New Haven: Yale University Press, 1999), 230.
8 Simmons, *The Victorian Railway*, 122–126.
9 F.S. Williams, *Our Iron Roads: Their History, Construction and Administration* (London: Bemrose and Sons, 1883).
10 "Literature," *Morning Post*, August 31, 1852, 7.
11 "Literary Notes," *Sheffield Independent,* October 23, 1884, 8.
12 E. Carlyle, "Williams, Frederick Smeeton (1829–1886), Congregational Minister and Railway Historian." *Oxford Dictionary of National Biography*, accessed August 8, 2018, www.oxforddnb.com/view/10.1093/ref:odnb/9780198614128.001.0001/odnb-9780198614128-e-29503.
13 Williams, *Our Iron Roads*, 227–249.
14 Wolfgang Schivelbusch, *The Railway Journey: The Industrialisation of Time and Space in the 19th Century* (Leamington Spa: Berg, 1986), 177.
15 "A Railway Trespasser," *Whitehaven News*, May 4, 1865, 8. UK Government, "Regulation of Railways Act 1868," Clause 23, 1166, legislation.gov.uk www.legislation.gov.uk/ukpga/1868/119/pdfs/ukpga_18680119_en.pdf
16 "Trial of George Gray and John Parker" July 6, 1868, *Old Bailey Proceedings Online*, accessed January 9, 2019, www.oldbaileyonline.org/browse.jsp?name=18680706.
17 London Bridge Terminus Notice, 1983-8831, collections of the National Railway Museum, York, United Kingdom.
18 Howard Chudacoff, *Children at Play: An American History* (New York: New York University Press, 2008), 16–17.
19 Julia Briggs, *A Woman of Passion: The Life of E. Nesbit 1858–1924* (New York: The Meredith Press, 1987), 33.
20 Edward Munro, *The "Navvies" and How to Meet Them: A Letter to a Friend* (London: Joseph Masters, 1857), 3–4.
21 Ian Carter, *Railways and Culture in Britain* (Manchester: Manchester University Press, 2001), 73.
22 Norris Pope, "Dickens's "The Signalman" and Information Problems in the Railway Age," *Technology and Culture* 42, no. 3 (2001): 437–438.
23 Pope, "Dickens's "The Signalman"," 441–444; Simmons, *The Victorian Railway*, 199–201.
24 Munro, *The "Navvies,"* 3.
25 Charles Dickens, "The Signal-Man," in *Christmas Stories*, ed. Charles Dickens (London: Chapman and Hall, 1894), 312–313.
26 Dickens, "The Signal-Man," 320.

27 Nicholas Daly, "Blood on the Tracks: Sensation Drama, the Railway, and the Dark Face of Modernity," *Victorian Studies* 42, no. 1 (1998–1999): 47–49; Paul Fyfe, "Illustrating the Accident: Railways and the Catastrophic Picturesque," in *The Illustrated London News', Victorian Periodicals Review* 46, no. 1 (2013): 61–91.

28 "Appalling Railway Disaster," *Northern Echo*, November 3, 1892; "Fatal Railway Collision," *Lloyd's Weekly Paper*, November 6, 1892.

29 "One of the Public", "The Railway Accident at Chester," *The Times*, July 12, 1878, 11.

30 Williams, *Our Iron Roads*, 318–320.

31 "The Signalman on the Midland," *Myra's Journal*, October 1, 1889, 518.

32 Compare to the very visible, and thus well-uniformed, roles of porters, guards, etc. Freeman, *Railways and the Victorian Imagination*, 185–186.

33 Arthur McIvor, *A History of Work in Britain 1880–1950* (Basingstoke: Palgrave, 2001), 44–47.

34 "Signalmen's and Switchmen's Society," *South London Press*, November 11, 1865, 6.

35 Frank McKenna, *The Railway Workers 1840–1970* (London: Faber and Faber, 1980), 70–72.

36 Helena Wojtczak, *Railwaywomen: Exploitation, Betrayal and Triumph in the Workplace* (Hastings: Hastings Press, 2005), 12–17, 20–26.

37 Charles Pearce, "Young Job: The Signalman's Son," *Young Folks*, February 3, 1877, 67–68.

38 "Saved by a Ghost: A Mystery of the Iron Road," *Illustrated Chips*, December 10, 1898, 3.

39 "Notices of New Publications," *The Western Times*, August 6, 1872, 8; "Literature," *Glasgow Herald*, August 15, 1872, 2.

40 "Literary Notices," *Worcestershire Chronicle*, July 15, 1876, 3.

41 Friedrich Engels, *The Condition of the Working-Class in England in 1844: With a Preface Written in 1892* (London: Swan Sonnenchein & Co., 1892), 43.

42 Hector Gavin, *Sanitary Ramblings: Being Sketches and Illustrations of Bethnal Green* (London: John Churchill, 1848).

43 Anthony Trollope, *The Prime Minister* (New York: Dodd, Mead, and Company, 1918), Volume III, 82–83.

44 Ibid., 85–86.

45 Émile Durkheim, *Suicide* (London: Routledge and Keegan Paul, 1966), 292.

46 Olive Anderson, *Suicide in Victorian and Edwardian England* (Oxford: Clarendon Press, 1987).

47 Charles Booth Notebooks, B375, 109, London School of Economics Archive, London, United Kingdom.

48 Medical Officer of Health for Rotherhithe, *Fourth General Report of the Vestry of Rotherhithe, Surrey, Presented to the Metropolitan Board of Works* (Rotherhithe: B. Batt, 1860), 5.

49 Thomas Barrow Emmanuel, "The Dwellings of the Working Classes," in *Transactions of the National Association for the Promotion of Social Science, Manchester Meeting 1866*, ed. George Woodyatt Hastings (London: Green, Reader and Dye, 1866), 731–740.

50 *The Railway News*, "Utilisation of Railway Arches for Workmen's Dwellings," November 3, 1866, 459.

51 Joachim Schlör, *Nights in the Big City: Paris, London, Berlin, 1840–1930* (London: Reaktion Books, 1998), 47–49.

52 Ike Matthews, *Full Revelations of a Professional Rat-Catcher After 25 Years Experience* (London: Friendly Societies' Printing Company Ltd, 1898), 48–49.

53 "A Daily Traveller", "The Accident at Ludgate Hill Station: to the Editor of the Times," *The Times,* January 28, 1879, 8.
54 Schivelbusch, *The Railway Journey,* 171–177.
55 Bradley, *The Railways,* 257.

Bibliography

1983–8831, London Bridge Terminus Notice, Collections of the National Railway Museum.
Anderson, Olive. *Suicide in Victorian and Edwardian England.* Oxford: Clarendon Press, 1987.
Bradley, Simon. *The Railways: Nation, Network, and People.* London: Profile Books, 2015.
Briggs, Julia. *A Woman of Passion: The Life of E. Nesbit 1858–1924.* New York: The Meredith Press, 1987.
Carlyle, E., and Frederick Smeeton Williams. "Congregational Minister and Railway Historian." *Oxford Dictionary of National Biography* (1829–1886). Accessed August 8, 2018. www.oxforddnb.com/view/10.1093/ref:odnb/9780198614128.001. 0001/odnb-9780198614128-e-29503.
Carter, Ian. *Railways and Culture in Britain.* Manchester: Manchester University Press, 2001.
Chudacoff, Howard. *Children at Play: An American History.* New York: New York University Press, 2008.
Coleman, Terry. *The Railway Navvies.* London: Pelican, 1972.
Daly, Nicholas. "Blood on the Tracks: Sensation Drama, the Railway, and the Dark Face of Modernity." *Victorian Studies* 42, no. 1 (1998–1999): 47–49.
Dickens, Charles. "The Signal-Man." In *Christmas Stories,* edited by Charles Dickens. London: Chapman and Hall, 1894.
Dow, Andrew. *The Railway: British Track since 1804.* Barnsley: Pen and Sword, 2014.
Durkheim, Émile. *Suicide.* London: Routledge and Keegan Paul, 1966.
Emmanuel, Thomas Barrow. "The Dwellings of the Working Classes." In *Transactions of the National Association for the Promotion of Social Science, Manchester Meeting 1866,* edited by George Woodyatt Hastings, 731–740. London: Green, Reader and Dye, 1866.
Engels, Friedrich. *The Condition of the Working-Class in England in 1844: With a Preface Written in 1892.* London: Swan Sonnenchein & Co., 1892.
Freeman, Michael. *Railways and the Victorian Imagination.* New Haven: Yale University Press, 1999.
Fyfe, Paul. "Illustrating the Accident: Railways and the Catastrophic Picturesque in *The Illustrated London News.*" *Victorian Periodicals Review* 46, no. 1 (2013): 61–91.
Gavin, Hector. *Sanitary Ramblings: Being Sketches and Illustrations of Bethnal Green.* London: John Churchill, 1848.
London School of Economics Archive. London: Charles Booth Notebooks, B375, 109.
Matthews, Ike. *Full Revelations of a Professional Rat-Catcher after 25 Years Experience.* London: Friendly Societies' Printing Company Ltd, 1898.
McIvor, Arthur. *A History of Work in Britain 1880–1950.* Basingstoke: Palgrave, 2001.
McKenna, Frank. *The Railway Workers 1840–1970.* London: Faber and Faber, 1980.
Medical Officer of Health for Rotherhithe. *Fourth General Report of the Vestry of Rotherhithe, Surrey, Presented to the Metropolitan Board of Works.* Rotherhithe: B. Batt, 1860.

Munro, Edward. *The "Navvies" and How to Meet Them: A Letter to a Friend.* London: Joseph Masters, 1857.

Oxford English Dictionary Online. Accessed January 16, 2019. www.oed.com/view/Entry/240547?redirectedFrom=permanent+way

Pope, Norris. "Dickens's "The Signalman" and Information Problems in the Railway Age." *Technology and Culture* 42, no. 3 (2001): 437–438.

Regulation of Railways Act 1868, Clause 23, 1166. www.legislation.gov.uk/ukpga/1868/119/pdfs/ukpga_18680119_en.pdf.

Schivelbusch, Wolfgang. *The Railway Journey: The Industrialisation of Time and Space in the 19th Century.* Leamington Spa: Berg, 1986.

Schlör, Joachim. *Nights in the Big City: Paris, London, Berlin, 1840–1930.* London: Reaktion Books, 1998.

Simmons, Jack. *The Victorian Railway.* London: Thames and Hudson, 1991.

"Trial of George Gray and John Parker" 6 July 1868. *Old Bailey Proceedings Online.* Accessed January 9, 2019. www.oldbaileyonline.org/browse.jsp?name=18680706.

Trollope, Anthony. *The Prime Minister*, Volume III. New York: Dodd, Mead, and Company, 1918.

Williams, F.S. *Our Iron Roads: Their History, Construction and Administration.* London: Bemrose and Sons, 1883.

Wojtczak, Helena. *Railwaywomen: Exploitation, Betrayal and Triumph in the Workplace.* Hastings: Hastings Press, 2005.

Publications and newspapers

Illustrated Chips
Journal of the Permanent Way Institution
Lloyd's Weekly Paper
Morning Post
Myra's Journal
Northern Echo
Sheffield Independent
South London Press
The Railway News
The Times
The Western Times
Whitehaven News
Worcestershire Chronicle
Young Folks

6 "Being poor is going to the Ritz on the bus"

The portrayal of buses and trams in popular culture

Martin Higginson

Introduction

This chapter compares the place of buses and trams in popular culture with that of trains and railways. Arguably, the perception is that buses and trams are less favourably presented and the aim is to establish whether or not this is the case, and if so, why. Because of the limited scholarly research on this subject, in the first instance we do however need to identify where buses and trams feature, and this chapter considers their appearance in literature, songs, poetry, music, journalism, the visual and audio media material and even in aspects of language. From this exploration, it will be suggested that buses and trams have not featured as strongly in popular culture in large part because of the nature of a large portion of their users.

Arguably, buses have been ignored, misunderstood or looked down upon because for much of the last century and a half they have not been used by the better off, who have their own private transport. Whether or not in 1986 Margaret Thatcher really said "A man who, beyond the age of 26, finds himself on a bus can count himself as a failure" is open to conjecture, but recollection of the allegation was strong enough for it to be cited in a House of Commons debate in 2003.[1] Similarly, the Conservative peer Baroness Trumpington quoted her mother as saying, in the context of the family losing its fortune in the 1929 stock market crash, that "Being poor is going to the Ritz on a bus".[2]

Reflecting this differential usage, buses, trams and their predecessors are historically 'popular' modes of transport and used by the population at large to meet their travel needs. They have been of particular value to persons unable to afford their own means of transport, an association that remains to this day. Less wealthy families are less likely to own a car and thus use public transport. As such, those creating cultural productions – usually from the upper and middle classes – were and are less apt to include and feature buses as they were not part of their own travel experience.

Usage of buses was and is also gendered, and this too has shaped their representation. Nineteenth century bus and tram travel was principally a male middle and working-class experience, linked to male dominance of employment and to women's perceived domestic role in society. As double-decker buses and trams evolved, it was also considered especially inappropriate for decent women to travel on the top deck. Nonetheless, in one of the rare pieces of academic work on buses' representation in popular culture, Shelley (2015) reviews the place of omnibuses in late nineteenth-century short stories and journalism, citing the role of bus travel in women's emancipation. Shelley concludes that, despite difficulties associated with omnibuses being a traditionally male preserve – both passengers and conductors – depictions of buses and trams in literature show that considerable numbers of women, including those from the middle classes, travelled by bus and increasingly breached former taboos by travelling alone and climbing the stairs to the top deck. Shelley cites authors such as Quiller-Couch to demonstrate '*how frequently omnibuses feature in fiction concerned with aspects of city life*' and how *fin-de-siècle* novels address the subject, especially in the context of female emancipation.[3]

Generally, however, in the post-war world such dynamics of bus usage changed, girls and women of all ages using them more than men and boys. When car ownership rose after the Second World War many families only had one, typically taken to work by the (usually male) principal breadwinner, leaving the spouse to rely on public transport for errands; which for most local trips means buses. This pattern of usage was also reinforced by the fact that more men than women held driving licences. Additionally, women, on average, also live longer than men, so have more years to use their bus passes, reliance on which may rise if they are widowed. Consequently, as these women have not been the predominant producers of popular culture, it can be suggested that their experiences of bus travel have been side-lined.

Similar is the case with the other major group of bus users, children. They use buses to travel both to and from school (with and without parents and guardians) and for leisure and recreation. This grows in importance as they grow up and achieve greater independence, although there are counter pressures from increased car availability (older teenagers driving themselves and parental lift-giving) and from reductions in evening and weekend bus services. Nonetheless, their travel experiences are again less likely to turn up in the pages of books or in journalism, meaning the bus features less.

Buses and trams have nonetheless always been a site of socialisation. Whilst the privacy of car travel is sometimes described as a benefit, the sociability of bus travel is a counter-attraction, where conversations with friends and acquaintances occur; friends work together on homework, or one can pass the time of the day with the driver, the latter especially on rural and smaller buses, where such interactions can be found. As will be shown, such interactions have been a source of creative inspiration, and thus this has led to some of the most prominent featuring of public road transport in popular culture. Additionally, where London is concerned, buses particularly have become woven into the fabric of the city's identity. As such, whilst frequently public road transport is featured incidentally in popular culture, this chapter will also foreground a good number of examples where it is the star of the show.

The written word

In contrast to the depiction of buses and trams, rail travel receives stronger and more favourable treatment in the written word. Conforming to the lines outlined above, trains are often used by the principal characters in novels, particularly the rich and famous, such as works by Agatha Christie,[4] Dick Francis,[5] Graham Greene[6] and Patricia Highsmith,[7] which feature railways and trains as glorious and romantic. Indeed, Emile Zola's *La Bête Humaine*[8] dramatises and humanises the steam locomotive. The train can also be central as a site of dramatic events, for example, Christie's *Murder on the Orient Express* and Francis's *The Edge*, set on a trans-Canadian train journey. There is also a genre of popular railway fiction, typified by Andrew Martin's detective novels, featuring Railway policeman Jim Stringer, where the railway and its operation themselves become a character.[9] Fictionalised accounts of real-life travel experiences are also more usually by rail travel, of which Paul Theroux's *The Great Railway Bazaar*[10] (1975) is a representative example.

Buses and trams are seemingly ignored by the authors of works centered on the high-born and the wealthy (Agatha Christie, Ian Fleming). Rather, bus and tram travel are often portrayed as mundane in written works. It can be a background component of the stories, illustrate events that either happened or were recalled during a bus journey, embracing escape, failure to escape, scene-setting and fond recollection, rather than being instrumental in the events. Similar to Shelley's work, public road transport before 1914 has been depicted as a middle-class means of mobility. The London bus, usually rendered as 'omnibus', is referred to on many occasions in Virginia Woolf's writings, as conveying middle-class citizens, for example, in *Mrs Dalloway*[11]: "*The British middle classes sitting sideways on the tops of buses with parcels and umbrellas, yes, even furs on a* [hot summer] *day like this.*" At Hampton Court, reached on the top of an omnibus, "*they were standing by the river, and he looked at it with a look which she had seen in his eyes when a train went by, or an omnibus – a look as if something fascinated him.*", the omnibus is associated not with an idyllic, romantic outing, but with a visit during which Mrs Dalloway finally accepts that her marriage is over.

In the post-war world, however, the shifts in who was using the bus towards women and the young are evident, but still the bus is incidental. Dexter's Inspector Morse detective novel *Last Bus to Woodstock* centres on the murder of a girl who had been waiting for a late evening bus home from Oxford. Pauline McLynn's romance *The Woman on the Bus*,[12] features buses only in the cover scene, which describes the heroine's escape by bus from her violent partner. Tony Judt's collection of short stories *The Memory Chalet* includes the autobiographical *The Green Line Bus*,[13] a descriptive and wholly sympathetic text highlighting the distinction between the '*average London bus*' and long distance Green Lines, with their '*cozy, reassuring, and rather warm feel*', which he was catching in his youth typically catching '*late at night…..returning from Zionist youth meetings or a tryst with a girlfriend*'. What draws these texts together is the focus on the mobility of those other than working-age men.

Public road transport has also received little attention in the fictionalised travel writing genre, and there are few examples of it. D.H. Lawrence was however a key exponent of it. Growing up in the industrial east Midlands gave him the opportunity to write about working-class travel from personal experience. Two examples from Lawrence's opus are each fictionalised accounts with strong factual backgrounds. The 1919 short story *Tickets Please*[14] is a fictional narrative of female emancipation, set on the real-life Nottingham & Derby tramway during the First World War, when "*the drivers are men unfit for active service: cripples and hunchbacks*" and female conductors – *fearless young hussies. In their ugly blue uniform* – have replaced the men who are away on active service. The narrative reads as an eye-witness account of travel on the tramway at that time, demonstrating that it was a means of mobility for women and those of less substantial means.

In a rare featuring of buses in travelogue literature, Lawrence's 1923 novella *Sea and Sardinia* includes a detailed review of a bus journey across rural Sardinia that demonstrates the bus's role in providing transport for poor and working-class people. A fellow-passenger, described as an '*old peasant*', bemoans the time he has '*wasted*' on this, his first ever omnibus trip. On its arrival in a village the bus is greeted by '*old half-broken houses of stone*'. People crowd round when the bus stops, '*many of them in very ragged costume. They look poor*'. Even the mail bag the conductor collects exudes poverty; it '*is usually a limp affair, containing about three letters*'.[15] This last example encapsulates the general position of buses; buses are served and frequented by the poorest of society.

In some sense, the idea that the buses are a form of transport principally frequented by those on lower incomes, or at least those outside of the richest in society, has remained to the present, as suggested by recent examples of journalism. The report of the highly paid Brazilian footballer Robson 'Robinho' de Souza and his girlfriend travelling by bus to and from Manchester's Trafford Centre is one such example, the interest coming from the fact that a highly paid football player was travelling on a form of transport not usually commonly frequented by such individuals.[16] Moreover, a 2006 six-page feature '*Aboard the budget buses*' in *the Guardian* about who travels by National Express coaches emphasised how they were used predominantly by mostly young, price-conscious people.[17]

Only in works of fiction for children have trams and buses portrayed in an almost universally positive light, usually as a trusty companion. Several of Rev. W Awdry's *Thomas the Tank Engine* books feature *Bertie the Bus*,[18] who is represented as friendly and amiable, despite being an upstart competitor to Thomas's branch line. Although losing an initial competitive foray, a co-operation agreement is eventually reached whereby Bertie will bring passengers to Thomas's train instead of trying to compete with it. *Trusty and the Toys*, 'A Father Tuck BIGGER little book' by Violet M Williams[19] is the story of a group of toys (doll, teddy, golly, etc.) who run away from a toyshop and are given a ride by Trusty to "a nice, friendly-looking house", whose occupants eventually buy them. The name 'Trusty' is significant, suggesting the bus as a mode of transport that is reliable and child-friendly:

> "What do you want my dears?", asked a big bus, as the toys stared up at him.
> "We want to go to the country," said Teddy.
> "Well, Trusty, the single-decker, over there, is a country bus. He may be able to help you."

Awdry's and Williams' stories are set contemporaneously and depict buses as friendly, flexible, obliging and, perhaps most importantly, relevant to contemporary lifestyles. Connecting with those who used buses on a day to day level, this arguably reflected the fact of buses being a source of familiar mobility for families and the young people who were reading the works. For the avid child reader, particularly, it would have been inappropriate to characterise a form of travel they experienced daily as the enemy or forbidding. These ideas are most explicitly reflected in Edinburgh artist and author Aileen Paterson's *Morningside Maisie*. Paterson's 30 books for children became a popular television series that led to Lothian Buses route 5 being named *Morningside Maisie* and operated by vehicles in an appropriate pictorial livery.[20]

This sense of public road transport being a positive and friendly thing, was reflected in the nostalgia some children's books had for it. Val Howels' picture book *Gordon's Tumbledown Tram*[21] tells how the composer Gordon Langford, a tram enthusiast as well as a composer and musician, acquired a derelict ex-London tram and organised its restoration to become No.14 in the Seaton Tramway fleet, linking visual art, literature and music in the story of buses and trams in popular culture.

Finally, the *Wonder Book* series, covering a range of technical and scientific topics for older children, was published from the 1920s to the 1950s. *Wonder Book of Motors*,[22] first published in 1926, included throughout its many editions chapters entitled *Motors for All: The friendly omnibus in town and country* and *By Bus Across Britain*. The articles' titles confirm the ubiquity and perceived personality of bus services before their role was attacked by the motor-car.

Poetry, songs and music

In poetry, songs and music railways are again treated more favourably, buses mostly being mentioned in passing. On the one hand trains are symbolic of progress and advancement, for instance *Coming Round the Mountain*, a railway navvies' song believed to have evolved from a spiritual, and *Are ye right there Michael* (Percy French, 1902), about an Irish excursion train. The Danish composer Hans Christian Lumbye (1810–1874) composed *Steam Railway Gallop* (1847) for the opening of Denmark's first railway. Arthur Honegger (1892–1955) wrote the 'mouvement symphonique' *Pacific 231* in 1923, a film version appearing in 1949. The Czech composer Antonin Dvořák (1841–1904), brought up opposite a railway station at the dawn of the railway age, was an enthusiast for railways and steam locomotives, his Humoresque No.7 and 7th symphony each having been influenced by railway rhythms and sounds.[23] There is also almost universal glorification and popularisation of railways by poets – such as W. H. Auden (*Night Mail*[24]) and song-writers, for example, Percy French (Are you right there Michael?[25]). Rail-related poetry includes the eulogistic *The Newport Railway* by William McGonagall (1825–1902). Particularly indicative of the relative inclusion of railways and public road transport, is the fact that D.H. Lawrence's poetry includes some 50 transport-related works, with most references being to railways, tramways and cars and only one briefly mentioning buses.

In poetry, songs and music buses and trams have nonetheless had varied representations, even if the established themes remain. Buses receive favourable treatment in popular songs, where the focus is leisure pursuits and the social life within its environment. As early as 1862, Geordie Ridley's music hall-style *Blaydon Races* features the vehicle overturning; an example showing the bus as the centre of an event that contrasts with its minor role in the works identified above:

> We flew past Airmstrang's factory, and up to the "Robin Adair",
> Just gannin' doon te the railway bridge, the 'bus wheel flew off there.
> The lassies lost their crinolines off, an' the veils that hide their faces,
> An' aw got two black eyes an' a broken nose gannin' te Blaydon Races.[26]

Leisure via buses remained a theme until the near current. The coach outing, although less popular than before mass car ownership, featured in folk music in the 1970s, with Debbie Cook's *Day trip to Bangor*, performed by Fiddler's Dram:

> Jumped on the bus, Flo said to us
> Oh isn't it a shame to go.

Music also expressed how public road transport was also a site of sociability, especially for working people. Fred. W. Leigh's (1871–1924) risqué music hall song, *Riding on Top of the Car*, about a mill girls' outing, is typically saucy for the genre:

> And when the conductor comes up for the fare,
> He punches our tickets then goes,
> But he gives us a wink as he pops down the stairs,
> Like some overgrown Cupid in clothes............

with the chorus repeated after each verse:

> We go go go for a ride on a car car car,
> Cause we know how cosy the tops of the tramcars are
> The seats are so small, there's not much to pay,
> You sit close together and 'spoon' all the way,
> And many a Miss will be Mrs some day
> Through riding on top of the car.

The inherent sociality of public road transport is therefore revealed, in this case young love, something more starkly emphasised in Roger McGough's 1967 *At Lunchtime*[27]: "*When the bus stopped suddenly, the young lady in the green hat sitting opposite, was thrown across me...*". Indeed, buses were not always seen as a struggle, but a joyful thing; Flanders and Swann's famous *Transport of Delight* featuring the immortal lines:

> That big six-wheeler scarlet-painted London Transport diesel-engined
> 97-horsepower, 97-horsepower omnibus.
> Hold very tight please! Ting-ting!

Nonetheless, clearly buses and trams are observed frequently as mundane and routinised forms of transport, lacking the glamour found with railway travel. Michael Nyman's opera *Man and Boy Dada*[28] (2004), an imaginary episode in the real life of the artist Kurt Schwitters (1887–1948), focussed on the hobby of collecting bus tickets. The opera centres on the shared interest of a lonely older man and a somewhat nerdish young boy in collecting discarded bus tickets.

> I don't want an orange one.
> Need a blue.
> A ticket to go here
> A ticket to go there
> You need a ticket
> To breathe the air

Betjeman in his poetry also chose to include the bus (and, unusually, the trolley-bus) as part of the mundane, daily routine of life, whilst emphasising the bus's role as a mode of transport for the less well-off. Indeed, the back-drop of run-down post-war austerity London served to emphasise how they served those in poverty and drudgery.[29] *St Saviour's, Aberdeen Park, Highbury, London N* (1948) poignantly evokes this:

> With oh such peculiar branching and over-reaching of wire
> Trolley-bus standards pick their threads from the London sky
> …
> Of weariest worn-out London, no cigarettes, no beer,
> No repairs undertaken – nothing in stock, alight.

Public road transport's position as a symbol of austerity and poverty remained for almost a decade after the end of the Second World War. *Business Girls* (1954) describes the impecunious lifestyle of *a thousand business women having baths in Camden Town; "All too soon the tiny breakfast, Trolley-bus and windy street".* But as austerity passed, a later poem, *In Beaumaris, December 21, 1963,* illustrates a more settled life-stage, but here the emphasis shifted to the bus being a source of mobility for newly married women without cars, undertaking their expected social role: *"With girlhood over and marriage begun: Queuing for buses and rearing children, Washing the dishes and missing the fun".*

Yet, the mundanity of the bus can be brought to life. D.H. Lawrence's *For a moment*[30] brings romance to the mundane life of a young tram conductor lifted to an imaginary moment of heroism in a verse that shows Lawrence observing the routine real-life event of turning the trolley pole at the terminus:

> For a moment, at evening, tired, as he stepped off the tram-car
> the young tram conductor in a blue uniform, to himself forgotten, –
> and lifted his face up, with blue eyes looking at the electric rod which
> he was going to turn round,
> for a moment, pure in the yellow evening light, he was Hyacinthus.

Mundanity is also not found where buses are featured in children's music, and for the reasons outlined above with regard to children's literature, they have been cast as a friendly and familiar mode of transport. Very young children can be introduced to buses through the nursery rhyme *Wheels on the bus*, which starts *"The wheels on the bus go round and round,"* subsequent verses covering the horn, the wipers, the money, the driver, the children, etc. in a similar vein. Indeed, the longevity of this particular rhyme has meant *Wheels on the bus* is available in audio and video format as part of BBC *Early Learning* and CBeebies programmes,[31] for which additional resources such as teachers' packs are available, and on social media. The rhyme is used in the British Council's *LearnEnglish Kids* English language tuition series,[32] whose associated documents include a download of the words, an activity pack to open discussion on individual words in the rhyme, suggesting the discussion topics "Do you like this song? Do you usually take the bus?", matching exercises (e.g. to link a picture of a bus with the written word 'bus') and an art exercise "Draw a picture of yourself on a bus!".

The visual arts

Once again, in the visual arts, the bus has featured far less prominently than the railway. Internationally renowned artists have regularly portrayed railways, but seldom buses, with the paintings themselves becoming very well known, representative of modernity and progress. One of the first to paint a railway scene was J.M.W. Turner (1775–1851), whose *Rain, Steam and Speed – The Great Western Railway* was exhibited at the Royal Academy in 1844. Claude Monet's oeuvre includes his *Gare St Lazare, Paris* series, whilst Vincent van Gogh's 1890 *Landscape at Auvers after the Rain* (Pushkin Museum, Moscow) shows a train crossing a rural landscape. *The Terminus, Penzance Station Cornwall* by Stanhope Forbes (1857–1947) is in the National Railway Museum, York.

By contrast, there are examples of buses featuring in paintings, but the artists and their works are less well known, although here again the same themes come to the fore. Victorian and Edwardian pictures, such as those by Blanche, Layng and Morgan, evidence the opulence and wellbeing that characterised the years before the First World War, with the London bus being a means of transport for the middle classes. Jacques-Emile Blanche (1861–1942) *Knightsbridge from Sloane Street, London (Fine December Morning)* portrays the bus in a prosperous-looking, sunny environment. Mabel Francis Layng (1881–1937) *The Top of the Bus, 1920s* is a double portrait of an elegantly dressed couple seated on a bus. By contrast *An Omnibus Ride to Piccadilly Circus: Mr Gladstone Travelling with Ordinary Passengers* by Alfred Edward Morgan (1835–1924), shows a group of seven smartly attired people ranged on inward-facing benches inside a horse-bus; the 'ordinary people' being members of the artist's family.[33]

Nonetheless, in the visual arts, for the most part buses have been considered a domain for those on lower incomes than the richest. The long-established *Punch*, with its predominantly wealthy and upper-class audience, tended to take a snobbish attitude to buses. *Punch* cartoons from the first decades of the twentieth century show bus drivers as surly, cocky, road-hogging cockneys and passengers to be stupid, ignorant people who didn't understand how to use buses. A typical example by JCB Knight is captioned "INDIGNANT DRIVER: Hi! 'Ow much more o' the blinkin' road d'yer want?" Bus drivers' reputation for sardonic humour was also noted, as in the caption to a cartoon showing a bus held up by a small stationary car[34]:

BUS-DRIVER. "Wotcher stoppin' for, mate?"
MIDGET-DRIVER. "I was just waiting for you to say something funny."

Passengers too could be the butt of critical humour[35]:

TIRESOME WOMAN. "and how shall I know when we come to Acacia Avenue?"
WEARY CONDUCTOR. "Oh, you'll 'ear me burst into song."

Not every humourist is critical of buses though. *Bus 49*[36] criticises the upstart and unreliable motor car, the protagonists preferring to take the bus:

> Daddy bought a motor-car
> Painted black and red;
> He keeps it in the garage,
> Which used to be the shed;
> It's such a silly motor-car
> That now the weather's fine
> Me and Mummie go outside
> Bus 49

And so on, for three further verses, each criticising the motorcar and each ending with the line *Bus 49*.

Once again, however, visual art works from the mid-twentieth century typically portray buses as part of the depressed, run-down post-war environment. Hammersmith-born Ruskin Spear (1911–1990) featured buses in *The Blackout* (1942) and *A London Street* (1944–1945). In *Winter* (1947) and *Hammersmith Broadway* (1950) he uses using the trolleybus wires to fill areas of the canvas otherwise dominated by pale skies. In these cases, they are portrayed as a part of the everyday, run-of-the-mill life during the austere aftermath of the Second World War, in a similar manner to John Betjeman in his poetry from the same era.

The nostalgia individuals today have about the double decker bus, and particularly those in London, which constitutes one of the key elements of London's outwardly projected persona as a city, have been in large part shaped by the role London Transport and its predecessors have played in the evolution of poster art depicting buses and trams. London General Omnibus Company examples include *The Open Road* [Walter Spradbery, 1914], *Barnes* [L MacLeish, 1914], which invites travel by General Route No.9, *The Country by Coach* [L.B. Black, 1926], *Chigwell 101B* [Fred Taylor, 1914] and *Abridge Route 10A From Elephant & Castle Station* [Clive Gardiner, 1930].[37] The latter and its companion *This is St Albans served by Route 84 from Golders Green Stn* [John Mansbridge, 1930] each carry the strapline '*Another General Busway*'; early instances of the use of a marketing slogan.[38] London County Council (LCC) was prolific in the production of pictorial posters promoting travel by its trams. General/London Transport commissioned well-known artists, such as Taylor and Spradbery, but the LCC sourced its artwork from '*the council's own art school*' and from the Central School of Arts and Crafts, under its first Principal, William Lethaby.[39]

In addition to selling public road transport, London's transport providers have also deployed buses visually to create positive popular narratives about their virtues. A 1965 poster by Heinz Zinram[40] illustrates the impact of traffic congestion by presenting the slogan "*these vehicles are carrying....69 people who could all....be on this one* bus" alongside photographs of the same street occupied by 69 cars, 69 pedestrians or one bus. Chandler's 1960s cartoon[41] of the bus proclaiming its superior capacity clearly demonstrates that London Transport's 'capacity' message has touched popular culture. The cartoon shows a bus bearing the slogan *I can carry 98 passengers. How many passengers travel in your car?* being passed by an overloaded car full of football supporters displaying a banner proclaiming the answer to be '13'. Such representations potentially have supported the London double decker bus's route to becoming an icon.

The iconic status of the London Bus is in large part why cartoons can use them as visual signifiers of broader issues. Drawing on the history of the London double decker, Steve Bell's 2012 *Guardian*[42] cartoon shows how even a new piece of equipment can almost immediately become a cultural icon, whether viewed as popular or unpopular. Here London's 'New Routemaster' ('Boris Bus'), a 'retro' body design evoking the original 1954 Routemaster, is assumed to be recognisable, and the danger of re-introducing open rear platforms worthy of comment. The cartoon's 'bubble' text reads "*Well I Don't get it – you bring in a few overpriced **retro-buses** with **two sets of stairs** to fall down and a **jump-off rear platform** you're not allowed to **jump off**...*". Implied in this is the foolhardiness of allowing nostalgia for the past to inform modern decision-making.

Public road transport has however frequently been depicted in artworks as a feature of an idealised past, artists romanticising about disappeared scenes from earlier eras. French post-impressionist Edouard Leon Cortès (1882–1969) depicted Parisian street scenes, representing horse and motor-buses and electric trams between the 1890s to the late 1930s, but probably painted in the 1950s. Cortès, a pacifist, when asked why his works still showed horse-drawn carriages and fashions from before 1930, responded that he "wished to stop history in 1939 before the Second World War".[43] Amateur Mancunian painter Arthur Delaney (1927–1987) was influenced by L.S. Lowry. His paintings recall his 1930s childhood "with its smoke-laden skies, rattling tramcars and gas lamps".[44] Such evocation of the past is not unique to posters though. Grayson Perry's sculpture, *Head of a Fallen Giant*[45] includes a model Routemaster among its British images. Although here the objective is not to romanticise the past, but is part of a recognition of how Britons hold certain symbols more dear 'than blinging diamonds', the sculpture being encrusted with various symbols of perceived 'Britishness' (Figure 6.1).[46]

The double decker buses particularly have become icons in the landscape of Britishnesses generally, evidenced by them being treated as canvases for

Figure 6.1 The bus that conveyed the 1987 Coventry City Football Association cup team. The bus on which they made their victory parade is in Coventry Transport Museum; a cartoon representation is prominently displayed in the museum foyer. A popular tradition has grown up whereby the team winning the FA Cup or other important trophies parades around its home town on an open-top bus. Photo Martin Higginson, permission given by the Coventry Transport Museum.

giant mobile art, thus suggesting that what is done to them has resonance. In 2009 Sir Peter Blake's *Art Bus* was launched by CCA Galleries as a mobile gallery.[47] Moreover, whilst 'all-over' pictorial liveries are more often associated with commercial advertising than with culture, exceptions are to be found, such as rainbow 'pride'-liveried vehicles celebrating the 10th anniversary of Transport for London's lesbian, gay, bisexual and transgender staff network group in 2018.

Figure 6.2 Double Decker Chocolate Bar Bus. Source: Author.

Further indication of acceptance of public road transport into the popular psyche is the extent to which a subject is featured an entourage of ephemera, found through everyday life. This includes confectionery such as Cadbury's *Double Decker*[48] chocolate bar, introduced in 1976 and still available in 2019, promoted by appropriately liveried former (Figure 6.2) and current London Transport vehicles.[49] Buses have also been found in the *Bus Stop* record label, featuring a London Transport-style roundel (e.g. *Celia* and *Billy – Don't be a hero)*,[50] greetings and postcards, advent calendars, key fobs and crockery. Buses are particularly over-represented on cards, it becoming a visual signifier for the city as powerful as the London Underground roundel, but other locations featuring on them include Liverpool by a Plaxton Panorama *'Magical Mystery Tour'* coach commemorating the Beatles,[51] a York City Sightseeing open topper outside the Minster by Chris Ceaser Photography[52] and Jennifer Thomson's *'Tour bus on the Mound'* featuring Edinburgh.[53] Children are catered for by toy buses (Dinky, Corgi: and for adults too more accurate models by EFE, Oxford Diecast and others) (Figure 6.3). Since the early twentieth century[54] several manufacturers have produced toy bus conductors' outfits and ticket machines,[55] such as the Lone Star Toy Bus Conductor Outfit: ("It PRINTS the ticket with the FARE") from around 1960. One therefore does not have to look far to find the bus, and perhaps less so the tram, in everyday life, even if they are perhaps not as prominent as trains.

Figure 6.3 Display of toy die-cast buses at Coventry Transport Museum. Photo Martin Higginson, permission given by the Coventry Transport Museum.

Film, television and theatre

Where film television and theatre are concerned, once again, the train dominates, perhaps because of its inherent glamour. Unsurprisingly, given the source material, a number of film versions of novels, including Christie's *Murder on the Orient Express* and Zola's *La Bête Humaine* and Highsmith's *Strangers on a Train*, have featured the train predominantly. Other popular railway films include *Titfield Thunderbolt* and *The Great St Trinians Train Robbery*. Alternatively, the railway has been depicted as a site of drama, for example, Arnold Ridley's (1896–1984) *The Ghost Train* (1923), originally written as a stage play, was subsequently filmed four times in English and in French.[56]

Moreover, on television, the railway has been romanticised as a source of nostalgia. The 1959–62 *Railway Roundabout* series by John Adams and Patrick Whitehouse supported the popular interest in steam as its demise approached. Since 2010, Michael Portillo has run successful railway journeys programmes on BBC2 and other channels, skilfully mixing interest in the rail journeys themselves with characteristics of the places they serve.

By contrast, buses and trams typically feature as background 'incidentals' in film, television or theatre, usually forming part of a street scene, or the occasional reference. Several cinema films feature buses or coaches in this manner, for instance the rock musical *Tommy*, in which coaches from Basil Williams' fleet are seen.[57]

When buses are more prominently featured, however, their depictions are varied in tone. The *Titfield Thunderbolt* (1953), while predominantly a railway film, also involves road passenger transport. An upstart competitive bus is introduced to try to put an antiquated railway branch line out of business, although ultimately unsuccessful nefarious actions by the villainous bus owner (played by Terry Thomas) give the story 'bite'. *The Runaway Bus* (1954), with Frankie Howerd as the driver, tells of a bus journey by a group of fog-grounded would-be airline passengers intent of getting to Ireland, who turn out to be bullion smugglers. In both these cases, the depiction of the bus accords with what is found above, against rail or air travel it is considered a lesser form of transport.

Nonetheless, positive representations of public road transport can be found elsewhere. A bus film par excellence is *Summer Holiday* (1963) starring Cliff Richard as the organiser of a trip across Europe in a former London Transport double decker. In the French film *My Afternoons with Marguerite* (2010), the female love interest is provided by Sophie Guillemin, who plays the part of a village bus driver. The bus's greatest success on film is arguably *On the Buses*, originally made for television by the BBC. Starring Reg Varney (1916–2008)[58] as the put-upon Inspector Blakey, the series ran to 74 episodes (1969–73) and spawned three films and a play. Realism was guaranteed by filming in a real-life bus depot, at Wood Green, North London. This series, while contemporaneous, has a great deal of affection for the bus depot. On stage, in 2006 Berwick Kaler, York Theatre Royal pantomime script writer and Dame, made his entry wearing a costume in the form of model FTR bus, the futuristic articulated vehicles having made their heavily publicised – and sometimes controversial – entry into service in the city that year. Each of these examples depict bus travel to be part of everyday life or of pleasure; and unlike other forms of popular culture, none suggest it to be infra dig to travel by bus.

Conclusion

This chapter has surveyed the many and varied ways in which public road transport has been found in popular culture, perhaps demonstrating how it is woven more imperceptibly into public life than trains. It is worth pausing for a moment to consider just how far this has gone; words and phrases relating to buses, trams and coaches have entered the English language, particularly as figures of speech. Some phrases have come and subsequently disappeared as technology has evolved: how many of today's population would know what a *'tram pinch'* is? Other phrases and terms have remained. These include *'busman's holiday'*, for leisure time spent doing what one normally does for a living, and *'miss the bus'*. Terms already in use in other contexts gained a 'bus' meaning: seats in forward-facing pairs either side of a central gangway were designated *'garden seats'*, while those in two back-to-back rows down the length of the vehicle were known as *'knifeboards'*.

Beyond this though, public road transport's appearances in popular culture have been a constant since their inception, and this chapter has shown the broad extent to which this is so in literature, poetry, the visual arts, film, theatre and television and in ephemera. Coverage, and the nature of that coverage, varies between different elements of popular culture, but for the most part trams and buses appear only as an element of the background; passing vehicles, sounds, visual props such as overhead wires or as a means of moving the action of the book from one place to another.

Railways have not been incidental to the same extent; the degree of attention given to them is greater than that afforded to public road passenger transport, with innumerable works for adults and for children being set in a railway environment and starring passengers, rail employees and even the trains themselves. This chapter has asked why buses, trams and omnibuses have been less favoured in popular culture. On the one hand, this may be because of the nature of the transport mode, the railways having greater physical presence in the landscape. But this piece has also shown how when public road transport has appeared, it had frequently been cast as a mode of travel for the lower echelons of society: the poor, manual workers, rural peasants and elderly people, and those without their own means of transport, whilst often staffed by members of the same social strata. In part, therefore, it can be suggested that with most of the creation of cultural productions not being undertaken by such individuals, what has emerged has not represented their experiences.

It is however worth acknowledging that despite having lesser number of appearances than the railways, public road transport has frequently been afforded favourable treatment or become central in a piece of popular culture. The visual presence of brightly painted trams and buses on the street, particularly in London, has found favour since the nineteenth century. Indeed, frequently they have been a source nostalgia for a bygone age, part of a world idealised and longed for. They have also become central in different productions, as sites of leisure, socialisation and fun.

Ultimately, this chapter through highlighting where the public road transport is featured incidentally and prominently in public culture, demonstrates how examining how it is represented can inform our knowledge of mobility in the past. There is much more to be explored.

Acknowledgements

The author would like to thank the following people for their contributions to this chapter: Richard Storey for his structural contribution, involvement in preparing the 2016 York University presentation, for ideas and for reading and checking the draft. Ian Yearsley for sharing his extensive knowledge of public transport and its surrounding culture. Ros Clayton, my wife, for contributions to the range of information, especially with regard to popular songs and poetry. David Turner at University of York for guiding the project. Matty Gray, my five-year old grandson, who, on being held up from his train seat to look at Durham Cathedral, instead looked down at the bus station and exclaimed "bus, bus!".

Notes

1 United Kingdom. Hansard Parliamentary Debates, House of Commons, 2 July 2003, Column 407, Statement by Mr. Don Foster (Bath).
2 Ibid.
3 Lorna Shelley, "Buses should...inspire writers: Omnibuses in *fin-de-siècle* Short Stories and Journalism," in *Transport in British Fiction*, eds. Adrienne E. Gavin and Andrew F. Humphries (Basingstoke: Palgrave Macmillan, 2015), 136–150.
4 Agatha Christie, *450 from Paddington* (London: William Collins & Sons, 1957); Agatha Christie, *Murder on the Orient Express* (London: William Collins & Sons, 1934); Agatha Christie, *The Mystery of the Blue Train* (London: William Collins & Sons, 1928).
5 Dick Francis, *The Edge* (London: Michael Joseph, 1988).
6 Graham Green, *Stamboul Train* (London: William Heinemann, 1932).
7 Patricia Highsmith, *Strangers on a Train* (New York: Harper & Brothers, 1950); *Strangers on a Train*, directed by Alfred Hitchcock (Warner Brothers, 1951), film.
8 Emile Zola, *La Bête Humaine* (Paris: Bibliothèque-Charpentier, 1890).
9 Andrew Martin, *The Last Train to Scarborough* (London: Faber & Faber, 2010). Andrew Martin, *The Necropolis Railway* (London: Faber & Faber, 2005). Andrew Martin has written other novels based on or around the railway.
10 Paul Theroux, *The Great Railway Bazaar: By Train Through Asia* (New York: Washington Square Press, 1975).

11 Virginia Woolf, *Mrs Dalloway* (Richmond: Hogarth Press, 1925), 15, 66.

12 Pauline McLynn, *The Woman on the Bus* (London: Headline, 2004).

13 Tony Judt, *The Memory Chalet* (New York: The Penguin Press, 2010), 57–63.

14 D.H. Lawrence, *The Complete Short Stories, Vol. 1* (New York: Viking, 1961).

15 D.H. Lawrence, *Sea and Sardinia*, 1923 (Harmondsworth, Middlesex: Penguin Books, 1944).

16 Aida Edemariam, "Is Robinho the richest man on the bus?" *The Guardian*, November 20, 2008, accessed June 30, 2018, www.theguardian.com/football/2008/nov/20/robinho-bus-shortcuts.

17 "Coach Class," *The Guardian*, October 13, 2005, accessed June 30, 2018, www.theguardian.com/world/2005/oct/13/transport.budget

18 W. Awdry, *Thomas and Bertie* in *Tank Engine Thomas Again* (Leicester: Edmund Ward, 1949), 48–62.

19 Violet M. Williams, *Trusty and the Toys* (London: Raphael Tuck, c.1950)

20 "Obituary: Aileen Paterson, author of the Maisie of Morningside books, artist, illustrator and teacher, Aileen Paterson," *The Scotsman*, April 9, 2018. www.scotsman.com/news/obituaries/obituary-aileen-paterson-author-of-the-maisie-of-morningside-books-artist-illustrator-and-teacher-1-4719783

21 Val Howels, *Gordon's Tumbledown Tram* (Seaton: Devon, 2013).

22 Harry Golding, *Wonder Book of Motors* (First edition, London: Ward, Lock & Co, 1928). Harry Golding, *Wonder Book of Motors* (Second edition, London: Ward, Lock & Co, 1930); Harry Golding, *Wonder Book of Motors* (Fourth edition, London: Ward, Lock & Co, 1948).

23 Keith Horner, "The Czech Quartet." *Music Toronto*, accessed December 2, 2018, http://music-toronto.com/train-spotting-with-a-famous-composer/

24 *Night Mail*, directed by Harry Watt and Basil Wright (General Post Office Film Unit, 1936), film.

25 Percy French, *Are Ye Right There Michael?*, 1902. This song was set on the West Clare Railway, Ireland.

26 As a present-day tribute to the song's enduring popularity, Go North East's Newcastle – Blaydon bus service is named the Blaydon Racer and the vehicles' livery is emblazoned with the phrase from the song's chorus: Gannin along the Scotswood Road.

27 Roger McGough, "At Lunchtime," in *Blazing Fruit: Selected Poems 1967–1987*, ed. Roger McGough (Harmondsworth: Penguin, 1990), 26–27.

28 Michael Nyman (music) and Michael Hastings (libretto), *Man and Boy Dada* (London, MN Records, 2005), Act 1, Scene 1.

29 John Betjeman, *John Betjeman's Collected Poems* (London: John Murray, 1958), 126, 181, 299.

30 D.H. Lawrence, *The Collected Poems of D.H. Lawrence* (Ware: Wordsworth Poetry Library, 1994), 562.

31 e.g. "The Wheels on the Bus," *Nursery Songs and Rhymes*, BBC, April 10, 2017, accessed June 24, 2019, www.bbc.co.uk/programmes/p038jj3n

32 "The Wheels on the Bus," *LearnEnglish Kids*, British Council, accessed November 27, 2018, http://learnenglishkids.britishcouncil.org/songs/the-wheels-the-bus

33 Alfred Edward Morgan, "An Omnibus Ride to Piccadilly Circus: Mr Gladstone Travelling with Ordinary Passengers," *Oil on Canvas* (Unknown Owner, 1885).

34 J.A. Hammerton, *Mr Punch in London Town, Vol. XI* (London: The Educational Book Company, 1930s), 106.

35 J.A. Hammerton, *Mr Punch in London Town, Vol. XV* (London: The Educational Book Company, 1930s), 198.

36 Hammerton, *Mr Punch in London Town, Vol. XI*, 188.

37 Michael F. Levey, *London Transport Posters* (Oxford: Phaidon; London: London Transport, 1976).

38 James Laver, *Art for All: The story of London Transport Posters* (London: Art & Technics Ltd, 1949).

39 Jonathan Riddell, *Tramway Art: The Distinctive Poster Art of the London County Council Tramways* (Crowthorne, Berkshire: Capital Transport, 2010).

40 Zoe Craig, "Exhibition Preview: Painting by Numbers @ London Transport Museum," *The Londonist*, January 5, 2012, accessed June 24, 2019. This page show's Heinz Zinram for London Transport, 1965.

41 Author, Birkbeck College collection: original source not traced.

42 Steve Bell, "Well I Don't get it – you bring in a few overpriced retro-buses with two sets of stairs to fall down and a jump-off rear platform you're not allowed to jump off...." *The Guardian*, September 18, 2012.

43 "Edouard Cortes – Paris: Part II," *Rehs Galleries Inc.*, 2000–2019, accessed June 15, 2018, www.rehs.com/cortes_virtex.htm.

44 Laurence Stephen Lowry, "Going to Work," *Oil on Canvass*, Imperial War Museum, London, United Kingdom, accessed June 24, 2018, www.iwm.org.uk/collections/item/object/17026.

45 Grayson Perry, *Head of a Fallen Giant*, Bronze, 2008.

46 "Pictures of the Day," *The Telegraph*, Undated, accessed May 26, 2019, www.telegraph.co.uk/news/worldnews/1928779/Pictures-of-the-day.html?image=6.

47 "Welcome to the CCA Art Bus," *CCA Galleries*, Undated, accessed June 30, 2018, www.ccagalleries.com/art-bus.html.

48 "Cadbury Double Decker," *Mondelez United Kingdom*, 2018, accessed June 24, 2018, www.Cadbury.co.uk/Cadbury-double-decker.

49 Martin Higginson, "Former London Transport RT2725 – Edinburgh Bus Station," (photograph, private collection, 4 September 1980). "In-service New Routemaster ('Boris Bus') LT532," (photograph, private collection, c. 2017).

50 Paper Lace, "Billy – Don't Be A Hero," Track 1 on *Celia*, Philips, 1974, Vinyl, 7", 45 RPM, Single.

51 Jo Gough, "The Beatles Magical Mystery Tour Bus with flowers Greeting Card," *Mementos of Home*, 2017, accessed June 30, 2018, www.mementosofhome.co.uk/standardprints/prod_6110633-Jo-Gough-The-Beatles-Magical-Mystery-Tour-Bus-with-flowers-Greeting-Card.html.

52 Chris Ceaser, "card 240 – York," *Chris Ceaser Photography*, Undated, accessed June 30, 2018, www.chrisceaser.co.uk/greetings-cards/other-7x5-inch-cards/card-240-york/.

53 Jennifer Thomson, "Cards," *Jennifer Thomson* Undated, accessed June 30, 2018, www.jenniferthomson.com/store/c7/Cards.html.

54 "Toy Ticket Punch, Early 20th Century, Original," *Object Lessons*, Undated, accessed September 23, 2018, www.objectlessons.org/childhood-and-games-20th-century-to-present/toy-ticket-punch-early-20th-century-original/s68/a1026/. This is an early example featuring a Bell Punch machine.

55 "Lone Star (UK) Bus Conductors "Roll Ticket Machine"," *Vectis Auctions*, Undated, accessed December 2018, www.vectis.co.uk/lot/lone-star-uk-bus-conductors-roll-ticket-machine_538777.

56 Alfred Hickling, "The Ghost Train – All Aboard for the World's Scariest Play," *The Guardian*, May 22, 2015, accessed June 24, 2019, www.theguardian.com/stage/2015/may/22/the-ghost-train-arnold-ridley-playwright-new-productions.

57 Alan Lambert, *Hants & Sussex: The Basil Williams Story* (Bromley, Kent Bowden Publishing, 2017), 187.

58 Dennis Barker, "Obituary: Reg Varney," *The Guardian*, November 17, 2008, accessed June 24, 2018, www.theguardian.com/culture/2008/nov/17/reg-varney-obituary-buses-television; "Letters: Last Bus for Reg," *The Guardian*, November 22, 2008, accessed June 24, 2018, www.theguardian.com/theguardian/2008/nov/22/european-commission-reg-varney-routemaster.

Bibliography

Awdry, W. *Thomas and Bertie* in *Tank Engine Thomas Again*. Leicester: Edmund Ward, 1949.

Barker, Dennis. "Obituary: Reg Varney." *The Guardian*. November 17, 2008. Accessed June 24, 2018. www.theguardian.com/culture/2008/nov/17/reg-varney-obituary-buses-television.

Bell, Steve. "Well I Don't get it – You Bring in a Few Overpriced Retro-buses with Two Sets of Stairs to Fall Down and a Jump-off Rear Platform You're Not Allowed to Jump Off....," *The Guardian*. September 18, 2012.

Betjeman, John. *John Betjeman's Collected Poems*. London: John Murray, 1958.

"Cadbury Double Decker." *Mondelez United Kingdom*. 2018. Accessed June 24, 2018. www.Cadbury.co.uk/Cadbury-double-decker.

Chris Ceaser. "card 240 – York." *Chris Ceaser Photography*. Undated. Accessed June 30, 2018. www.chrisceaser.co.uk/greetings-cards/other-7x5-inch-cards/card-240-york/.

Christie, Agatha. *450 from Paddington*. London: William Collins & Sons, 1957.

———. *Murder on the Orient Express*. London: William Collins & Sons, 1934.

———. *The Mystery of the Blue Train*. London: William Collins & Sons, 1928.

"Coach Class." *The Guardian*. October 13, 2005. Accessed June 30, 2018. www.theguardian.com/world/2005/oct/13/transport.budget

Craig, Zoe. "Exhibition Preview: Painting By Numbers @ London Transport Museum." *The Londonist*. January 5, 2012. Accessed June 24, 2019.

Edemariam, Aida. "Is Robinho the Richest Man on the Bus?" *The Guardian*. November 20, 2008. Accessed June 30, 2018. www.theguardian.com/football/2008/nov/20/robinho-bus-shortcuts.

"Edouard Cortes – Paris: Part II," *Rehs Galleries Inc*. 2000–2019. Accessed June 15, 2018. www.rehs.com/cortes_virtex.htm.

Francis, Dick. *The Edge*. London: Michael Joseph, 1988.

French, Percy. "King Laoghaire: The Home of Irish Ballads and Tune," *Are Ye Right There Michael?* 1902. Accessed June 15, 2018. www.kinglaoghaire.com/lyrics/947-are-ye-right-there-michael.

Golding, Harry. *Wonder Book of Motors*. First, second and fourth editions. London: Ward, Lock & Co, 1928, 1930 and 1948.

Gough, Jo. "The Beatles Magical Mystery Tour Bus with flowers Greeting Card." *Mementos of Home*. 2017. Accessed June 30, 2018. www.mementosofhome.co.uk/standardprints/prod_6110633-Jo-Gough-The-Beatles-Magical-Mystery-Tour-Bus-with-flowers-Greeting-Card.html.

Green, Graham. *Stamboul Train*. London: William Heinemann, 1932.

Hammerton, J.A. *Mr Punch in London Town, Vols. XI and XV*. London: The Educational Book Company, 1930.

Hickling, Alfred. "The Ghost Train – All Aboard for the World's Scariest Play." *The Guardian*. May 22, 2015. Accessed June 24, 2019. www.theguardian.com/stage/2015/may/22/the-ghost-train-arnold-ridley-playwright-new-productions.

Higginson, Martin. "Former London Transport RT2725 – Edinburgh Bus Station." *Photograph*. Private Collection, September 4, 1980.

Highsmith, Patricia. *Strangers on a Train*. New York: Harper & Brothers, 1950.

Horner, Keith. "The Czech Quartet." *Music Toronto*. Accessed December 2, 2018. http://music-toronto.com/train-spotting-with-a-famous-composer/.

Howels, Val. *Gordon's Tumbledown Tram*. Seaton: Devon, 2013.

"In-service New Routemaster ('Boris Bus') LT532." *Photograph*. Private collection, c. 2017.

Jennifer, Thomson. "Cards." *Jennifer Thomson*. Undated. Accessed June 30, 2018. www.jenniferthomson.com/store/c7/Cards.html.

Judt, Tony. *The Memory Chalet*. New York: The Penguin Press, 2010.

Lambert, Alan. *Hants & Sussex: The Basil Williams Story*. Bromley: Kent Bowden Publishing, 2017.

Laver, James. *Art for All: The story of London Transport Posters*. London: Art & Technics Ltd, 1949.

Lawrence, D.H. *Sea and Sardinia*. Harmondsworth, Middlesex: Penguin Books, 1944.

———. *The Collected Poems of D.H. Lawrence*. Ware: Wordsworth Poetry Library, 1994.

———. *The Complete Short Stories, Vol.1*. New York: Viking, 1961.

"Letters: Last bus for Reg." *The Guardian*. November 22, 2008. Accessed June 24, 2018. www.theguardian.com/theguardian/2008/nov/22/european-commission-reg-varney-routemaster.

Levey, Michael F. *London Transport Posters*. Oxford: Phaidon; London: London Transport, 1976.

"Lone Star (UK) Bus Conductors "Roll Ticket Machine."" *Vectis Auctions*. Undated. Accessed December 2018. www.vectis.co.uk/lot/lone-star-uk-bus-conductors-roll-ticket-machine_538777.

Lowry, Laurence Stephen. "Going to Work." *Oil on Canvass*. London: Imperial War Museum. Accessed June 24, 2018. www.iwm.org.uk/collections/item/object/17026.

Martin, Andrew. *The Last Train to Scarborough*. London: Faber & Faber, 2010.

———. *The Necropolis Railway*. London: Faber & Faber, 2005.

McGough, Roger. "At Lunchtime." *Blazing Fruit: Selected Poems 1967–1987*, edited by Roger McGough. Harmondsworth: Penguin, 1990.

McLynn, Pauline. *The Woman on the Bus*. London: Headline, 2004.

Morgan, Alfred Edward. "An Omnibus Ride to Piccadilly Circus: Mr Gladstone Travelling with Ordinary Passengers." *Oil on Canvas*. Unknown Owner, 1885.

Night Mail. directed by Harry Watt and Basil Wright. General Post Office Film Unit, 1936. Film.

Nyman, Michael (music) and Michael Hastings (libretto). *Man and Boy Dada*. London, MN Records, 2005. Act 1, Scene 1.

"Obituary: Aileen Paterson, Author of the Maisie of Morningside Books, Artist, Illustrator and Teacher, Aileen Paterson." *The Scotsman*. April 9, 2018. Accessed December 31, 2018. www.scotsman.com/news/obituaries/obituary-aileen-paterson-author-of-the-maisie-of-morningside-books-artist-illustrator-and-teacher-1-4719783.

Paper Lace. "Billy – Don't Be A Hero." Track 1 on *Celia*, Philips, 1974. Vinyl, 7", 45 RPM, Single.

Perry, Grayson. *Head of a Fallen Giant*. Bronze, 2008.

"Pictures of the Day." *The Telegraph*. Undated. Accessed May 26, 2019. www.telegraph.co.uk/news/worldnews/1928779/Pictures-of-the-day.html?image=6.

Riddell, Jonathan. *Tramway Art: The Distinctive Poster Art of the London County Council Tramways*. Crowthorne, Berkshire: Capital Transport, 2010.

Shelley, Lorna. "Buses should…inspire writers: Omnibuses in *fin-de-siècle* Short Stories and Journalism." In *Transport in British Fiction*, edited by Adrienne E.

Gavin and Andrew F. Humphries, 136–150. Basingstoke: Palgrave Macmillan, 2015.

Strangers on a Train. Directed by Alfred Hitchcock. Warner Brothers, 1951. Film.

Theroux, Paul. *The Great Railway Bazaar: By Train Through Asia*. New York: Washington Square Press, 1975.

"The Wheels on the Bus", *Nursery Songs and Rhymes*. BBC. April 10, 2017. Accessed June 24, 2019. www.bbc.co.uk/programmes/p038jj3n.

"Toy Ticket Punch, Early 20th Century, Original." *Object Lessons*. Undated. Accessed September 23, 2018. www.objectlessons.org/childhood-and-games-20th-century-to-present/toy-ticket-punch-early-20th-century-original/s68/a1026/.

"Welcome to the CCA Art Bus." *CCA Galleries*. Undated. Accessed June 30, 2018. www.ccagalleries.com/art-bus.html.

Williams, Violet M. *Trusty and the Toys*. London: Raphael Tuck, c.1950.

Woolf, Virginia. *Mrs Dalloway*. Richmond: Hogarth Press, 1925.

Zola, Emile. *La Bête Humaine*. Paris: Bibliothèque-Charpentier, 1890.

7   Canals in nineteenth-century literary history

Jodie Matthews

In a rare novelistic foray to the north, Charles Dickens described the great industrial 'Coketown' in *Hard Times* (1854), based partly on Preston. While trains as a means of conveying passengers to and from Coketown steam through the narrative, the railway is largely distant from, rather than integral to, the town's industry. Those travelling by express at night see the great factories illuminated 'like Fairy palaces' rather than experiencing the noise and smoke. Mrs Sparsit's journey sees her 'borne along the arches spanning the land of coal-pits *past* and present, as if she had been caught up in a cloud and whirled *away*'. Deep within the 'town of machinery and tall chimneys', however, is its 'black canal', a blackness implicated in the town's name and polluted existence. The canal is one of the attributes 'inseparable from the work by which [Coketown] was sustained'. The products 'which found their way all over the world' to consumers who cannot bear the thought of Coketown itself and its role in their luxury are transported around Britain and to ports for trans-shipment via that very canal.[1] Dickens's responses to the railway are often discussed, but his allusions to canals are rarely, if ever, mentioned.[2]

In *Dombey and Son* (1848), Dickens's attempt to communicate the speed and terror of the railway in a breathless account of the landscape through which the train rattles includes a canal and a barge floating, syntactically abutting the place 'where the dead are lying', as if to accentuate the sense of train travel leaving the waterways to the past.[3] For Simon Bradley in his 2015 epic history of the railway, Britain is railway-haunted territory.[4] Other chapters in the present collection ably describe some of those hauntings in detail. But the railway, now regularly a feature of discussion in analyses of nineteenth-century literature, has its own, watery, ghost: the canal network. Despite vivid popular and literary associations between the Victorians and the age of steam, Bradley also reminds us that more miles of canal were built than railways in the 1830s, and Victorian goods continued to be transported around the country and to ports by navigable waterway.[5] Indeed, the Manchester Ship Canal opened in 1894, indicating the longevity of major investment in British water transport infrastructure. In the same region, despite competition from the Manchester & Leeds Railway, the Rochdale Canal was still carrying 750,000 to 900,000 tons of goods per year in the 1880s (though lost significant income from tolls).[6] Steam narrow boats came into limited use in the 1860s, with a 'fly' boat, travelling day and night, scheduled to make the 151-mile journey from the Regent's Canal to Birmingham in 44 hours.[7] The waterways' central role in Britain's industrialised and urbanised economy was rarely celebrated by the mid-nineteenth century. In an edition of the *Edinburgh Review* from 1882, an article assessing a number of works on the waterways complained that 'the services rendered to mankind by the canal engineer have of late been signally undervalued in England'.[8] This value is even more rarely commented on in Literary Studies today. This chapter moves with the hydrological turn in Humanities research to address the absence of canals in transport-, industry- and economic-related literary research. This comparatively neglected focus might enable, therefore, further exploration of an important feature of the nineteenth-century physical, commercial, social and textual landscape.

The canals' technology 'freed them from the tyranny of natural hydrology that limited the value of rivers'.[9] Many histories of Britain's industrial canals commence in the eighteenth century with James Brindley, an often-overlooked engineer today. In 1836, Brindley was seen retrospectively as having been one of the first of a new class of professional men whose opportunity to succeed was tied to 'increased national means' made possible by visionary capitalist speculation. Without the opportunity to bestow the benefits of his enterprise on the whole country, his skills may only have been put to use in his 'immediate district'. Brindley was seen in the nineteenth century as a product of, and provider for, the nation. His skill was seen as innate, 'guided by natural bias', but this might have lead nowhere without the good fortune of his being called to advise the Duke of Bridgewater, who wanted a waterway to move coal from his mines in Worsley to Manchester.[10] The *Edinburgh Review* saw this as 'the commencement of a great revolution in the material welfare of the country'.[11] Though not designed initially as a national network, as canals were gradually linked up to form a long-distance inland haulage system, connecting coal to industry and goods and materials to and from the sea, they changed Britain. There was an immediate social impact quite apart from the changes that industrialisation wrought through urbanisation and mechanisation.[12] They developed links that moved people and things between towns and cities that had previously seemed a long way away or to which people had no real reason to travel. As Charlotte Mathieson notes, canals 'served an important conceptual function, creating links through which the most isolated of rural regions were both physically and imaginatively connected to the wider world'.[13]

Adrienne Gavin and Andrew Humphries posit, in their introduction to *Transport in British Fiction*, 'transport's often unnoticed but integral role in literature'.[14] That collection focuses on technological change between 1840 and 1940 and attendant shifts in cultural perspective, on optimism about and fear of the new. It does not, therefore, consider the canals, a familiar technology by 1840. The waterways were still important to the core concerns of the Victorian period, though, to its industry, economy, and society, and should become, I argue, less marginal within nineteenth-century literary scholarship. In a *Guardian* review of Alys Fowler's recent memoir afloat, *Hidden Nature*, Alice O'Keeffe rightly noted that Fowler 'follows in the slipstream of generations of writers and artists who have been drawn to Britain's canals'.[15] O'Keeffe suggested that the tradition of the canal travelogue stretches back to 1911 – but is rather belated in citing that date. The fact that it is so easy, if erroneous, to think of canal literary history as beginning with *The Flower of Gloster* shows how under-studied and under-advertised this channel of writing is. In fact, the nineteenth century saw many canal travelogues, including J. Hassell's *Tour of the Grand Junction* (1819) and works described later in this chapter.[16] Richard Warner's 1802 *Tour Through the Northern Counties of England* notes a number of canals, and the busy 'manufactories' on their banks.[17] By the mid-nineteenth century the canal was discursively (if not necessarily industrially) marginalised and, like ripples on water, the effects of that have grown with the passage of time, so that canal literature is almost completely submerged.

In comparing literary attention to the railways with that of canals, I do not suggest simply using the study of railways as an exact model for waterways research. While both are interested in mobility and industry, trains in nineteenth-century literature are symbols of speed, change, and modernity. Canals signify in other ways. I want, here, to draw attention to the ways in which waterways research might bring together a recycling of the class-focused literary analysis more often seen in the later twentieth century than today (because canals are uniquely implicated in developing industrial capitalism), and the urgent hydrological concerns of twenty-first century ecocriticism (which grapples with the catastrophic consequences of industrial capitalism). Railways as a nineteenth-century literary trope are fascinated by water in the form of steam, while my approach to canals in nineteenth-century literary history prioritises the liquid.

In examining fiction and narrative, I take a cue from Rosemarie Bodenheimer, who is not simply interested in the ways in which literature from this period reflects or distorts working-class life, or literature's contiguousness with nonfictional documentations of industrialisation, but is on the lookout for 'patterns of contradiction and paradox which characterise the formal fantasies of people living through a period of unprecedented social change'.[18] The word 'navigate' is often deployed to describe the subject's experience of such periods, and this term comes from travel by water; a 'navigation' is also a canal. Canals in nineteenth-century literature can be seen, therefore, as not simply a reflection of the realities of industrial networks at this time, but a literary means of navigating a route 'through highly charged ideological territories' as narratives attempt to 'bring order and meaning to situations characterised exactly by their lack of established historical meaning, or by acute conflicts about the meanings assigned to them in public discourse'.[19]

A focus on canals helps explore questions such as 'what did it mean to be mobile and working class?' 'How did canals connect the nation, and the nation to the world?' 'What is the place of water – in technology, as transport, as idea, and as socio-cultural connection – in modernity?'

Jamie Linton has examined the ways in which water has been modernised as an abstraction, divorced from 'ecological, cultural, or social factors'. However, the history of water, he maintains, 'is a story of how people have drawn meanings, ideas, representations, and powers from water'.[20] In contrast to the abstraction Linton details as an archaeologist of knowledge, my approach is to consider literature as a social hydrological discourse and specifically, as social, a discourse in which class is implicated. As the editors of a collection of essays about *Water in Social Imagination* note, this way of thinking has the potential to 'rehabilitate knowledge and modes of perception left marginalised if water is perceived only in physical and technological terms and left alienated from its social significance'.[21]

The rest of this chapter considers three texts chronologically over a mid-century span of 25 years, in order to offer a sense of the ways in which this nineteenth-century literature engages water's social significance to discuss class and work. The first is an often-overlooked 'social problem' novel by Charlotte Elizabeth Tonna. *Helen Fleetwood* (1841) has perhaps not tempted many potential later readers because of its strong religiosity, paternalism, and furious anti-Socialism. Nevertheless, it speaks clearly to the ways in which Bodenheimer describes literary narratives working out the social conflicts of industrialised urban life. The second text returns us to Dickens, with an anonymous article in his *Household Words* from 1858. The final text is George Eliot's 1866 novel, *Felix Holt: The Radical*, a work which, intriguingly for an analysis that touches on the canal as a route to the past, looks back to an earlier period before the Reform Act of 1832.

Helen Fleetwood was initially serialised in the *Christian Lady's Magazine* (which Tonna edited), and the novel wears its author's evangelicalism heavily. It shares much in theme and imagery with Elizabeth Barrett Browning's more famous but later poem, 'The Cry of the Children' (1843), and anticipates the social problem novels of Disraeli and Gaskell. In 1970, Ivanka Kovačević and S. Barbara Kanner were able to point to 'an almost total conspiracy of silence' surrounding Tonna and her work, but she has been the subject of feminist scholarly retrieval since then. These critics, while noting that the novel is 'unashamedly propagandistic and self-consciously reliant upon the dry bones of parliamentary and other reports', see it as 'a genuinely moving assault upon the reader's conscience in its graphic account of what it is like to be a woman or child forced by compulsions of poverty to work in a factory'.[22]

Helen is a 'simple country girl' adopted by a widow and brought up with the widow's grandchildren. On the expiry of a lease on their cliff-top cottage, the family are persuaded by officials keen to avoid their becoming a burden on the parish to move to Manchester for work in the cotton mills.

Most criticism focuses, understandably, on the Manchester portion of the novel, for here is found in Helen a fully realised female factory worker as heroine. The conditions in which she and her family must work are appalling, an explicit indictment of the factory system. The girls are beaten and mocked; their cousin is gravely injured by machinery. They work in an environment where they are 'excluded from the free air, and almost from the pure light of day'; they are 'shut up in an atmosphere polluted by clouds of fetid breath, and all the sickening exhalations of a crowded human mass, whose unwashed, overworked bodies were also in many cases diseased'. Such conditions lead, insists the narrator, to 'perversion of mind and corruption of morals'. Helen's adopted brother despairs that the factory system 'fattens [the rich] and melts the flesh off our bones'. Like the goods produced in Coketown, 'it brings all indulgences within their reach, and kills the industrious creatures whose toil provides them'.[23] The descriptions of factory life are realistic and upsetting. I am most interested, however, in the details of the family's migration to Manchester.

The novel makes absolutely clear: these are 'altered times'. Tonna, as well as using literature as campaigning material for the Ten Hours Bill (aiming to limit the working hours of women and young people), attempts to make sense of these new conditions, and sees the Greens and Helen navigate their way from a rural, agricultural existence to an industrial urban one. They do this by canal. They leave their village with only bedding and blankets, tightly packed for the party to sit on for the 'long, tedious, uncomfortable' journey. With the boatmen they have their first experience of 'mercenary strangers' and 'contemptuous rudeness', having been respected and looked after in their native village. The journey itself performs the painful movement from village to urban centre, cliff-top garden to Cottonopolis, but the boatmen also 'dropped hints' of the change the family will see. It is not particularly common to read accounts of migrations by canal, and I suggest that Tonna's motivation in selecting this mode of transport is more literary than her repeated appeals to factual evidence and real-life testimony would suggest. This slow passage marks a transition from one mode of life to another, not just for these individuals but for the nation. The village is no idyll as they leave it, but life there is infinitely preferable to the bare survival of their existence in Manchester.

Tonna uses this passage by water to mark social transition. I propose that she also selects this transport in particular to evince another enforced journey by boat from a life of freedom to one of servitude: the Middle Passage of the transatlantic slave trade. In so doing, she recognises water as what we can call today a 'social hydrological discourse' in order to make a political statement about the factory system as white slavery. Britain's role in the system of transatlantic slavery officially ended on 1 August 1834, following the previous year's Slavery Abolition Act, though the apprenticeship system remained in place until 1838. Cotton produced via American slavery was imported to Manchester until 1865. From a twenty-first-century perspective we might resist drawing straightforward equivalences between the slaves who picked cotton and the exploited workers who wove it, but from where Tonna stood this was a powerful argument – with the further implication that the capitalist system for making cloth from cotton hurt everyone involved, including the factory owners so distanced from God.[24] As the Greens and Helen make their journey, the narrator comments that

> The waste of human life in the factories, like that in the plantations of the west, occasions so pressing a demand for a supply of new labourers, that it gives rise to a traffic not very dissimilar to the slave trade.

The journey by canal is, therefore, the factories' Middle Passage. Tonna not only wrote about transatlantic slavery as an analogy for the British factory system; as well as poetry on the subject, she had published a novel, *The System: A Tale of the West Indies* in 1827, though the slaves' passage to these islands is not detailed therein.[25] This novel, too, privileges didacticism over narrative, and views insurrection as a crime. Tonna's literary connection between a canal migration and the Middle Passage, an example of water as social, political, and historical, inspires further probing. For instance, in what ways are the proceeds of slavery implicated in canal ownership? The UCL *Legacies of British Slave-ownership* project provides some clues: Thomas Bond of Lancaster, a West Indies plantation owner, used this income to buy shares in the Lancaster Canal; the manager of that same canal company was Samuel Gregson, who owned slaves in the Virgin Islands; George Hyde Clarke, who inherited an estate and 220 slaves in Jamaica invested in and promoted the Peak Forest Canal Company; George Daubeny III, slave-owner on Montserat, owned 30 shares in the Worcester and Birmingham Canal; William Hendrie made money from his estate in Tobago, which he was able to invest in (amongst other projects) the Coventry and Grand Junction canals.[26] These indicative examples demonstrate, along with Tonna's impulse to use the canal as an after-image of the Middle Passage to emphasise the fate of her working-class characters, the fact of the waterways as economically and discursively implicated in capitalist systems of human exploitation. What Tonna's hydrological gesture in representing the labouring poor also reveals is the way that the meaning of the waterways as a feature of national power and industry (as with so much British history) should, as Paul Gilroy puts it in his classic *The Black Atlantic*, be understood within 'a complex pattern of antagonistic relationships with the supra-national and imperial'.[27] In other words, Tonna's use of the canal to engage abolitionist discourse in the service of Manchester's white factory workers is not an anomaly, but a startling reminder of the supranational and imperial political and economic networks into which the canals are locked.

As if to make this realisation unavoidable, a three-part piece in *Household Words* about an inbound canal trip in August 1858, 'On the Canal', begins its narrative voyage by describing a transatlantic passage. The ostensible purpose of the article's broad horizon is to extol the virtues of exploring home territory, every corner of the nation, but its effect is to connect the placidity of the Grand Junction Canal to the author's feared Atlantic. While my reading of the previous literary example focused on privation, the *Household Words* triptych features want of a wholly different order: the middle-class canal tourists unable to satisfy their gastronomic whims while on board a narrowboat. They are separated from the bounty of the agricultural land and countryside whilst simultaneously passing through it. The canal figures as passage, from urban centre to urban centre, from present to past, and from city to country, while never existing satisfyingly as a place *in itself.*

Having 'nearly exhausted the land of [his] birth', the author of the article (labelled only within the text as 'Must'r Olly', as anonymity was the norm in *Household Words*) takes to water 'in its placidist condition' for his next intrepid adventure. While noting that the railway cannot match the fly-boat for transporting heavy goods not requiring rapid transit, the author asserts that they have 'gone at one bound a century back in the history of conveyance'. Almost immediately, he draws attention to his appetites, alluding, for comic effect, to the spectacle of 'accommodating [his] vast bulk to the confined space afforded by the crowded cabin of a Grand Junction Canal Company's fly-boat'. At the commencement of the journey, he places himself 'in a cab by the side of a friend ['Cuddy'] and a large meat pie, who were to attend me on the journey'. The name that the author gives to his friend also points to food: a cuddy is a cabin in which officers and cabin-passengers take their meals.[28]

The author, Cuddy, and the pie board the fly-boat *Stourport*, a reminder to the reader, with that name, of early canal towns. Stourport-on-Severn, on the Staffordshire and Worcestershire Canal, grew out of James Brindley's decision to house basins, wharves and warehouses there. Leaving the basin, the canal moves through the Islington tunnel, 'between the silent houses of Camden Town', past London Zoo and 'to the termination of the Regent's Canal, and the commencement of the Grand Junction Canal' at Paddington. Here, at 2am, Cuddy cannot be restrained from attacking the meat pie. Meanwhile, 'the victualing of the vessel consists in shipping a sack of potatoes, a quantity of inferior tea, and about 50 pounds of meat'. Eight-pound loaves of bread are acquired en route.[29] At 4am, Cuddy is at the pie once more. The disappointingly inferior tea is no more appetising once brewed for breakfast, served as it is weak, sugared, in a cup without a saucer 'and, above all, without milk'.[30]

From the metropolis, the *Stourport* glides along the 'artificial river', and the passengers' 'admiration for the picturesque beauty of the country' as seen from this vantage increases. There are views of woods and meadows, parks and gardens running down to the water, brooks and sparkling waterfalls. However, 'man cannot be fed on scenery' alone.[31] Soon, the author and Cuddy are hankering for 'rural luxuries' rather than the stale bread and boiled beef on board. 'Where were the new-laid eggs? where were the fowls that laid them? where were the autumnal fruits? where was the delicate bacon? the cottage bread? the cream thick as paste?'[32] They have money to spend, but nothing to spend it on. Captain Randle is no use to them in locating a market: 'familiar as he was with the line of route, he knew less than an infant about the commercial provision-supplying capabilities of the towns and stations on the canal'. In lieu of useful information about where to purchase the consumables they desire, Randle tells them about the vast quantity of beasts his butcher slaughters. He 'can't be messed about wi' a lot o' small butchers'.[33] The rural farmer has been supplanted by the large-scale meat processor. Randle can take them *through* the countryside, carrying them *on* the canal, but there is no 'at' to this journey, no association with a particular place – especially a place they might source food. Certainly, the Captain's land home in Stoke, Staffordshire, is mentioned in the second part – like Stourport a clear reminder of the canals' early history and the social changes it engendered. A 'boatman's village' near Braunston in Northamptonshire is described with anthropological detail. It is 'the only place' on the journey 'where the people on the land seemed to belong to the people on the water'. This sense of belonging lies not just in the conversation, ritual, and specialist shops, but the fact that the author is able to buy several pounds of beefsteak. Canal towns and other locales with which canal communities were associated, such as Banbury on the Oxford Canal, are what one might call places of the canal; I do not suggest that canals in some way lack a sense of place because of their function as passage. However, the waterway as represented in *Household Words* is not experienced, for the most part, as place. It is a channel, and the passengers and captain have little knowledge of nor real access to the land that they pass, as evidenced by the small yet lively exception to be found near Braunston. The author and Cuddy on one walk meet an old man carrying pails of fresh milk and attempt to buy it, not understanding that even a shilling a pint will not be enough; it is not for sale to passing trade. The same happens later with a leg of mutton that cannot be bought for two shillings a pound. They find that their 'canal journey had brought [them] to a land where the ordinary relations of buyer and seller were reversed; where it was looked upon as a favour granted when an article was sold'. They eventually obtain enough eggs to make a 'tolerable breakfast', but then 'some demon' whispers to Cuddy: 'have a fowl for dinner'. The demon of consumer desire has followed them into their simple 'canal-existence'. The quest for fowl takes up a considerable portion of the third instalment of 'On the Canal'.

As Charlotte Boyce explains, the 'so-called "consumer revolution" of the eighteenth century' meant that 'the inhabitants of nineteenth-century Britain had access to a greater range of foodstuffs than ever before'. As well as 'technological advances in food production and preservation', those who had plenty also benefited from 'trans-global trading networks' – and the waterways were a vital part of these networks.[34] The canals thus contribute to the diversity of food that the author and Cuddy expect, yet make it impossible to purchase while they are afloat. This image is also very clear when the author complains about the cutlery on board, which 'must have come from Sheffield, when that distinguished town was first struggling with the earliest rudiments of its staple manufacture'. Sheffield's luxury silver-plate trade followed Thomas Boulsover's invention of the material in 1742.[35] By 1819, the Company of Cutlers (governing the quality of Sheffield blades since the seventeenth century) ensured that the Sheffield Canal came into the city centre. South Yorkshire's canals were integral to the development of Sheffield's cutlery industry and to the middle-class author's access to such refinement. Whilst on the canal itself, however, he is forced to eat with what he imagines must be an older, rougher version of the implements. This diffi-culty, a water-borne obstacle to obtaining food and its accoutrements, high-lights how these middle-class passengers find themselves, as do the urban working-class, 'increasingly dislocated from agricultural food sources' and, indeed, from manufactured goods.[36] The author and Cuddy may feel that they had stepped back 100 years when choosing to voyage by canal but, once more, this mode of transport insists on the reader considering the ways in which the travellers navigate the cultural conditions they inhabited in the nineteenth century. As Cuddy and the author prepare to disembark in Bir-mingham, they must reckon with the 'floating dead dogs and factory scum of the inky canal' on the return to industrialised Victorian urban life. But Cuddy and the author are paradoxically more at home in the city, despite its death and scum. It is a location where they at least know where their next meat pie is coming from, unlike the picturesque hunger they suffered as they passed through the countryside.[37] The social significance of the waters of the canal in this text is as a symbol for the nineteenth-century consumer's alienation from food production in a urbanised industrial capitalism.

As *Household Words* suggests that travelling by canal is also like travel-ling back in time, so George Eliot's *Felix Holt* looks to forms of transport as a way of characterising the past, in this case the days of coach travel. Eliot compares the sights and sounds of that long, slow journey to a future where travel will more likely resemble a 'bullet' being 'shot [...] through a tube'.[38] The canal is part of that older way of life, but it is also what marks the opening of change; not just a passage for water, but a passage to the fu-ture. It becomes, in literature, a way of signalling the navigation of religious, political, and cultural transition in England.

Felix Holt's Treby Magna was an 'old-fashioned, grazing, brewing, wool-packing, cheese-loading' type of market town, until:

> there befell new conditions, complicating its relation with the rest of the world, and gradually awakening in it that higher consciousness which is known to bring higher pains. First came the canal; next, the working of the coal-mines at Sproxton, two miles off the town; and thirdly, the dis-covery of a saline spring, which suggested to a too constructive brain the possibility of turning Treby Magna into a fashionable watering-place.

So daring an idea was not originated by a native Trebian, but by a young lawyer who came from a distance, knew the dictionary by heart, and was probably an illegitimate son of somebody or other.[39]

Traditional, agrarian existence alters once the canal allows the exploitation of the coal mines. In turn, this brings new economic and social opportunities but also new pains. A world outside Treby Magna begins to influence life there. The 'non-native', Jermyn, with his suspiciously broad vocabulary, has ideas for capitalist speculation that will further line the pockets of the aristocracy. The hint of illegitimacy points us towards an obsession of the novel and, indeed, of Victorian fiction: who has fathered whom. This can be understood as an anxiety connected to knowledge of the community: unknown new-comers are harder to vouch for; we do not know their families. It is not just that Jermyn brings secrets with him; he digs away at old ones, makes a cut – another word for a canal, in fact – beneath the solid foundations of old English families. The spa project fails, however, and 'some attributed the failure to the coal-mines and the canal'.[40] Even as they appear to usher in prosperity, the industrial canals are thought of as dirty. These new, canal-motivated conditions of Treby Magna and the non-native who exploits them can be seen as a synecdoche for provincial relationships with imperial metropoles and Britain's relationships with the world; and the novel makes these connections clear. Felix Holt himself returns from medical training in Glasgow to suspend his mother's sale in quack medicines. His scientific and political enlightenment threatens their family income. Harold Transome returns from Smyrna – a port of the Ottoman Empire, which, after 1839, was, like Britain, attempting to modernise rapidly and exploit international trade links – with a half-Greek son and radical ideas. He represents, in many ways, 'the East' in an Orientalist vision of the world (albeit an 'empty, economic Orientalism' as Alicia Carroll describes it), and 'is an ingenious fashioning of what much of Victorian England feared and desired in 1832 [the time of the novel's setting] and in 1867 [the context of its publication]'.[41] These changes in the village and its denizens contribute to a sense that people, ideas and capital are being moved around in new, and perhaps troubling, ways. This is changing Treby Magna and changing Britain. As the novel's Mr Nolan has it, 'the prosperity of the country is one web', a network now (in 1832) connected by improved roads and canals, and in 1867, by rail.[42]

Eliot connects the canals, via Treby Magna's industrialisation, with the national social tumult of the 1830s (as her readers navigated the changes threatened by the Reform Bill), with reconfigurations of class and power. Carolyn Lesjak asserts, in a consideration of the form of the industrial novel, that, paradoxically, 'a central precondition for [the] symbolic resolution of conflict is the exclusion of work and working-class struggle from representation'. She suggests that 'to mute class conflict and the disparities of wealth which divide the productive sphere', working-class characters are 'represented in the pub or the home' so that workers are defined in terms of pleasure/non-work rather than 'productive activity'.[43] Felix, Eliot's protagonist apparently wholly concerned with the realities of the class struggle, manages to turn the canals from a site of work to a site of leisure *and* domesticity at once. As he walks alongside the canal, he considers its 'Sunday peacefulness', a peace 'hardly broken if a horse pulled into sight along the towing-path, and a boat, with a little curl of blue smoke issuing from its tin chimney, came slowly gliding behind'. Though the narrator admits that this is a 'boyish impression', Felix retains the idea 'that the days in a canal-boat were all like Sundays'. The labour described in *Household Words* disappears altogether, supplanted by the perennial Sabbath of Felix's conception.

As Lesjak anticipates, Felix follows this branch canal to the coal pits and then to the pub, 'Chubb's', where the reader finds the colliers and navvies – precisely where the electioneering agents also want to find them when they try to rouse a mob in support of one candidate or another. It is where Felix hopes to find them even as he tries to convince them to join him in agitating for political representation. And as for the people inside the boat with its little curl of blue smoke issuing from the tin chimney? Entirely absent. The narrative coherence of the industrial novel and the fragile web of national prosperity are both reliant on the suppression of work and of working-class struggle; Felix Holt eventually calms down in order to marry, and his wife, Esther, resigns her claim to the Transome fortune. I suggest that this representational suppression can be seen very tellingly in Felix's blindness to the labour of canal transport. *Felix Holt* may not be a novel *about* canals, but following that waterway enables an exploration of the novel's ideological navigations.

By examining three literary texts in terms of the canals they feature, using those waterways as a point of reference for the navigations of the characters and, indeed, nineteenth-century readers, through a voracious industrialised capitalism is a novel direction for the hydrological turn in the Humanities. Throughout all of the texts, and countless more from this period, water can be understood for its literal role in industry and technology, and as a figurative connection between the working classes in different nineteenth-century contexts of oppression. The plight of Manchester's cotton manufacturers is connected via a canal journey with American slaves; this connection makes the links between industrial wealth and slavery legible. A middle-class writer's comic search for decent food while on a canal journey prompts the reader to consider access to food in an economically reorganised Britain, with the implication that the urban working classes were, unlike their rural counterparts, alienated from the means to find nourishment as producers rather than consumers (and consumers with little means to purchase what they required). Felix Holt's inability to understand the canal boat as a place of labour rather than rest is of a piece with industrial fiction's location of the working class away from the labour that defines them, a representation that ideologically suppresses the power of the worker in a regionally and internationally networked nation. These interpretations assert the potential for reading the waterways, with a canal focus drawing new sets of texts and contexts together to understand the ways in which literature navigates the nineteenth century.

Notes

1 Charles Dickens, *Hard Times: For These Times*, ed. by Kate Flint (London: Penguin, 2003), 6, 202, 27–8. Emphasis added.
2 See, for instance, Daragh Downes, ""Excellent Monsters": The Railway Theme in Dickens's Novels," *English: Journal of the English Association* 61, no. 235 (2012): 382–393.
3 Charles Dickens, *Dombey and Son*, ed. by Andrew Sanders (London: Penguin, 2002), 9.
4 Simon Bradley, *The Railways: Nation, Network and People* (London: Profile, 2015), 6.
5 Ibid., 9.
6 Peter Maw, "Water Transport in the Industrial Age: Commodities and Carriers on the Rochdale Canal, 1804–1855," *Journal of Transport History* 30, no. 2 (2009): 200–228.
7 Anthony Burton, *The Canal Pioneers: Canal Construction from 2,500 BC to the early 20th Century* (Barnsley: Pen and Sword, 2015), 209.
8 "Inland Navigation," *The Edinburgh Review* 156 (1882): 439.
9 Gerard Turnbull, "Canals, coal and Regional Growth During the Industrial Revolution," *Economic History Review* 2nd ser. 40, no. 4 (1987): 537–560.
10 "Obituary: James Brindley, 1716-1772," *ICE Transactions* 1 (1836): 6–8. For more on Brindley's career and influence see Christine Richardson, *James Brindley: Canal Pioneer* (Burton-on-Trent: Waterways World, 2005) and Victoria Owens, *James Brindley and the Duke of Bridgewater: Canal Visionaries* (Stroud: Amberley, 2015).
11 "Inland Navigation," *The Edinburgh Review*, 439.
12 See Liz McIvor, *Canals, The Making of a Nation: A Journey into the Heart of Industrial Britain* (London: BBC Books, 2015).
13 Charlotte Mathieson, *Mobility in the Victorian Novel: Placing the Nation* (Houndmills: Palgrave, 2015), 5.
14 Adrienne Gavin and Andrew Humphries, *Transport in British Fiction: Technologies of Movement, 1840–1940* (Houndmills: Palgrave, 2015).
15 Alice O'Keeffe, "*Hidden Nature* by Alys Fowler Review – A Life Crisis on the Canals," *The Guardian*, April 1, 2017, accessed 2018, www.theguardian.com/books/2017/apr/01/hidden-nature-by-alys-fowler-review.
16 J. Hassell, *Tour of the Grand Junction* (London: Published Privately, 1819).
17 Reverend Richard Warner, *A Tour Through the Northern Counties of England, and the Borders of Scotland* (Bath: Cruttwell, 1802).
18 Rosemarie Bodenheimer, *The Politics of Story in Victorian Social Fiction* (Ithaca, NY and London: Cornell University Press, 1991), 5.
19 Ibid, 4.
20 Jamie Linton, *What is Water? The History of a Modern Abstraction* (Vancouver and Toronto: UBC Press, 2010), 8, 34, 88.
21 Jane Costlow, Yrjö Haila, and Arja Rosenholm, eds., *Water in Social Imagination: From Technological Optimism to Contemporary Environmentalism* (Leiden and Boston: Brill Rodopi, 2017).
22 Ivanka Kovačević and S. Barbara Kanner, "Blue Book into Novel: The Forgotten Industrial Fiction of Charlotte Elizabeth Tonna," *Nineteenth-Century Fiction* 25, no. 2 (1970): 152–173.

23 Charlotte Elizabeth Tonna, *Helen Fleetwood* (London: Seeley and Burnside, 1841), 2, 165, 393.
24 Tonna was not, of course, alone in making this uneasy comparison. Richard Oastler, for instance, another abolitionist and campaigner for the Ten Hours Bill at home, and whose name adorns the University of Huddersfield building in which I write, referred to 'Yorkshire slavery', insisting that this was 'more horrid' even than colonial slavery. See Oastler, "Slavery in Yorkshire," *Leeds Mercury*, October 16, 1830. *British Library Newspapers*, http://tinyurl.galegroup.com/tinyurl/5fwKC0, accessed December 15, 2017. On the complexities of understanding shared transatlantic exploitation and international radicalism, especially when assessing the later Lancashire Cotton Famine of the 1860s, see Alan Rice, "The Cotton that Connects, the Cloth that Binds," *Atlantic Studies* 4, no. 2 (2007): 285–303.
25 Charlotte Elizabeth Tonna, *The System: A Tale of the West Indies* (London: Westley and Davis, 1827).
26 "Commercial Legacies", *Legacies of British Slave-Ownership*, University College London, 2018, accessed December 15, 2017, www.ucl.ac.uk/lbs/commercial/.
27 Paul Gilroy, *The Black Atlantic: Modernity and Double Consciousness* (Cambridge, MA: Harvard University Press, 1993), 11.
28 "On the Canal: First Stage," *Household Words*, September 11, 1858, 289–293.
29 Ibid.
30 "On the Canal: First Stage," *Household Words*, September 18, 1858, 318–323.
31 Ibid.
32 "On the Canal: First Stage," *Household Words*, September 25, 1858, 354–360.
33 Ibid.
34 Charlotte Boyce and Joan Fitzpatrick, *A History of Food in Literature: From the Fourteenth Century to the Present* (Abingdon: Routledge, 2017), 201–202.
35 Maxine Berg, *Luxury and Pleasure in Eighteenth-Century Britain* (Oxford: Oxford University Press, 2005), 161.
36 Boyce and Fitzpatrick, *A History of Food in Literature*, 201–202.
37 "On the Canal: Stage the Third," *Household Words*, 360.
38 George Eliot, *Felix Holt: The Radical*, ed. Lynda Mugglestone (London: Penguin, 1995), 3.
39 Ibid., 46.
40 Ibid., 47.
41 Alicia Carroll, "The Giaour's Campaign: Desire and the Other in Felix Holt: The Radical," *NOVEL: A Forum on Fiction* 30, no. 2 (1997): 247, 250. Carroll's article is a nuanced and exceptionally-well contextualised reading of Orientalism in this novel.
42 Eliot, *Felix Holt*, 208.
43 Carolyn Lesjak, "A Modern Odyssey: Realism, the Masses, and Nationalism in George Eliot's *Felix Holt*'," *NOVEL: A Forum on Fiction* 30, no. 1 (1996): 78–97.

Bibliography

Primary

"Commercial Legacies." *Legacies of British Slave-Ownership*. University College London, 2018. Accessed December 15, 2017. www.ucl.ac.uk/lbs/commercial/.
Dickens, Charles. *Dombey and Son*, edited by Andrew Sanders. London: Penguin, 2002.
———. *Hard Times: For These Times*, edited by Kate Flint. London: Penguin, 2003.

Eliot, George. *Felix Holt: The Radical*, edited by Lynda Mugglestone. London: Penguin, 1995.

Hassell, J. *Tour of the Grand Junction*. London: Published Privately, 1819.

Tonna, Charlotte Elizabeth. *Helen Fleetwood*. London: Seeley and Burnside, 1841.

———. *The System: A Tale of the West Indies*. London: Westley and Davis, 1827.

Warner, Reverend Richard. *A Tour Through the Northern Counties of England, and the Borders of Scotland*. Bath: Cruttwell, 1802.

Secondary

Berg, Maxine. *Luxury and Pleasure in Eighteenth-Century Britain*. Oxford: Oxford University Press, 2005.

Bodenheimer, Rosemarie. *The Politics of Story in Victorian Social Fiction*. Ithaca, NY and London: Cornell University Press, 1991.

Boyce, Charlotte, and Joan Fitzpatrick. *A History of Food in Literature: From the Fourteenth Century to the Present*. Abingdon: Routledge, 2017.

Bradley, Simon. *The Railways: Nation, Network and People*. London: Profile, 2015.

Burton, Anthony. *The Canal Pioneers: Canal Construction from 2,500 BC to the early 20th Century*. Barnsley: Pen and Sword, 2015.

Carroll, Alicia. "The Giaour's Campaign: Desire and the Other in Felix Holt: The Radical." *NOVEL: A Forum on Fiction* 30, no. 2 (1997): 237–268.

Costlow, Jane, Yrjö Haila, and Arja Rosenholm, eds., *Water in Social Imagination: From Technological Optimism to Contemporary Environmentalism*. Leiden and Boston: Brill Rodopi, 2017.

Downes, Daragh, ""Excellent Monsters": The Railway Theme in Dickens's Novels." *English: Journal of the English Association* 61, no. 235 (2012): 382–393.

Gavin, Adrienne, and Andrew Humphries. *Transport in British Fiction: Technologies of Movement, 1840–1940*. Houndmills: Palgrave, 2015.

Gilroy, Paul. *The Black Atlantic: Modernity and Double Consciousness*. Cambridge, MA: Harvard University Press, 1993.

Kovačević, Ivanka, and S. Barbara Kanner. "Blue Book into Novel: The Forgotten Industrial Fiction of Charlotte Elizabeth Tonna." *Nineteenth-Century Fiction* 25, no. 2 (1970): 152–173.

Lesjak, Carolyn. "A Modern Odyssey: Realism, the Masses, and Nationalism in George Eliot's *Felix Holt*." *NOVEL: A Forum on Fiction* 30, no. 1 (1996): 78–97.

Linton, Jamie. *What is Water? The History of a Modern Abstraction*. Vancouver and Toronto: UBC Press, 2010.

Mathieson, Charlotte. *Mobility in the Victorian Novel: Placing the Nation*. Houndmills: Palgrave, 2015.

Maw, Peter. "Water Transport in the Industrial Age: Commodities and Carriers on the Rochdale Canal, 1804–1855." *Journal of Transport History* 30, no. 2 (2009): 200–228.

McIvor, Liz. *Canals, The Making of a Nation: A Journey into the Heart of Industrial Britain*. London: BBC Books, 2015.

"Obituary: James Brindley, 1716–1772." *ICE Transactions* 1 (1836): 6–8.

O'Keeffe, Alice. "*Hidden Nature* by Alys Fowler review – a Life Crisis on the Canals." *The Guardian*. April 1, 2017. Accessed 2018. www.theguardian.com/books/2017/apr/01/hidden-nature-by-alys-fowler-review.

Owens, Victoria. *James Brindley and the Duke of Bridgewater: Canal Visionaries.* Stroud: Amberley, 2015.

Rice, Alan. "The Cotton that Connects, the Cloth that Binds." *Atlantic Studies* 4, no. 2 (2007): 285–303.

Richardson, Christine. *James Brindley: Canal Pioneer.* Burton-on-Trent: Waterways World, 2005.

Turnbull, Gerard. "Canals, Coal and Regional Growth During the Industrial Revolution." *Economic History Review* 2nd ser. 40, no. 4 (1987): 537–560.

Periodicals and newspapers

Household Words
Leeds Mercury
The Edinburgh Review

Part 3
Methodologies

Part 2

Methodologies

8 Reading historical archive film through sensory ethnography

Peter Cox

Introduction

Recent work in sensory ethnography, especially as applied to the study of mobilities, makes extensive use of video recording as a means of making field notes. A body of literature has built up around these mobile methodologies and the practices of interpretation connected with using this data. Drawing on these approaches to mobile methods and visual research the author undertook a six-month study to explore the sensory experiences of cycle riders as urban (and peri-urban) travellers.

At the same time, investigations were undertaken using conventional analyses of photographic and written archive materials to locate current practices in historical contexts. During the course of this investigation it became clear that there were also film documentary sources that could inform this research. This then raised a question as to whether existing historical film sources could be "read" and interpreted as a form of 'naturally occurring data' using the same analytical frameworks deployed for the interpretation of the video field notes captured in the investigation of sensory experiences.

This chapter outlines the methodological procedures involved in this analysis and the result of initial attempts to deploy these in relation to historical sources. By connecting approaches developed in the context of digital recording of mobile experience to extant analogue film sources it considers whether such connections can enable a richer understanding of historical mobile subjects. While visual analysis suggests that film-makers' intentions, especially in framing and editing their subject matter, are always inescapable, interpretative practices applied to digital recordings of public space today suggest there may be value in considering incidental "background" mobilities in historical documentary film and incidentally explains how a critical sociologist comes to be developing historical research tools.

Thinking about film as method

Considering transport practices and technologies in a broader context of mobilities studies has opened a wide range of considerations both of subject and method. These expanded interests are reflected in the changes to content and approach in publications such as the long-established *Journal of Transport History* and newer journals such as *Transfers: interdisciplinary journal of mobility studies*. These stand alongside the focus on transport in *Mobilities* and *Applied Mobilities*. While much of this work remains firmly focused either on the present or on historical work dedicated to conventional explorations of written archive sources, increasing use is made of cross-disciplinary approaches. These blur boundaries between historical investigations and sociological and anthropological research, further drawing on methods pioneered in literature and arts studies, as well as using these practices as sources.[1] Important strands in this multidisciplinary armoury of research techniques and practices are those concerned on the one hand with visual research methods and on the other with the concurrent possibilities offered by digital technologies.

As Marion and Crowder succinctly point out, the social sciences have a long tradition of using cameras in research.[2] Indeed, both sociological and anthropological fields of study and documentary photography are born out of parallel concerns in nineteenth-century modernity to record and understand the world. Early debates on subjectivism versus objectivism in the visual image continue to be central to any analysis of visual material.[3] The unresolved tensions between these poles requires us, as researchers, to acknowledge the degree to which all our methods are reliant upon often under-examined epistemological foundations and assumptions concerning the constitution of truth, verity, facticity and meaning. The contested place of visual imagery and its potential for manipulation (in both production and reception) highlights the importance of critical analysis of sources, not just for provenance, but for how we derive knowledge from them.

While ethnographic and anthropological use of photographic material, both still and moving image, is well established, a more strictly sociological dimension is a more recent innovation.[4] Part of the reason for this is critical sociology's positive engagement with social constructionism.[5] Constructionist scepticism of (naïve) realism highlights the ways in which meaning cannot and should not be taken for granted in any form of source data, whether visual, written or recorded by other means. Every method of generating data is a form of intervention and thus needs to be considered critically.[6] In historical terms, one needs especially to bring in to play the means by which the artefact, whether film or not, was not just brought into being, but also the implications of its preservation. Indeed, film's deliberate creation as a communication tool raises serious questions as to the limits within which it can be understood as naturally occurring data.

The framing and selection of image by the photographer or film-maker is a deliberate and constructed act. Compositional elements, visual clues, even focus and depth of field all are tools to create images not simply to record an objective reality but to form a particular way of seeing that image.

Viewers engaged with the material are persuaded to read it in particular ways through presentational schemes. An early and important example of this kind of visual sociology was highlighted in Beatrix Campbell's 1984 study, *Wigan Pier Revisited*, in which she undertook an investigation into conditions of working-class life in the north of England. As reflecting her findings against Orwell's, she also juxtaposed these thoughts with the way in which well-known works photographic works provided particularly enduring images of social reality. She showed how the visual image acted as a powerful narrative of its own, often overpowering and excluding more complex and multifaceted readings of social life.[7] As well as highlighting Orwell's relative blindness to the gendering of social class inequalities, she also show how Bert Hardy's image of a flat capped man leaning on a street corner, head bowed and looked on by two children, published in *Picture Post* had subsequently become "part of the iconography of unemployment in the 30s". Such was the ubiquity of Hardy's photograph at the time of her writing that a parodic image was reutilised in 1983 as an advertisement for high fashion. Setting the two photographs side by side allowed her to question how visual representations powerfully shape our historico-social imaginations asking "which is fact, which is fantasy?" Baudrillard's parallel work on the simulacrum only heightens the pertinence of this question and indicates the caution we need to use in any visual investigation.[8]

When it comes to reading moving images as text, the problems are just as intensive. As Sian Barber reminds us in her excellent and practical introduction to those considering use of film as a research resource notes, "film is a crafted artefact".[9] Documentary film is equally, if not more so, in that its very intention is to persuade the viewer into a particularly determinate reading. The crafting of documentary film engages all the processes of still photography and multiplies them with shot selection, editing, juxtaposition and transition. Further, film, as a medium "generated for the purposes of being seen" is further mediated at each stage of production, distribution and consumption.[10] The power and ubiquity of the visual today and its legacy in propaganda through the twentieth-century lands a credibility to any reluctance to try and use film as a resource for historical enquiry (except in and of itself as an historical artefact). Film studies as a wider discipline has opened up our understanding of the medium and our capacity to read the moving image, but as viewers we are nevertheless constrained only to see what the filmmaker wants us to see. Pointing out that film is a flawed source is only of limited value, however. All sources are flawed. What any source demands of the academic researcher is rigour in method and analysis and openness of process in order that the limitations of those methods be fully understood. We need to consistently ask how the present of the film is being represented, by whom, for whom and with what purpose.

Digital videography and mobilities studies

The rapid expansions of digital photography and capacities for online sharing in the twenty-first century have dramatically changed the location of the visual in our academic research methods. Possibilities offered by digital recording of mobile practices allow different forms of investigation of those practices.[11] The portability and disposability of digital video coupled with its linkage to other information sources, including social media, opens up profound new spaces for academic investigation. Notwithstanding important debates about the deployment and utility of novel methods on mobilities research and whether they provide a privileged understanding or are simply another tool through which to see and understand, the use of digital recording methods has vastly increased awareness of the importance and possibilities of visual researches.[12]

My own specialist subfield of research within mobilities studies centres on vélomobilities: the systematic practices concerned with cycling.[13] In common with other researchers, my work has used digital video recording to investigate mobile practices of cycling.[14] Investigating people's mobile experiences when actually on the move, traditional ethnographic approaches have expanded to engage strongly with the kinaesthetic dimensions of mobility.[15] Within studies on cycling as a mobile practice, therefore, making and using visual resources as part of the investigative process has become a notable feature. My initial interest in understanding how design affects mobility practices and possibilities expanded into consideration of how the spatial is part of a triad of elements that make up mobile subjectivity. The traveller is not just a person utilising a machine as a mode of transport but the traveller can be deemed as co-constituted by both the person and the mode of travel. Furthermore, the third, spatial, element involved in co-constituting the travelling subject is the space for travel, both as provided by the vehicular mode, and by the infrastructures associated with it, in the landscape through which it moves. For example, the rail passenger as traveller is a shaped by the infrastructure, not just the machinery of the train and carriage, but through the stations: what are the experiences that a particular station engenders: is it cold or warm, welcoming or hostile, beautiful or ugly, showing care and attention to detail or neglected? Understanding the travelling subject requires research sensitivity therefore to the experiential dimensions of travel. To do this required familiarisation with a broader literature on spaces, cultures senses and attention to the politics of these spaces, as well as finding appropriate research methods through which to investigate the lived experience rather than just its written reflection.[16] Exploring these possibilities resulted in a research project to apply these methods to the cycle traveller. Before considering how I came to address historical documentaries as a source for understanding prior mobility practices, some explanation of my research project is necessary.

Designing research and identifying methods

My underlying research question at the outset of research project was "how do people ride, when bicycling is a mundane phenomenon?". In order to do this, I was located in a city (Munich) where every day cycling as a utilitarian mode of transport is a relatively mundane phenomenon. This is not to make any claims about the conditions or the desirability of the current cycling practices, infrastructures or transport regimes in the city, but just as observable fact according to the modal trip distribution.[17] To investigate and to try and make sense of how people move around, it is first necessary to observe. To this end, the research process began by exploring quotidian journeys to work, using a handlebar mounted video camera. Because the original subject of my own study was mundane behaviour in public spaces, it was considered that filming journeys made, for the purposes of research only, and within the confines of the research context, would be justified as a legitimate means to investigate these practices. There are proper ethical concerns about filming in public environments as a tool for research. Careful consideration of existing guidance on both public space research and digital research published by the British Sociological Association (Britsoc. co.uk, as my professional oversight body) and given that the film was not to be shared in any public forum suggested that the film making process would not breach any trustor expectations of confidentiality.

For data recording on the move, the integrated capacity of proprietary Garmin cycling devices was used. A (VIRB) digital camera with GPS function designed for sports use was mounted on the handlebars to provide a simple wide angle point of view recording and synchronised with a dedicated bicycle GPS unit (Garmin 1000).[18] Similar in appearance to a smartphone, this unit records speed, elevation, temperature and a host of other spatial and environmental details and unites these with biometric data in the form of heart rate information from a chest monitor and from power metering pedals (Vector) both wirelessly connected. From this combination a single data source is produced in the form of a unified digital output which can be recalled as a video image overlaid with selected data readings. Since the camera also records sound, field notes in conventional ethnographic fashion could be narrated along the way. Repeated recordings were made of daily journeying, as well as one-off trips exploring the city and its surrounding areas. These were then replayed and analysed to produce a series of codings to help understand the ways in which environments both physical and social affect how people travel by bike.

Visual and sensory ethnographies: developing coding

Analysing the resulting films was a time-consuming (not to say deeply tedious) process. As with any coding exercise, I was looking for patterns and for clues. First, I was looking for the obvious fixed data, numbers and relative density of travellers, the use and allocation of road space (and of dedicated infrastructures where appropriate). Forms and types of interaction between road users were also important, both when sharing the same mode of locomotion and when there were interactions between different modes.

Second, there were more subjective issues around the quality of the environment. Some, like the quality of surface and its impact on travel were easily identifiable. Others, like the ways in which certain types of road surface, space or interaction made one feel more, or less, confident and comfortable, initially relied more strongly on correlation between the visual and verbal note taking and through repeated travel in those same spaces. Repetition of travel is vital to understand the effects of familiarity, but through the repeated journeying, more subtle visual clues could be discerned, especially in the way in which other cyclists move through the spaces.

The third level of analysis of the augmented video concerned the interactions of cyclists: with the infrastructure, with each other, and with other modes of travel: buses, cars, trams, powered two wheelers and pedestrians. Visual observation of other's actions could be combined with my own body-monitoring and audio notes. What were the physical cues and behaviours that indicated apprehension or relaxation? Which patterns of action either of self or of external actors (especially other vehicles) raised the heart rate in fear and which patterns of action were associated with observations of pleasure. By cross-referencing the different data sources correlations could be made between specifically visual actions and the experiential and perceptual states associated with them. Much of this information is simply what we take for granted in everyday navigation of our lives. What the analysis provided was a replicable dataset to prove this intuitive knowledge and to provide quantifiable data on the degree to which certain specific scenarios were conducive to cycling or proven hostile to it.

Watching the same journey, repeated daily, sensitised me as a viewer to subtle details in the way that other cyclists moved around me. As viewer, details of interaction emerged that had been invisible to me as rider, because of the necessary concentration on the processes of travel. Differences from one day's film to another, cross-tabulated with the biometric information from the film and the oral notes allowed me to "read" the actions of other cyclists in ways of which I had not previously been conscious. As well as developing a considerable sense of how my own actions were developed and altered by the physical and social spaces of the city, I was able to observe how these forms of agency affected others.

Simultaneously with the digital augmented video recording process, I was also engaged in more conventional archival research. Studying the material artefacts of cycling and the literatures associated with them, allowed an insight into historical representations of cycling.[19] Advertising material, manufacturers' catalogues and travellers' narratives combined to build a sense of how cycling practices were seen and understood, and how the cyclist as traveller was perceived politically and socially in Germany in the first half of the twentieth century.[20] Seeking broader understanding of the background contexts to some of these materials, I began to explore recently restored video news reel and documentary sources. Whilst viewing these it occurred to me that the same visual interpretative language could be applied to documentary film, however stylised or designed for propaganda, where the footage included naturally occurring background information regardless of the subject.

Historical documentary as source

A useful way to begin thinking about the place and purpose of historical (documentary) film sources in the research process is to treat them (despite their status as deliberately crafted artefact) as naturally occurring data. Documentaries, whether film or television, as Kiyamba, Lester and O'Reilly point out, allow us an insight into "social, cultural and historic trends in how particular ... issues are portrayed".[21] Non studio based film frequently, and of necessity, includes background information not pertaining to the theme intended by the film-maker. Unless the filming is undertaken in closed conditions, all photographic sources, still and moving, record background information that can potentially be treated as naturally occurring data. Recognising the limitations of interpretation mentioned above, location footage and the actions of those in the streets provide a data source that can be interpreted and read with the same attention as the video ethnographic material recorded in my own research. Applying the three levels of analysis to a purely visual historical source must necessarily be treated with a high degree of caution. Nevertheless, as a means to supplement or be supplemented by other historical sources, it appeared to be a fruitful line of investigation for understanding cyclists use of and experience of the city.

The interest in these documentary films is not in the film's subject, nor the film itself as an object of study, but instead as a naive source. That is, as a recorded artefact containing details necessarily observed in the filming, but not the subject or focus of the camera. Transport researchers may more obviously be drawn to the extensive archives of, for example, *British Transport Films*.[22] These and other films provide ample representation of the public faces of transport themes and are of interest for what they tell us about the representation of transport at this time. The focus of my analysis, however, is on films made not concerning transport themes as their subject. Instead, this study began to look at documentaries of other forms of public life to consider how the background action in the streets behind the subject being filmed might be read in light of the coding developed in my own augmented video work.

In the process of restoration and reproduction, archives such as Munich's Filmmuseum, package and present not only distributed prints of films but also where possible, unedited or rough-cut materials as additional extras to enable film scholars to study the processes by which individual film-makers work. One such example is the Filmmuseum's 2006 DVD release of Ella Bergmann-Michel's work between 1931 and 1933.[23] This comprises all extant footage, including the three documentary films completed by the artist together with her unfinished study of the last free German elections in 1933.

To provide an example of the process of using historical documentary as a source for investigation of mobility practices, we can examine her work in depth.

Analysing the documentary film of Ella Bergmann-Michel

Ella Bergmann-Michel (1896–1971) was part of a wider international movement of artists in the 1920s and 1930s who saw their work as contributing to a greater project of social change. Drawn first to photography and then to film she was a pioneer of avant-garde modernism, committed to exploring and promoting new social relations of "liberated living" especially affecting the re-organisation of domestic sphere (Luke 2017).[24] The discussion that follows concerns her third (and first independently made and financed) film *Fleigende Händler in Frankfurt Am Main* (*Travelling Hawkers in Frankfurt Am Main*) which exists in both a 21 minute work print and a 46 minute (silent) rough cut. The work print uses editing techniques that echo Joris Iven's work of the same period, depicting the rapid mobilities of everyday life.[25] Of greater value for the analytical methods described here is the longer footage in the rough cut.

Ella Bergmann-Michel herself recalled the shooting of the film as enabled by the handheld 35 mm camera, with which she could film unseen.[26] Hence, this particular documentary is unusual in that it was deliberately made as a covert recording on the streets of the city, in amongst the everyday actions with which she was concerned. The rough cut, while edited to indicate her favoured juxtaposition of scenes and to establish a particular narrative contains a number of longer views of streets. Camera shots last up to 20 seconds and several, while separated in the cut, are clearly filmed in almost continuous sequence, allowing the viewer concerned with background action much greater information than contained in a fully edited film. In addition to the specific details recorded and analysed in a raw digital point of view camera recording, the purposeful creation of a documentary entails its creator establishing the mis-en-scène of the piece. The framing and location selections are part of the narrative process inducing the viewer to see what the filmographer 'sees' not just visually but in the way that they want the viewer to interpret what they see. In this case the limitations of the camera technology and filming opportunities require relatively broad views and a common single lens focus lending a naturalistic feel to the film, as is clearly the intention of the author. As in her previous documentaries on housing and on soup kitchens, she wants the viewer to engage with and empathise with the subjects.

Concentrating on the background during the opening sequence, one is struck by the relative lack of traffic. The stillness of the scene selection is clearly deliberate to accentuate the flapping of awnings and newsstand displays as they move in the wind, the focus of the camera. The greyness of the print means that there is little indication of the time of day this is shot.

In five seconds of film, the viewer can see two static and one moving motor car, together with two separate, solitary, cyclists. Traffic counts can be useful but this is too brief a glimpse to be meaningful. What is more interesting is the low speed differential of the traffic modes: pedestrians stride briskly across the road and the car only slowly edges alongside the cyclist in view. These are insignificant background details in shot, but provide a ground for comparison with other sequences. Later, a lorry driven through the streets, unimpeded by other traffic, moves at the same speed as the cyclists on the road around it.

Other important visible background details that enable us to think carefully about the mobility practices and experiences of the city are the qualities of road surfaces revealed in successive shots. Mobility is not just shaped by vehicular activity but the qualities of the spaces in which these occur. Paving slabs in some street sections are incised with gridded patterns, presumably providing drainage and ensuring less slippery conditions underfoot than from smooth paviours. Road surfaces vary. Some are paved with small brick type cobbles with visible gaps. In these cases, the road also has strongly cambered edges again presumably from concern with drainage. These shape how and where road traffic, motorised, pedestrian or cyclist moves. They also provide convenient parking for two wheeled handcarts, crossways to the traffic flow (and used as a seesaw by children able to play in the streets with no trams or motor traffic, during a 20 second shot in which four cyclists pass). Similarly, the height of the kerb from the road surface allows bicycles to be parked (unlocked) unsupported except by a pedal on the kerb. Other surfaces appear smooth and the demarcation between surface types at intersections shows a smooth (asphalted?) surface to the large of roads, while side streets remain with cobbles or block setts.

The handcarts hauled by the street hawkers share the road with motor traffic, trams and cyclists. In a 15 second shot of a handcart holding up the passage of a tram, one motor car passes and six cyclists are visible, along with the same number of pedestrians. While some of the shots of the hawkers are clearly staged, especially those that unfold the plot of their evasion from the police,[27] the action takes place against a background of unremarkable activity and thus of greatest interest for the analysis here. At a busy intersection of smoothly surfaced roads (though the pavement has gridded paviours) pedestrians, cyclists and motor traffic wend in and out of the spaces. Again, short, establishing shots enable only impressionistic glimpses, and are subject to the deliberate choices of the filmmaker to establish the tone and theme of the material. From a transport perspective, however, what is notable is the diversity of modes: a range of hand drawn or pushed carts of various sizes for different loads: flat-bed and box-sided, two- and four-wheeled, all the way down to different shaped perambulators, some clearly handmade. These, plus animal traction carts, motor cycles and sidecars and even motor tricycles alongside trucks, tractors pulling multiple trailers combine to create an impression of vehicles each designed and

selected for specific purposes. Bergmann-Michel is interested in the handcarts inasmuch as they provide the mobility for the hawkers and traders
whose story she is telling. A sustained sequence at the exit to a print works
consciously echoes Auguste and Louis Lumière's first film, *La Sortie de
L'Usine Lumière à Lyon*.[28] She shows distributors departing with bundles of
newspapers, some stacked chin high on the front of a (ridden) bicycle, others
carried in shoulder bags or backpacks, tucked underarm or on rear racks or
simply balanced on handlebars. Pedestrians carry stacks of print underarm
or in bags, and in handcarts and perambulators. Traffic types and moving
practices are the obvious products of first level analysis.

Connecting to my own video work on cycling, certain themes become
important as we see incidental cycle traffic. Among them are the wide range
of cycle speed variations, from the very rapid to little more than walking
pace. Luggage is carried under arm, in back packs or on front carriers.
Each arrangement affords different capacities and affects the speed and
mobility of the cyclist. Speeds correspond to the spaces and the traffic with
which they share the spaces, pedestrian or vehicular. In early morning shots
(judged by the length of shadow) the pace of movement is generally higher
than later in the day as shadows shorten. These are patterns that might be
expected from experience and are demonstrated as data in the film studies
explained above. They are still visible in Munich today, but it is valuable to
see the same temporally shaped rhythmic patterns of city life confirmed in
the 1930s.[29] Cycle transport is further aided by the occasional specially designed carrier bike, in one instance with very large wicker baskets front and
rear. A series of 20-second long shots at a junction (in morning light) allow
some comparative number counts. In the first, ten bicycles to one care and
one tram pass. In the second, two cars, a truck, two (goods carrying) motor
tricycles and six cyclists.[30] What is more noticeable, however, is the manner
in which cyclists travel. No hint of hesitation is shown, the cyclists proceed
at their own chosen pace, weaving in and out of pedestrians and motor vehicles as necessary. Carrying loads underarm or balanced on handlebars
up to the chin in a manner that necessarily limits control over the bike is
clearly not seen as a problem from the frequency with which such practices
are visible. The environments of travel are clearly conducive to a confidence
and an ease of cyclists movement. This is also reflected in the interactions of
riders, side by side, clearly deep in conversation.

Pedestrians likewise negotiate the road space with ease, not with hesitation. The confidence that cyclists show is confirmed in one particular passing shot while the filmmaker is focused on the trader, a figure rides past in
the background and even with the lack of focus on a momentary passing
figure, a window cleaner with ladders over his shoulder and bucket slung
on his arm can be made out.[31] To ride in the road space thus encumbered
requires a considerable degree of trust in other road users. Although the
heavily laden cyclists wobble while starting off, once moving, they proceed
smoothly along the roads.

Combining these series of sequences, all shot from the same point and at the same time of day, enables the background viewer to watch traffic (vehicular and pedestrian) interact at a crossroads, with no visible road signage or marking and to glimpse how uninterrupted flows depend on mutual recognition. In my own filming, interactions of this kind only take place in the context of modally identical traffic, pedestrian, cycle or (more rarely) motor. Where modes are mixed in today's transport systems there are clear assumptions of priority made by all actors in the system, usually based on the perceived fear of relative damage potentially involved in any collision. In Bergmann-Michel's film the equality of mobile subjects is noticeable. With relatively little traffic, the whole of the available road space is also used, cyclists do not necessarily ride close to the gutter, enabling better anticipation of any interactions necessary.

Cycling and mobility in Joris Ivens and Henri Storck: *Borinage*

By way of a contrast, a second short example can be drawn from *Borinage* (1934) produced by of Joris Ivens and Henri Storck. Joris Ivens (1898–1989) is widely regarded as one of the most influential documentary makers, producing films from the 1920s onwards, most of his output reflecting his commitment to radical left politics. *Borinage* documents and dramatises the lives of striking and unemployed Belgian Miners, depicting their labour struggles within a broader framework of a worldwide crisis of capitalism. It was expressly intended "to call attention to the desperate conditions in the area and to stimulate European public support for the miners' cause".[32] Visually, the film deliberately avoids the aestheticisation of poverty that marks other documentary explorations of the life of the urban or rural poor of the time, and is framed as a series of vignettes showing aspects of life. Ivens himself explained the care that had to be taken in shot framing and selection in order not to achieve this.[33] This reflection only emphasises the caution we need to take when assuming the images we see on film are representative reflections of reality.

In transport terms we note the proximity of housing to places of labour, the cinder surfaces streets and general lack of mobility of the workers, contrasted with the mobility of police. Brief views are given of an entire squad of rapidly cycling police officers, apparently travelling to break up a demonstration. Elsewhere police disembark from trucks to disperse the assembled miners. In the scenes of miners' own assemblies, there are small numbers of workers with bicycles. These workers assemblies contrast consciously with the factory gates scenes previously mentioned. Ivens' crowds of workers are not in employment but gathered to protest their unemployment or working conditions and reduced pay, static masses rather than flowing, liquid crowds. There is no background traffic or trade to speak of in these shots. One scene, which Waugh points out as a deliberate reconstruction of a case highlighted in a report on the hunger and food shortages in the region, is especially worth noting.[34] A fellow worker lends one unemployed miner a bicycle in order that he can undertake a four-mile ride to collect a loaf of bread from his mother-in law. The mobility provided is precious and life saving but also opens up views on what is denied in the ghettoisation of the worker's everyday lives. In another mood-establishing sequence of interiors of temporary housing for the unemployed, among the few possessions that the family have taken with them through evictions can be seen a bicycle, perhaps indicating the potential value of that mobility. On the surface, *Borinage* is a film with little obvious relevance to thinking about transport and traffic. A careful reading of the glimpses we are shown and awareness of the contexts of travel and the use of spaces, as well as those symbolic and value dimensions that become apparent, allows us to enrich and complexify our understanding of transport modes and uses in historical context.

Conclusions

Limited glimpses into the streets of a city or people provided by documentary film as described here, can only provide a snapshot into the travel and transport worlds of the past. However, by focusing on the background, and treating film background as naturally occurring data, new insights may be gained to enrich the understanding of twentieth-century mobilities outside of our own experiences or lacking in data rich sources. This is not to say that film depicts naturally occurring events. Nor is it to suggest that film shows us 'real' events and actions. To call background and incidental information 'naturally occurring data' is, however to suggest that unstaged filmed action may provide informative insight into specific conditions and interactions that are of value to the transport historian. More importantly, comparing historical footage with analytical techniques used to read today's digital sources allows us insight into the quality of interactions of road users. Thus, we are offered a possible glimpse into the experiential world of mobile subjects. This case study has been conducted as an experiment to demonstrate how these techniques may be applied to provide a richer understanding of travel than can be gained simply from numerical or narrative data alone. It cannot supplant our primary sources, but it can help to illuminate and perhaps to humanise our thinking about travel and how it creates its own subjectivities. It allows us to perceive affective factors that may be significant, but which do not appear in mere technical descriptions of traffic, transport and mobility.

Notes

1 See, for example, Gijs Mom, *Atlantic Automobilism: Emergence and Persistence of the Car, 1895–1940* (Oxford: Berghahn, 2014).
2 Jonathon S. Marion and Jerome W. Crowder, *Visual Research: A Concise Introduction to Thinking Visually* (London: Bloomsbury, 2013).

3 Gillian Rose, *Visual Methodologies* (London: Sage, 2001); Claudia Mitchell, *Doing Visual Research* (London: Sage, 2011).
4 Douglas Harper, *Visual Sociology* (London: Routledge, 2012).
5 Peter Berger and Thomas Luckmann, *The Social Construction of Reality* (Harmondsworth: Penguin, 1966); Vivenne Burr, *Social Constructionism* (second edition, London: Routledge, 2003).
6 J. Bonham and C. Bacchi, "Cycling Subjectivities in On-Going-Formation: Interviews as Political Interventions," (conference paper, paper presented to Foucault and Mobilities symposium, University of Lucerne, Switzerland, January 6–7, 2013).
7 Beatrix Campbell, *Wigan Pier Revisited: Poverty and Politics in the 80s* (London: Virago, 1984). Following quotations from unpaginated photo section. Original image of "A street corner in Wigan" by Bert Hardy, first published in *Picture Post* November 11, 1939, juxtaposed with 1983 photograph by Gloria Chalmers.
8 Jean Baudrillard, *Simulacra and Simulation* (Ann Arbor, MI: University of Michigan Press, 1994[1981]).
9 Sian Barber, *Using film as a Source* (Manchester: Manchester University Press, 2013), 4.
10 Barber, *Using Film* 13.
11 Sarah Pink, "Walking with Video," *Visual Studies* 22, no. 3, (2007): 240–252; Monika Büscher, John Urry, Katian Witchger, eds., *Mobile Methods* (London: Routledge, 2010); Ben Fincham, Mark McGuinness and Lesley Murray, *Mobile Methodologies* (London: Palgrave Macmillan, 2010); Malene Freudendal-Pedersen, Katrine Hartmann-Petersen and Emmy Laura Perez Fjalland, eds., *Experiencing Networked Urban Mobilities: Practices, Flows, Methods* (Abingdon: Routledge, 2018).
12 Peter Merriman, "Rethinking Mobile Methods," *Mobilities* 9, no. 2 (2014): 167–187.
13 Peter Cox, *Cycling: Toward a Sociology of Vélomobility* (Abingdon: Routledge, 2019).
14 Katrina Brown and Justin Spinney, "Catching a Glimpse: The Value of Video in Evoking, Understanding and Representing the Practice of Cycling," in *Mobile Methodologies*, eds. B. Fincham, M. McGuinness and L. Murray (Farnham: Ashgate, 2010), 130–151; Justin Spinney, "A Chance to Catch a Breath: Using Mobile Video Ethnography in Cycling Research," *Mobilities* 6, no. 2 (2011): 161–182.
15 Justin Spinney, "Cycling the City: Non-place and the Sensory Construction of Meaning in a Mobile Practice," in *Cycling and Society*, eds. Dave Horton, Paul Rosen and Peter Cox (Aldershot: Ashgate 2007), 25–46; S. Pink "Sensory Digital Photography: Re-thinking 'Moving' and the Image," *Visual Studies* 26, no. 1 (2011): 4–13; Kat Jungnickel and Rachel Aldred, "Sensory Strategies: How Cyclists Mediate their Exposure to the Urban Environment," *Mobilities* 9, no. 2 (2013): 238–255; Tim Jones, "The Velomobilities Turn," in *Experiencing Networked Urban Mobilities: Practices, Flows, Methods*, eds. Malene Freudendal-Pedersen, Katrine Hartmann-Petersen, and Emmy Laura Perez Fjalland (Abingdon: Routledge, 2018) 139–143.
16 Phillip Vannini, ed., *The Cultures of Alternative Mobilities. Routes Less Travelled* (Farnham: Ashgate, 2009); Tim Cresswell and Peter Merriman, eds., *Geographies of Mobilities: Practices, Spaces, Subjects* (Farnham: Ashgate, 2010); Phillip Vannini, Dennis D. Waskul, and Simon Gottschalk, *The Senses in Self, Society and Culture* (Abingdon: Routledge, 2014); Peter Merriman, *Mobility, Space, Culture* (Abingdon: Routledge, 2012); Sarah Pink, *Doing Sensory Ethnography* (London: Sage, 2009); Sarah Pink, Phil Hubbard, Maggie O'Neill and Alan Radley, "Walking Across Disciplines: from Ethnography to Arts Practice,"

Visual Studies 25, no. 1 (2010): 1–7. Sarah Pink, "Sensory Digital Photography: Re-thinking 'Moving' and the Image," *Visual Studies*, 26, no. 1 (2011): 4–13.

17 The six months project was funded by Leverhulme Trust International Academic Fellowship (IAF-2014–2016) and entitled 'Developing Cross-Disciplinary Research into Bicycling and the Environment'. It was undertaken in 2014/15 at the Rachel Carson Center for Society and Environment (RCC) an interdisciplinary research centre focusing on environmental history

18 These commercially available units, designed for sports use were selected because they are relatively discrete in use, and allow the overlay of data in the editing process.

19 Thanks here to the staff at the Deutsches Museum for guiding me through the intricacies of the archives.

20 Special mention needs to be made of Katherine Ebwert's important work on cycling in pre-war Germany: Anne-Katrin Ebert, *Radelde Nationen: Die Geschicht des Fahrrads in Deutschland und den Nederlanden bis 1940* (Frankfurt: Campus Verlag, 2010).

21 Nikki Kiyamba, Jessica Nina Lester, and Michelle O'Reilly, eds., *Using Naturally Occurring Data in Qualitative Health Research: A Practical Guide* (Cham: Springer International Publishing, 166).

22 www.britishtransportfilms.co.uk/. Many, but not all, are distributed by the BFI. The full BTF archives also include, for example, training films that provide different levels of insight for transport history research.

23 Ella Bergmann-Michel, *Dokumentarische Flime 1931–1933. Edition Filmmuseum 09* (München Film & Kunst / Deutsches Filmmuseum Frankfurt am Main, 2006). The Kinamo also used and championed by Joris Ivens "permitted the young filmmakers to shoot in the streets with a spontaneity and mobility that the larger studio-oriented cameras could not achieve". Thomas Waugh, *The Works of Joris Ivens: The Conscience of Cinema* (Amsterdam: Amsterdam University Press, 2016), 70.

24 Megan R. Luke, "Our Life Together: Collective Homemaking in the Films of Ella Bergmann-Michel," *Oxford Art Journal* 40, no. 1 (2017): 27–48.

25 Iven's early documentaries, especially *Études des mouvements à Paris*, use vivid intercutting and editorial techniques to give an impressionistic view of the frantic pace of street life. While powerfully persuasive, they are not particularly useful; as sources to understand the wider practices of Parisian mobility at the time but better understood as an exercise in modernist portrayals of speed, according to Waugh (2016).

26 Bergmann-Michel, interview January, 20, 1967, translation printed in accompanying DVD booklet. Original text, Sprengel Museum Hannover Inv. Nr. A 40..04-c-01.

27 Jutta Hecher: notes accompanying DVD edition.

28 Reading this sequence against Bruce Bennett' insightful analysis of the Lumière films reveals much about Bergmann-Michel's own self-consciousness as a film-maker.

29 Tim Edensor, "Commuter: Mobility, Rhythm and Commuting," in *Geographies of Mobilities: Practices, Spaces, Subjects*, eds. Tim Cresswell and Peter Merriman (Farnham: Ashgate, 2011), 189–203. Edsnor develops Lefebvre's rhythm analysis to provide a valuable discussion of these changing patterns of movement through the day.

30 Street scene observations on main thoroughfares from Bergmann-Michell's unfinished footage of the 1933 elections reveals a similar dominance of pedestrian traffic, with numerous bicycles and the very occasional motor vehicle. This balance is to be expected in what was at the time, one of the least motorised of industrial nations.

31 The shot is at 24:28.

32 Waugh, *The Works of Joris Ivens*, 175.
33 Ivens, 88 *The Camera and I*, ed. Jay Leydam (Berlin and New York: International Publishers, 1969) cited in Waugh, *The Works of Joris Ivens*, 182.
34 Waugh, *The Works*, 185.

Bibliography

Barber, Sian. *Using Film as a Source*. Manchester: Manchester University Press, 2013.

Baudrillard, Jean. *Simulacra and Simulation*. Ann Arbor, MI: University of Michigan Press, 1994 [1981].

Berger, Peter, and Thomas Luckmann. *The Social Construction of Reality*. Harmondsworth: Penguin, 1966.

Bergmann-Michel, Ella. *Dokumentarische Flime 1931–1933. Edition Filmmuseum 09*. München Film & Kunst/Deutsches Filmmuseum Frankfurt am Main, 2006.

Bergmann-Michel, interview January, 20, 1967, translation printed in accompanying DVD booklet. Original text, Sprengel Museum Hannover Inv. Nr. A 40.04-c-01

Bonham, J., and C. Bacchi. "Cycling Subjectivities in On-Going-Formation: Interviews as Political Interventions." *Paper presented to Foucault and Mobilities Symposium*, University of Lucerne, Switzerland, January 6–7, 2013.

"British Transport Films." *British Transport Films*. Undated. www.britishtransportfilms.co.uk/

Brown, Katrina, and Justin Spinney. "Catching a Glimpse: The Value of Video in Evoking, Understanding and Representing the Practice of Cycling." In *Mobile Methodologies*, edited by B. Fincham, M. McGuinness and L. Murray, 130–151. Farnham: Ashgate, 2010.

Büscher, Monika, John Urry, and Katian Witchger, eds., *Mobile Methods*. London: Routledge, 2010.

Burr, Vivenne. *Social Constructionism*. Second edition, London: Routledge, 2003.

Campbell, Beatrix. *Wigan Pier Revisited: Poverty and Politics in the 80s*. London: Virago, 1984.

Cox, Peter. *Cycling: Toward a Sociology of Vélomobility*. Abingdon: Routledge, 2019.

Cresswell, Tim, and Peter Merriman, eds., *Geographies of Mobilities: Practices, Spaces, Subjects*. Farnham: Ashgate, 2010.

Edensor, Tim. "Commuter: Mobility, Rhythm and Commuting." In *Geographies of Mobilities: Practices, Spaces, Subjects*, edited by Tim Cresswell and Peter Merriman, 189–203. Farnham: Ashgate, 2011.

Ebert, Anne-Katrin. *Radelde Nationen: Die Geschicht des Fahrrads in Deutschland und den Nederlanden bis 1940*. Frankfurt: Campus Verlag, 2010.

Fincham, Ben, Mark McGuinness, and Lesley Murray. *Mobile Methodologies*. London: Palgrave Macmillan, 2010.

Freudendal-Pedersen, Malene, Katrine Hartmann-Petersen, and Emmy Laura Perez Fjalland, eds., *Experiencing Networked Urban Mobilities: Practices, Flows, Methods*. Abingdon: Routledge, 2018.

Harper, Douglas. *Visual Sociology*. London: Routledge, 2012.

Jones, Tim. "The Velomobilities Turn." In *Experiencing Networked Urban Mobilities: Practices, Flows, Methods*, edited by Malene Freudendal-Pedersen, Katrine Hartmann-Petersen, and Emmy Laura Perez Fjalland, 139–143. Abingdon: Routledge, 2018.

Jungnickel, Kat, and Rachel Aldred. "Sensory Strategies: How Cyclists Mediate their Exposure to the Urban Environment." *Mobilities* 9, no. 2 (2013): 238–255.

Kiyamba, Nikki, Jessica Nina Lester, and Michelle O'Reilly, eds., *Using Natu-rally Occurring Data in Qualitative Health Research: A Practical Guide*. Cham: Springer International Publishing, 166.

Luke, Megan R. "Our Life Together: Collective Homemaking in the Films of Ella Bergmann-Michel." *Oxford Art Journal* 40, no. 1 (2017): 27–48.

Marion, Jonathon S., and Jerome W. Crowder. *Visual Research: A Concise Introduc-tion to Thinking Visually*. London: Bloomsbury, 2013.

Merriman, Peter. *Mobility, Space, and Culture*. Abingdon: Routledge, 2012.

———. "Rethinking Mobile Methods." *Mobilities* 9, no. 2 (2014): 167–187.

Mitchell, Claudia. *Doing Visual Research*. London: Sage, 2011.

Mom, Gijs. *Atlantic Automobilism: Emergence and Persistence of the Car, 1895–1940*. Oxford: Berghahn, 2014.

Pink, Sarah. *Doing Sensory Ethnography*. London: Sage, 2009.

———. "Sensory Digital Photography: Re-thinking 'Moving' and the Image." *Visual Studies* 26, no. 1 (2011): 4–13

———. "Walking with Video." *Visual Studies* 22, no. 3 (2007): 240–252.

Pink, Sarah, Phil Hubbard, Maggie O'Neill, and Alan Radley. "Walking Across Dis-ciplines: from Ethnography to Arts Practice." *Visual Studies* 25, no. 1 (2010): 1–7.

Rose, Gillian. *Visual Methodologies*. London: Sage, 2001.

Spinney, Justin. "A Chance to Catch a Breath: Using Mobile Video Ethnography in Cycling Research." *Mobilities* 6, no. 2 (2011): 161–182.

———. "Cycling the City: Non-place and the Sensory Construction of Meaning in a Mobile Practice." In *Cycling and Society*, edited by Dave Horton, Paul Rosen, and Peter Cox, 25–46. Aldershot: Ashgate, 2007.

Vannini, Phillip, ed., *The Cultures of Alternative Mobilities. Routes Less Travelled*. Farnham: Ashgate, 2009.

Vannini, Phillip, Dennis D. Waskul, and Simon Gottschalk. *The Senses in Self, So-ciety and Culture*. Abingdon: Routledge, 2014.

Waugh, Thomas. *The Works of Joris Ivens: The Conscience of Cinema*. Amsterdam: Amsterdam University Press, 2016.

9 The trajectories of railway kinship families in Victorian York

Philip Batman

Introduction: migration into Victorian York

This chapter examines how the development of railway centres in the nineteenth century had a profound effect on settlement through the development of communities of railway workers. The focus of the chapter is the City of York – a major railway centre for the North Eastern Railway. We target families that were tempted to move to York with close relatives in houses nearby. We then examine their origins and their occupation of particular streets, and speculate why such relatives should have chosen to migrate together.

In the two centuries before the railway's construction, York was an agricultural and social centre of northern England.[1] The York and North Midland Railway arrived in York in 1839, and thereafter the population of the city grew fourfold by 1901 from its size at the start of the century.[2] The city had formerly been occupied by 'resident gentry who relied for their connections with the outer world upon posting and coaches'.[3] With the arrival of the railway the gentry could now travel and they left the city. River transport, which for centuries had played to York's advantage, was largely superseded by the railways which allowed goods to be transported easily to all inland towns. With the railway boom new industries came to York including agricultural engineering and confectionery.[4] The arrival of the railway also brought with it an expanding workforce to service this new burgeoning industry.

In the nineteenth century, the building of streets in the suburb of Holgate coincided with the arrival of the railway, and some came to be occupied almost entirely by railway families. In many cases neighbouring houses were headed by people related by birth or marriage. Having found and tracked these so-called kinship families across the censuses, the forces which pushed and pulled these family trajectories in different directions will be described in this chapter. Most railway kinship family members moved together into houses near each other, occasionally moving in a chain reaction to be reunited in the same street. An attempt is made also to draw comparisons between the kinship patterns of railway families and the wider local community.

Railway families

Employment on the railways was an attractive proposition for working men of Victorian England. The railway industry offered job security in the form of career prospects and higher wages than other occupations, and in some cases better accommodation. Revill has argued that in Derby, as was the case elsewhere, these inducements pulled migrants in to form the bulk of the railway workforce.[5] Studies of other industries in the nineteenth century have also shown that skilled posts in general attracted long-distance migrants from the more well-established industrial areas of the country.[6] Workers with specialist ironwork skills, for example, were more inclined to relocate to Victorian Middlesbrough over long distances.[7] Skilled migrants made a core component of artisan railway elite, middle-ranking clerical grades and a few senior managers. Local men were only recruited for the less skilled jobs including labourers and porters. Indeed, in Brighton only about a quarter of engine drivers had been born locally, but a half had migrated from other areas of the British Isles. The most likely employees of all to be born elsewhere were some workshop men, engineers, fitters and turners, and boilermakers. Major sources of engineers and fitters in Brighton were Yorkshire (particularly Leeds), Lancashire, Cheshire, Northumberland and Durham. Relevant experience was clearly an inducement to move to work in Brighton.[8] As will be seen, the industry in York also attracted some working kinship families from northern industrial towns.

Another facet of railway work found also in York was its tendency to run in families. Relatives were attracted to move together or follow in each other's footsteps. Recruitment to the railway workforce was governed by patronage, a system that possibly accounts for the prevalence of some family connections in railway service. The railway company required a testimonial from a person of good standing, and young men from integrated kinship networks may have found it easier to obtain such a reference than individuals from less well-connected families. Families could provide continuous employment in the railway industry, and company records suggest that long service was typical of railway work.[9] The tendency for sons to follow father's footsteps into the railway industry was particularly prominent with skilled working men, as was found in Derby.[10] Similarly, in Brighton jobs on the railway could attract other family members and former workmates.[11] Sheppard found that blacksmiths employed by the railway in Brighton in the 1860s were the sons of Sussex rural blacksmiths, or had at least been trained by them. Gant identified an indigenous core group of workers in a society of Welsh railway villages, into which new minority groups integrated easily, perhaps because of their linkages.[12] New arrivals in a town could therefore build important kinship networks of benefit to further immigrants.

Generally, about a fifth of working-class households at mid-century remained at the same address for as long as a decade, as seen in Huddersfield and in some York families in 1844.[13] Middle-class families, those with house ownership or a secure income and the wherewithal to pay regular rent, were less likely to move. Such patterns have been seen amongst railway workers.

Most lived close to their jobs in the stations, depots and workshops. These employees, however, included such a diverse mix of lower- and middle-class status that even the most high-status areas of a district in some Victorian cities could be dominated by the 1870s by railway workers. New houses tended often to be occupied by families moving into a town.[14] Railway employees benefited from a structural career setting and secure housing tenure. There tended also to be residential and family or kinship segregation within the railway workforce. For these reasons, clusters of households from key employment sectors in the railway community often remained in the same houses between censuses. Long-serving staff, particularly managerial, clerical and artisan grades, showed remarkable stability, possibly because their employer was also effectively their landlord. In the Derby railway workforce, employees were less prone to move house than might be expected in comparison with other occupational groups.[15] Traffic staff was the core of long-term residents, whilst engine drivers were by far the most stable grade of the workforce. Similarly in Gant's study of three railway villages, an analysis of occupational grades and homes of railway staff showed preferential location of engine drivers in one residential area.[16] In line with these trends, this chapter finds in the Holgate suburb of York segregation of the railway workforce and stability of households in the working-class terraces.

Four streets of Holgate: the hub of railway York

The Holgate area of York experienced considerable upheaval during the nineteenth century that transformed a rural backwater just outside the city walls into a railway community. Railway workers migrated rapidly into York in the 1840s, when the city was connected to a host of new lines and became an important railway junction. The number of railway employees rose from 41 in 1841 to 513 ten years later and by 1855 more than 1200 men were employed in the station and engine works. By the end of the nineteenth century 5,500 men worked in the engine, wagon and carriage works and the station and offices of the North Eastern Railway company. York became an established railway town with the extension of wagon and coach-building shops between 1873 and 1876, a new station built in 1877, and the station hotel and offices in 1906.[17]

The effect of these developments on Holgate was severe, creating a wilderness of criss-crossing supplementary tracks, carriage works and engine sheds. The approach to the city not only intersected the land, it determined the future of the surrounding housing. It influenced the social mix of the streets around, and guided their direction and rates of growth. By cutting through agricultural land on the approach to York station, the railway avoided the demolition of overcrowded housing and creation of slums seen in some other industrial towns and cities.

In this chapter we explore the working-class terraced housing of St Pauls Terrace and adjoining Railway Terrace, and the more prosperous and elite housing of Holgate Road and St Paul's Square. All four streets were built or developed as a result of the railway boom in England during the period between 1830 and 1849. They lie within a few yards of each other alongside the railway approach to York station at the south-west boundary of the city. Figure 9.1 shows the Holgate district of York in the early twentieth century, long after the building of railway housing had been completed. The area including Railway Terrace, St Paul's Terrace and St Paul's Square is circled, and Holgate Road, the main thoroughfare from Leeds and the Ainsty of York, is found at the bottom of the map. The two terraces and St Paul's Square form dense housing abutting the approach railway lines, marshalling yards and works and sheds, while Holgate Road has more open housing planning.

Holgate Road predated the other streets by some centuries. It is, and always has been, a major arterial route into the city. The Bishop Fields in the eighteenth century lay on either side of the road. At the beginning of Victoria's reign the land around Holgate Road was almost entirely pasture for cattle. Houses had been built towards its junction with the main thoroughfare into York (Blossom Street), together with a few houses further out from the city. The road thereafter showed linear development with time away from the city. The coming of the railway in the late 1830s encouraged York Corporation to sell land on the north side of Holgate Road. There was considerable development in the construction of houses of the villa type in Holgate Road for residential purposes for the wealthier citizens. Behind this were built streets and houses before the arrival of the railway workforce.

St Pauls Terrace comprises terraced houses (and a school) on both sides of the street. The houses on one side of the street back onto St Pauls Square,

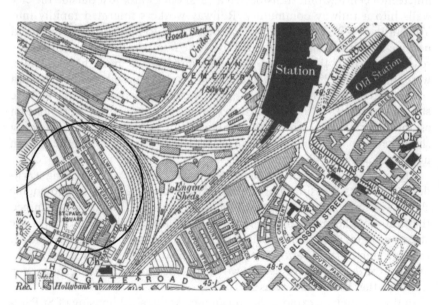

Figure 9.1 Roads in Holgate, Ordinance Survey Map, 1910. Reproduced with the permission of the National Library of Scotland.

and on the other side onto the similar terrace of Railway Terrace. St Paul's Square was built between 1851 and 1867. Both St Pauls Terrace and Railway Terrace were constructed between 1867 and 1872, relatively late in the development of housing adjoining the railway in this area of Holgate.[18] The railways thus contributed to the urban growth in York and the building of working-class housing. We see an overview of these terraces in Figure 9.2.

Figure 9.2 Terraced railway housing including St Paul's Terrace and Railway Terrace photographed in the 1950s. (c) City of York Council, Local Studies Collection.

Railway and St Paul's Terraces were linear two-storey housing, separated by small back yards. St Paul's Square was also terraced housing, but the properties were three-storeyed with gardens to the rear and faced a central tree-lined communal lawn. The houses along Holgate Road were detached, relatively large spacious accommodation, and built with generous gardens. Shops and businesses were interspersed with the houses, and also an increasing number of several high-status villas potentially attractive to railway managers or entrepreneurs.

Persistent and kinship families of Holgate: surname indices

We now locate and track kinship railway families in these four streets. Kinship families in this study are defined as two or more households in a street led by people with the same surname who were related by birth or marriage.[19] In contrast isolated families refer to those households headed by an individual with a surname unique in the neighbourhood. With this method of plotting families, the number of specific surnames of household heads (i.e. *not* the number of heads with a particular surname) is related to the total number of heads in the population. A population with a small number of surnames relative to its size may contain a large number of kin-related heads with the same surname; by contrast, a population with a large number of surnames relative to its size may contain relatively few kinship networks. An index was used to provide a means of assessing whether a community could have harboured a relatively large or small number of kinship families. This 'surname index' was defined as the number of surnames of household heads divided by the total number of household heads, and the figure multiplied by 100.

As an extreme hypothetical example, if we find only one surname in the household heads in a street or neighbourhood of 100 households, we may assume that all these heads probably belong to one kinship family (a low index). On the other hand, if we find 100 surnames in this group, we may assume that there are 100 isolated families but no kinship families (a high index). Thus, the lower the index, the lower is the density of isolated surnames; or the larger is the potential size or number of separate kin groups. The higher the index, the greater is the probable concentration of isolated families with few kin networks. Whilst these indices provide only a number which can be used to compare populations, and no information about specific families, a falling index over time suggests the possible growth or immigration of household heads from the same or other generations of the same family. By contrast, a rising index indicates their departure.

The surnames of all the heads of household of the four streets in Holgate were retrieved from the decennial census returns, and a surname index of the household heads in each street at each census was calculated. The indices show the likelihood of finding household heads in the street with the same surname derived through family connections. We can further subdivide these kinship families in Holgate into those that had an employment connection on the railway, and those that did not.

Figures 9.3–9.6 show the changes in the number of households and in surname indices in Holgate Road, St Paul's Terrace, Railway Terrace and St Paul's Square until the end of the century.

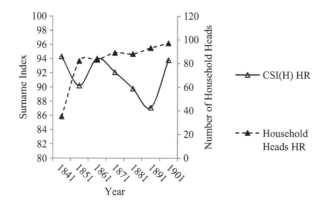

Figure 9.3 Surname index derived from census household heads (CSI(H)) and number of household heads in Holgate Road (HR); collated from The National Archives, English and Welsh Census, 1841–1901.

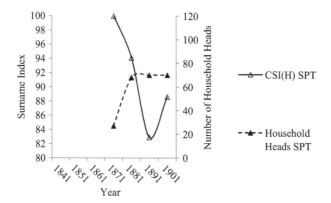

Figure 9.4 Surname index derived from census household heads (CSI(H)) and number of household heads in St Paul's Terrace (SPT); collated from The National Archives, English and Welsh Census, 1841–1901.

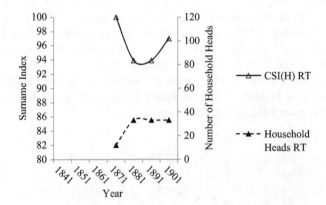

Figure 9.5 Surname index derived from census household heads (CSI(H)) and number of household heads in Railway Terrace (RT); collated from The National Archives, English and Welsh Census, 1841–1901.

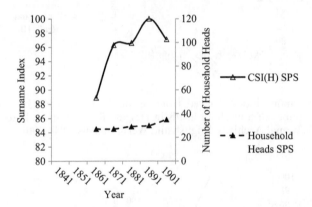

Figure 9.6 Surname index derived from census household heads (CSI(H)) and number of household heads in St Paul's Square (SPS); collated from The National Archives, English and Welsh Census, 1841–1901.

The surname indices show similar trends in three of these streets, namely Holgate Road, St Paul's Terrace and Railway Terrace, but a reversal of this pattern in St Paul's Square. In the 20 years after 1841 the surname index of Holgate Road residents varied, but thereafter until 1891 the index fell as household heads with shared surnames tended to grow in number at the expense of isolated families. The surname indices in St Paul's Terrace and Railway Terrace in 1871, when the streets were under construction, were 100, that is all of the household heads had a unique surname. This was a new fledgling community in 1871, no kinship families having been attracted

to the terraces. After this date the indices fell as heads with shared surnames concentrated in the houses of these two streets over the first 20 years
of their existence until 1891. The final ten years of the nineteenth century
witnessed a reversal of this trend in each of these three streets when indices
rose to an extent as heads with shared surnames tended to decline. We see
the opposite pattern in the indices in St Paul's Square. The surname index
derived from the household heads in the square rose until 1891, and then fell
in the last decade of the century. Isolated families tended to dominate in the
square throughout the century, and in 1891 there were no resident kinship
families at all.

The indices from these four streets in the Holgate district suggest, in
short, that kinship families may have been attracted over most of the period to the two terraces of working-class railway employees and to Holgate
Road. Whilst unclear, it is possible that the rental accommodation here and
its lower costs, combined with the presence of family members, meant they
were more attractive to working-class kinship families, than they were for
middle-class families, even though these terraced houses were more expensive than other forms of housing in the city.[20] By contrast, for the middle-
class occupants of the more affluent St Paul's Square, home ownership
meant the realisation of that independent status coveted by working people.[21] Furthermore, just as there was variability in surname densities in the
streets of this neighbourhood, so there was some difference in household
composition. Households in Holgate Road grew larger over the half century,
but families in the other three streets became smaller over time or remained
the same size. In line with the national fall in birth rate from the late 1870s,
fewer children on average lived in all these households by the turn of the
century.[22]

Having tracked across the censuses the proportions of heads of household
with shared surnames that lived in separate houses in the Holgate area of
York, we turn our attention now to families that gave the neighbourhood its
sense of community by their residence for prolonged periods of time. Families had lived along Holgate Road for more than a century, but the adjacent
square and terraces had been built in the 1860s and 1870s to accommodate
the new railway workforce. The two figures below show us how many heads
of household that remained in the same street for at least a decade. Figure
9.7 shows the number of heads in the censuses of 1881 and 1891 that had lived
in each street since at least the previous census and/or were destined to live
in the same street until at least the next census, that is to say the number of
heads that persisted in each neighbourhood for a minimum of ten years.
Figure 9.8 shows the number of these persistent heads expressed as a percentage of the total number of households.

In 1881 the number of these persistent heads was greatest in Holgate
Road, with a drop in their numbers in St Paul's Terrace, Railway Terrace
and St Paul's Square. However, within a decade by 1891, the persistent

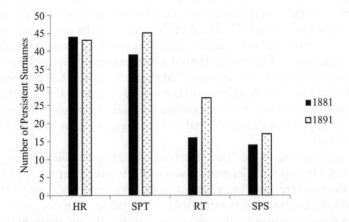

Figure 9.7 Number of persistent heads of household in Holgate streets in 1881 and 1891; collated from The National Archives, English and Welsh Census, 1841–1901.

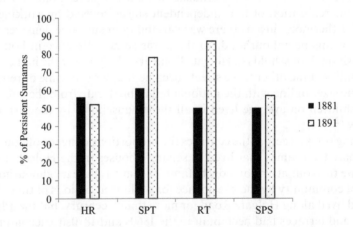

Figure 9.8 Persistent heads of household in Holgate streets in 1881 and 1891 expressed as percentage of total number of households; collated from The National Archives, English and Welsh Census, 1841–1901.

heads had fallen slightly in number in Holgate Road but risen in the other three streets. Markedly different numbers of houses existed in these streets of course, and a somewhat different picture emerges when we compare persistent heads with the total number. At least half of the heads in any street in 1881 were resident for at least a decade, and the proportion was at its greatest in St Paul's Terrace. These percentages had risen in each street bar Holgate Road by 1891, predominantly in the working-class railway terraces and most dramatically in Railway Terrace where nearly 90% of the heads were long-stay residents. The residential stability of these working-class families in the terraces is reinforced further when we explore the households in more detail. About half of the newly arrived heads in the terraces in 1881 were set to stay for at least a further ten years, and a similar proportion of the arrivals in 1891 were living in the very same house ten years later. Indeed, about a third of the newcomers in 1881 were in the same house in St Paul's Terrace and Railway Terrace for more than 20 years. The peak concentration of long-stay families in the two terraces in 1891 also coincided with the maximum concentration of kinship family household heads over the last three decades of the century.

Evolving differences emerge in the complexion of Holgate families when we compare the streets at their first census enumeration in our period and the heyday of the persistent families in 1891. Most of the heads of household present in Holgate Road in 1841 had agricultural jobs, such as farmer, wheelwright and cowkeeper. Few agricultural families arrived within the next ten years, but several skilled artisans and small businessmen moved into the street and these families were destined to stay. The road had a rural atmosphere in the 1860s, when there were working water- and wind-mills, horticultural produce worthy of winning prizes, heaps of manure in the gutters and newsworthy petty theft of apples and strawberries from gardens.[23] By 1891, however, a significant proportion of the heads of household were wealthy middle-class men, but this was a mixed community where few were employed by the railway. Some, notably engine and carriage builders and track workmen, were manual workers in this industry but men of higher status in the railway had arrived too. Some large residences of the moneyed and business middle classes in Holgate Road before the coming of the railway became the homes of some high-status individuals linked to the railway business. The Holgate Lodge estate, a magnificent villa, was occupied by Henry Thompson, uncle of Sir Harry Stephen Meysey-Thompson, chairman of York and North Midland Railway Company and then chairman of the North Eastern railway. It was also occupied by Charles Todd Naylor, with income gained by railway speculation.[24] Nonetheless, many families were not related to the railway industry. Several families in the final decade of the century in fact drew no wage of any sort, deriving their income from annuities, rents, or other independent means. Numerous educated and skilled workers included the clergy and teachers, a solicitor and surveyor, a photographic artist, and engineers. Skilled artisans lived along Holgate Road, namely a gunsmith, a joiner and cabinet maker, and a telephone wireman. There were also plentiful small businessmen and shopkeepers, including a market gardener. A charwoman was the only unskilled individual among the household heads. The residents of Holgate Road at the end of the nineteenth century had indeed evolved into an affluent and diverse community (Figure 9.9).

The new arrivals of 1861 in St Paul's Square were also relatively wealthy and educated, and railway workers were few in number. They included no

Figure 9.9 Entrance to Mount Terrace from Holgate Road in 1922. (c) City of
York Council, Local Studies Collection.

manual working-class families and only three railway employees, a goods
manager, the manager of the sack department, and a cashier. They lived
alongside several tradesmen and merchants, notably a tea dealer and comb
manufacturer, some of whom were retired. The educated included solici-
tors, a teacher, an architect and surveyor, and a vicar and a clergyman's
widow. These were 'comfortable homes in a respectable neighbourhood'.[25]
A third of the resident householders, both men and women, were people of
independent means, fundholders, landed proprietors and annuitants. The
early isolated inhabitants of St Paul's Square had moved in from other parts
of York and other Yorkshire towns in the main, and there were few new-
comers from further afield. This pattern of occupations and arrivals was
maintained in the square until at least the start of the twentieth century. The
long-stay families of 1891 were a mix of the retired or those of independent
means and the professional or managerial elite. Arguably the affluence of
this street meant that it attracted only a few of the more highly paid railway
employees.

The families of newly built St Paul's Terrace and adjoining Railway Terrace made a community of quite different character from their neighbours
in Holgate Road and St Paul's Square. We see in them the full influence of
the influx of railway employees. The 1871 census of these two terraces shows
that only about a third of the final total of houses had been built at that time

or at least were occupied. The heads of these households were all working married men who had moved into their new terraced homes with wives and young children. They had all also moved into the city from elsewhere, principally from towns and villages in Yorkshire and also from the North East, namely Durham and Northumberland. They had been attracted to this new development by the railway itself; barring two shopkeepers and a cab driver, all these men were employed by the railway. Some were joiners working in the railway works. About half of them were engine drivers or firemen, the elite of the railway workforce and mobile workers who valued no doubt living so close to the station. The majority of the engine drivers moved into these streets before building was completed. Those heads that arrived in St Paul's Terrace when the street was first built and were destined to remain included about a half of the railway engine drivers that ever lived there until the end of the century.[26]

Railway families had consolidated by 1891, when long-stay families were at their peak. These families still lived in four out of every five of the houses, even though most of the engine drivers had left.[27] These terraces were built then for working-class railwaymen and their families after the height of the railway mania in York, and therefore retained this character throughout the rest of the century. It was these families predominantly who had put down deeper roots than their more affluent neighbours, tending to arrive with related kin and staying for prolonged periods of time.

We have charted thus far the movement of groups of families into and within these York streets. The evidence presented has shown that the area had grown and been transformed by the arrival of the railway. Holgate Road, once a sleepy rural rutted track into the walled city of York, had evolved into a community of small businessmen and men of higher status. St Paul's Square was the province of the more private gentrified echelons of society. The nearby residential areas of St Paul's and Railway Terraces were the much more homogeneous streets. These were the enclave of the working-class families, whose menfolk spent their long days in the adjacent railway engine sheds and shunting yards.

We switch our focus finally to the individual kinship families in these Holgate streets and the forces that shaped their life cycles and trajectories. Kinship families are defined for our purposes as those families made of two or more households in the same street with a head of the same surname and who were related by birth. There were 18 such families in total.[28] There were similarities in the social standing and occupations of the heads of households between Holgate Road and St Paul's Square, but a marked difference in the density and number of kinship families. They were plentiful in Holgate Road and the opposite in St Paul's Square. There were only four families with a surname common to more than one head of household in the square across the second half of the nineteenth century, and only one such family with a proven kinship link. This was a family of two actuaries. William Newman, actuary to the Yorkshire Life Assurance Company, moved to Holgate from the fashionable residences of St Marys about a mile away, to be joined there by his son recently qualified from Cambridge University, who shortly took the house next door. They lived in the relatively affluent community of St Paul's Square alongside families who shared no ties with their neighbours through blood or marriage.

There are stark differences in family trajectories in the other three streets depending upon whether or not their livelihoods were gained by employment on the railway. Working-class kinship families, in which at least one and usually both relatives worked on the railway, settled only in the affordable houses of St Paul's and Railway Terraces. The more affluent and middle-class families, whose income did not come from the railways, came to live near each other only in Holgate Road and St Paul's Square. We see these two groups of kinship families in Tables 9.1 and 9.2.

The working-class railway kinship families of St Paul's Terrace and Railway Terrace in the nineteenth century were either fathers and their sons, or pairs of siblings. Similar relations took up residence in Holgate Road; for instance, a vicar's widow and her daughter and some cousins also migrated into Holgate Road. Arrivals into the working-class terraces had been born mainly in the industrial regions of the North East and Lancashire, such as Gateshead and Darlington, Liverpool and Skerton near Lancaster. A small number of railwaymen in these kinship families had moved into Holgate from York itself and the villages within a few miles of the city. Rural origins were the norm, however, for the kinship families of Holgate Road, most of them arriving from villages in the vicinity of York. Only one family came from further afield, the vicar's widow and daughter making the long journey from a parish in rural Oxfordshire to the ecclesiastically dominant city of York.

The stock from which the working-class families of the two terraces emerged was manual or semi-skilled labour. The father of William and John Middleton was the sexton at Malton cemetery in North Yorkshire, the father of Elizabeth and Samuel Rotherham was a millwright and wheelwright of Liverpool, and James Byrne with his two sons had migrated from Dublin to Lancashire, presumably in flight from the potato famine in Ireland. These families were not socially mobile. The kinship families of Holgate Road, by contrast, showed some signs of social climbing, and some settled in this more affluent community in retirement. The Daniels, a wealthy farming family in a village outside the city, moved into York on retirement, and cousins John and Parker Pickering came from a farming heritage to Holgate Road following careers as a woollen merchant and solicitor's cashier. Others established trades and businesses along the road, rising from more humble origins on the land, such as the Harrison brothers' joinery and bricklaying businesses next door to each other and the Hawkins brothers' market gardening and provisions concerns.[29]

Dependent on their occupation, railway kinship families often moved to York from various distances away, following the same trend as shown

Table 9.1 Railway kinship families of railway terrace and St Paul's terrace

	Relationship	Surname	Place of birth	Place from where migrated to York	Residence within York before kinship family home	House no.
Railway Terrace (RT)	Siblings	Middleton	Malton Malton	Leeds		14 1
	Father & Son	Rennison	Acomb York	Askham Richard	2 addresses in Walmgate 2 addresses in Walmgate then 32 RT	32 33
	Siblings	Rotherham	Liverpool Liverpool	Hull, then Chester Hull, then Chester	5 Cambridge St 5 then 4 Cambridge St	5 4
St Paul's Terrace (SPT)	Father & Son	Alport	Gateshead Gateshead	Hetton le Hole Durham, then Gateshead, then Darlington Darlington	29 SPT 29 SPT	39 34
	Father & Son	Birch	Durham Gateshead	Not known Not known	Union Street, then 55 Price St Union Street, then 55 Price St	22 21
	Siblings	Byrne	Skerton Skerton	Not known Not known	Dale St, then Bilton St, then St Cecilia Place, then 63 SPT Dale St, then Bilton St, then Newbegin St, then Charlton St	44 56
	Father & Son	Hall	Darlington Darlington	Stockton, then Darlington	Bainbridge Sq Price St Bainbridge Sq Price St, then 17 Price St	70 11
	Father & Son	Hutton	Bishopthorpe Moor Monkton	Moor Monkton	5 SPT 5, then 55 SPT	55 14
	Father & 2 Sons	Malthouse	Ripon Manchester York	Knaresborough, then Ripon Not known Not known	Oxford St, then SPT, then 51 SPT Oxford St, then SPT, then 51 & 52 SPT SPT, then 52 SPT	52 31 51
	Siblings	Simpson	York York		Eldon St, then Lowther St, then 76 Lowther St, then Newbigin St Lowther St, then 76 Lowther St, then 97 Lowther St	22 then 53 23

Collated from The National Archives, English and Welsh Census, 1841–1901.

Table 9.2 Non-railway kinship families of Holgate road and St Paul's square

	Relationship	Surname	Place of birth	Migration before York	Residence within York before kinship family home	House number	Occupation
Holgate Road	Siblings	Daniel	Yorks Whixley Yorks Whixley Yorks Whixley	Green Hammerton		HC 3 then 2 HT 3 HT	Living on own means Retired farmer Living on own means
		Day	York York	Newton on Ouse	Spurriergate	HC HT	Linen draper Linen draper
	Mother & Daughter	Forbes	Durham Wellington Banbury Oxon	Neithrop, Oxfordshire Neithrop, Oxfordshire		10 then 53 HT 10 then 53 HT	Rents of houses Not stated
	Siblings	Harrison	Yorks Gilling Yorks Wheldrake	Wheldrake	Oxford Street	76 HR 77 HR	Joiner Bricklayer
	Father & Son	Hattie	Yorks Stainforth Yorks Adwick le Street	Adwick le Street, then Barnby upon Don, then Gate Fulford Barnby upon Don, then Gate Fulford		21 WP 2 HR	Telegraph clerk Telegraph worker
	Siblings	Hawkin/s	Poppleton Poppleton	Huby, then Oulston Yorkshire Darton, then Barugh Yorkshire		79 HR 4 HR	Dairyman & Grocer, then Coal merchant Fruiterer & Gardener, then Photographic artist
	Cousins	Pickering	Acaster Malbis Bishopthorpe	Matlock	The Mount, then Mount Parade	HH 59 HH	Retired woollen merchant Cashier to Solicitor, then Annuitant
SPS	Father & Son	Newman	York York	Leeds	St Helen's Square, then St Marys St Marys	22 22, then 23	Retired actuary Actuary

Collated from The National Archives, English and Welsh Census, 1841–1901.
HC: Holgate Crescent; HH: Holgate Hill; HR: Holgate Road; HT: Holgate Terrace; WP: West Parade.

by Sheppard and others. These distances occasionally were short, even from one village to the next, but sometimes longer from one town or city to another.[30] Some men who were destined to work on the railways in the working-class terraces of Holgate moved initially from one industrial base to another: a joiner who moved from Malton to Leeds; a fitter and turner who moved from Liverpool to Chester via Hull; a blacksmith who moved from Gateshead to Hetton-le-Hole, Durham, then Darlington; a boiler-smith who moved from Darlington to Stockton then back to Darlington again; and a wheelwright who moved from the rural village of Bishopthorpe just outside York to a neighbouring village. Some of these individuals migrated as children with their labouring families. Likewise some tradesmen, professional persons and farming stock migrated via places other than York before settling there as kinship families. The wife of the vicar in Neithrop, Oxfordshire, was born in Durham. The telegraph workers of Holgate Road settled in several small places in Yorkshire before arriving in York, as did the progeny from workers on the land. These more affluent arrivals in Holgate Road had tended to leave their birthplaces as working adults, not as children as the working-class families of Holgate were prone to do. Seemingly the working-class kinship families of the two terraces in Holgate had migrated to affordable and available housing at an earlier stage in their life cycle than the middle-class families of Holgate Road.

Having arrived in York, all but one of the families destined to settle as kinship groups in the railway terraces of Holgate changed addresses in the city, usually more than once and up to four times. These houses were invariably similar working-class terraces as those they came to inhabit in Holgate. Sometimes relatives moved into Railway Terrace or St Paul's Terrace in the same or separate houses, only to move again along the street as head of household in a new home. In five of the ten kinship families who came to inhabit these two terraces, father lived next door to his son or brother next door to his sibling. The retirees, tradesmen, businessmen and professionals of Holgate Road and St Paul's Square, on the other hand, had tended not to live elsewhere within the city before arrival in Holgate. But, just like their working-class neighbours a few streets away, kinship family members tended to inhabit adjacent well-to-do houses. Family ties, both in working- and middle-class households, were pivotal to the Victorian frame of mind.[31]

Conclusions: migration into Holgate

We can speculate now on the motives and forces that brought these families into the four streets of Holgate, and in particular we can question if and why kinship families should have migrated together to York in preference to individual families moving on their own. Figure 9.10 shows the surname indices plotted against the total population of all four streets combined between 1841 and 1901. The indices fell in four of the six decades of this half century. In other words, household heads with shared surnames tended to grow in

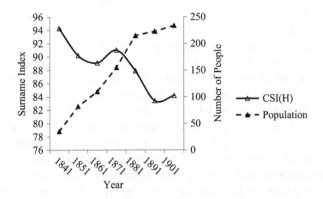

Figure 9.10 Surname index derived from census household heads (CSI(H)) and total population of four streets in Holgate; collated from The National Archives, English and Welsh Census, 1841–1901.

proportion over heads with surnames unique to the neighbourhood over most of the period in these Holgate streets. Heads related by birth or marriage and with the same surname were more likely to occupy houses than heads with no such relatives in the streets. Probably, as many other studies have shown, people often moved in family groups to ease the practical and emotional problems of migration.[32]

The community in Holgate blossomed during a phase of rapid growth of the railway industry. The kinship families that tended to move into Railway and St Paul's Terraces in the second half of the nineteenth century were motivated by economic forces and attracted by employment on the railway into the new working-class terraces that had been built specifically to house them. Rural decline may have pushed a few urban newcomers the short distance into York from neighbouring villages. Most railway kinship families arrived from other northern industrial towns outside Yorkshire, and only a few from York or surrounding villages. On the other hand, the majority of the non-railway kinship families arrived from the non-industrial settings of York and nearby villages, and only one wealthy family took a long-distance migration to York.

Ernst Ravenstein, one of the pioneers of migration studies writing in the late nineteenth century, found that working-class migrants tended to travel short distances in a stepwise manner, that more skilled migrants tended to travel further, and that the major impetus to uproot was economic necessity.[33] Our study of some streets in Railway York bears out these conclusions. No kinship families arrived in the terraces of Holgate when they were first built. Subsequently, however, the majority of railway kinship family members moved together into houses near each other in the two terraces. Occasional relatives moved in a chain reaction. Sons tended to follow fathers into this burgeoning industry, presumably the lustre of secure employment in a hub of the railway world enticing entire working families. Similarly, the non-railway kinship families tended to arrive in Holgate Road together or sequentially, again tending to live in close proximity.

The detached houses and more spacious terraced houses of Holgate Road and St Paul's Square attracted more wealthy kinship families than the railway workforce, but fewer of them. They were the established tradesmen or professional men, and retired and independent people. These more mature kinship families were presumably drawn by the better standard of housing they were able to afford, the prospect of a joint enterprise for their business ventures, and the hope of mutual emotional support in their declining years.

In summary, this chapter has shown that the economic boom of the arrival of the railway in Victorian York clearly attracted kinship family members who chose to live alongside their workmates and in close proximity to one another.

Notes

1 Peter Brears, "York and the Gentry: The York Season and the Country House," in *Feeding a City: York. The Provision of Food from Roman Times to the Beginning of the Twentieth Century*, ed. Eileen White (Totnes: Prospect Books, 2000), 150–167.
2 Hugh Murray, "Rebirth and Growth: Nineteenth-Century York," in *Feeding a City: York – The Provision of Food from Roman Times to the Beginning of the Twentieth Century*, ed. Eileen White (Totnes: Prospect Books, 2000), 187–202.
3 B. Seebohm Rowntree, *Poverty: A Study of Town Life* (London: Macmillan and Co., 1901), 9.
4 Alan Armstrong, *Stability and Change in an English County Town: A Social Study of York 1801–51* (Cambridge: Cambridge University Press, 1974), 16–46.
5 George Revill, "'Railway Derby": Occupational Community, Paternalism and Corporate Culture 1850–1881," *Urban History* 28, no. 3 (2001): 378.
6 Richard Lawton, "Mobility in Nineteenth-Century British Cities," *Geographical Journal* 145, no. 2 (July 1979): 211–213.
7 Minoru Yasumoto, *The Rise of a Victorian Ironopolis: Middlesbrough and Regional Industrialisation* (Woodbridge: Boydell Press, 2011), 101.
8 June A. Sheppard, "The Provenance of Brighton's Railway Workers, 1841–61," *Local Population Studies*, 72 (2004): 16.
9 P.W. Kingsford, *Victorian Railwaymen: The Emergence and Growth of Railway Labour 1830–1870* (London: Frnk Cass, 1970), 7–9.
10 Revill, "Railway Derby," 393.
11 Sheppard, "The Provenance of Brighton's Railway Workers, 1841–61," 26–31.
12 Robert Gant, "Railway Villages in South East Monmouthshire 1850–1965: A Community Perspective," *Local Population Studies*, 90, no. 1 (2013): 49–72.
13 Richard Dennis, *English Industrial Cities of the Nineteenth Century: A Social Geography* (Cambridge: Cambridge University Press, 1984), 255–268.
14 Ibid., 267.
15 Revill, "Railway Derby," 378–402.
16 Grant, "Railway Villages in South East Monmouthshire 1850–1965," 49–72.
17 F.W. Brooks, "Victorian and later York," in *The Noble City of York*, ed. Alberic Stacpoole (York: Cerialis Press, 1972), 321–330; Charles Brunton Knight, *A History of the City of York* (York: Herald Printing Works, 1944), 719–720.
18 Knight, *A History of the City of York*, 617, 657 and 668–669.

19 The surname indices in this chapter apply a measure along the chain migration of kinship families. Kinship is a societal concept, however, that is far broader than the links forged between people by family connections. Family and friendships within and between households in former times were important social alignments, but kinship did not correspond neatly to ties of blood and procreation. The definition of kinship used here is numeric and narrow, and excludes many family members and associates in a community who were regarded as kin. Surname indices notably exclude kinship women members who had changed surname by marriage.

20 Andrew August, *The British Working Class, 1832–1940* (Harlow: Pearson Education Ltd, 2007), 17–21; Standish Meacham, *A Life Apart: The English Working Class 1890–1914* (London: Thames and Hudson, 1977), 38.

21 David Englander, *Landlord and Tenant in Urban Britain 1838–1918* (Oxford: Oxford University Press, 1983), ix–xviii.

22 Eilidh Garrett, Alice Reid, Kevin Schürer, and Simon Szreter, *Changing Family Size in England and Wales: Place, Class and Demography, 1891–1911* (Cambridge: Cambridge University Press, 2001), 1.

23 The *York Herald* reported these facts and incidents: *York Herald*, May 26, 1860; May 11, 1861; June 16, 1861; August 10, 1861; August 23, 1862; Y.H., 10.8.1861; June 27, 1863.

24 Geoff Hodgson, *A History of Holgate (in five parts): Part Four Nineteenth Century Holgate* (York: G.H. Hodgson, 1999), 4.

25 Joseph Cockhill, a tradesman '... took a house in St Paul's Square. ... His profession called him a good deal from home, and he wished to take a house in a neighbourhood, where his wife would be comfortable, and also to have a comfortable home to come to off his voyages.' *York Herald*, February 2, 1860.

26 The terraces housed some of these drivers and their new young families during the precarious times of the strike of the North-Eastern line during 1867, when 1500 men walked out with demands of a 10-hour day and enhanced pay. Tensions could run high in the community as management brought in men from manufacturing and mining districts to maintain the service. One striker assaulted a replacement engine driver. Some details of the strike of 1867 are chronicled in the *York Herald*, e.g. The Apprehended Strike of 20,000 Engine Drivers and Firemen, *York Herald*, March 16, 1867; North Eastern Railway Half-Yearly Report, *York Herald*, August 10, 1867; Richard Dean, 'until very recently in the employ of the North-Eastern Railway Company, and one of the men who left the employ of the company without giving notice' was found guilty of violent assault upon Henry Nicholls who 'had lately entered their service as an engine driver', *York Herald*, May 18, 1867.

27 Household heads employed on the railway lived in 67 of the 84 houses in these two terraces in 1891. Only five of these men were engine drivers.

28 Family connections were sought in the censuses and baptismal records for all those heads of household who shared a surname with at least one other head in the same street over the second half of the nineteenth century. Heads related by birth were found in 7 of the 12 groups of heads with the same surname in Holgate Road; corresponding figures for St Paul's Terrace were 7 of 9; for Railway Terrace 3 of 4; for St Paul's Square 1 of 4.

29 The gross value of the estate of William Newman at his death, resident of St Paul's Square, was about £2000, equating to more than £200,000 in today's terms (registered at the District Probate Registry of York on 12 January 1903). The estate of the vicar's widow was valued at about £2700 in 1897, equating to more than £300,000 in today's terms (registered at the District Probate Registry of York on 8 June 1897). Mary Daniel, a spinster and annuitant on leaving farming,

left an estate valued at £11,324 in 1894, a figure in excess of a million pounds in today's terms (registered at the District Probate Registry of York on 2 January 1894).

30 Most migrants moved less than 1 km in the nineteenth century. Groups of migrants with short average distance moved were unskilled manual workers and agricultural labourers; employment which gave easier access to transport (such as in the case of railway workers) may have eased migration for some (Colin Pooley and Jean Turnbull, *Migration and Mobility in Britain since the Eighteenth Century* (London: Routledge, 1998), 53–71, 172).

31 See Claudia Nelson, *Family Ties in Victorian England* (Westport: Greenwood Publishing Group, 2007). See pages 1–14 for a discussion of the Victorian frame of mind and their attitudes to the family.

32 See, for example, Pooley and Turnbull, *Migration and Mobility in Britain since the Eighteenth Century*, 299–317.

33 D.B. Grigg, "E.G. Ravenstein and the Laws of Migration," in *Time, Family and Community: Perspectives on Family and Community History*, ed. M. Drake (Oxford: Wiley-Blackwell, 1994), 147.

Bibliography

Armstrong, Alan. *Stability and Change in an English County Town: A social study of York 1801–51.* Cambridge: Cambridge University Press, 1974.

August, Andrew. *The British Working Class, 1832–1940.* Harlow: Pearson Education Ltd, 2007.

Brears, Peter. "York and the Gentry: The York Season and the Country House." In *Feeding a City: York – The Provision of Food from Roman Times to the Beginning of the Twentieth Century*, edited by Eileen White. Totnes: Prospect Books, 2000.

Brooks, F.W. "Victorian and Later York." In *The Noble City of York*, edited by Alberic Stacpoole. York: Cerialis Press, 1972.

Englander, David. *Landlord and Tenant in Urban Britain 1838–1918.* Oxford: Oxford University Press, 1983.

Gant, Robert. "Railway Villages in South East Monmouthshire 1850–1965: A Community Perspective." *Local Population Studies* 90, no. 1 (2013): 49–72.

Garrett, Eilidh, Alice Reid, Kevin Schürer, and Simon Szreter. *Changing Family Size in England and Wales: Place, Class and Demography, 1891–1911.* Cambridge: Cambridge University Press, 2001.

Grigg, D.B. "E.G. Ravenstein and the Laws of Migration." In *Time, Family and Community: Perspectives on Family and Community History*, edited by M. Drake, 147–164. Oxford: Wiley-Blackwell, 1994.

Hodgson, Geoff. *A History of Holgate (in Five Parts): Part Four Nineteenth Century Holgate.* York: G.H. Hodgson, 1999.

Kingsford, P.W. *Victorian Railwaymen: The Emergence and Growth of Railway Labour 1830–1870.* London: Frnk Cass, 1970.

Knight, Charles Brunton. *A History of the City of York.* York: Herald Printing Works, 1944.

Lawton, Richard. "Mobility in Nineteenth-Century British Cities." *Geographical Journal* 145, no. 2 (July 1979): 206–224.

Meacham, Standish. *A Life Apart: The English Working Class 1890–1914.* London: Thames and Hudson, 1977.

Murray, Hugh. "Rebirth and Growth: Nineteenth-Century York." In *Feeding a City: York – The Provision of Food from Roman Times to the Beginning of the Twentieth Century*, edited by Eileen White. Totnes: Prospect Books, 2000.

Nelson, Claudia. *Family Ties in Victorian England*. Westport: Greenwood Publishing Group, 2007.

Pooley, Colin, and Jean Turnbull. *Migration and Mobility in Britain since the Eighteenth Century*. London: Routledge, 1998.

Revill, George. "'Railway Derby': Occupational Community, Paternalism and Corporate Culture 1850–1881." *Urban History* 28, no. 3 (2001): 378–404.

Seebohm Rowntree, B. *Poverty: A Study of Town Life*. London: Macmillan and Co., 1901.

Sheppard, June A. "The Provenance of Brighton's Railway Workers, 1841–61." *Local Population Studies* 72 (2004): 16–33.

Yasumoto, Minoru. *The Rise of a Victorian Ironopolis: Middlesbrough and Regional Industrialisation*. Woodbridge: Boydell Press, 2011.

Newspapers and publications

York Herald

10 Identification of the urban infrastructure of nineteenth-century horse transport

A case study of Worksop, Nottinghamshire, UK

Megan Doole

"The major development in urban transport in the Victorian Age was not the introduction of mechanical traction but the greater supplementation of human by animal power".[1] In Britain, from the mid-nineteenth century, a new societal activity of large-scale horse-powered transport developed – horses and horse-drawn vehicles moving large numbers of people and quantities of goods within towns and cities, for commerce, public service, employment, and leisure. At the beginning of the nineteenth-century, horse-powered land transport in towns was the preserve of those who could, or needed to, afford to utilise this expensive activity – private or hired coaches and carriages for the rich, saddle-horses, and carts and waggons for trade.

Knowledge of this transport form, including its infrastructure, is incomplete and seldom celebrated, certainly less than that of other nineteenth-century transport forms. In many accounts of the development of British land-based transport during the last 250 years horse-powered goods transport within urban areas is usually passed over briefly amongst descriptions of waggon-trains, canals, stage and mail coaches, railways, underground railways, electric trams, and various steam or petrol-powered vehicles. Its stable mate, horse-powered mass passenger transport, receives more consideration with descriptions of commercial networks in larger towns, for example, omnibus and horse-tram routes, however, other uses of horse-powered transport that existed in settlements country-wide are still overlooked, for example, cabs or wagonettes.

In the 1970s and 1980s some economic historians developed research interests in all horse-powered transport post-1840 and explored various aspects, for example, trends of amount of horse use including the final decline, and hay and horse supply, while drawing attention to the crucial role of the horse in the functioning of nineteenth-century British economy and society, especially for urban areas.[2] One declared that "The road haulage business... formed the central contribution of the horse to the nineteenth-century economy."[3] Since then, there has been little new investigation about this transport form from transport historians except in the case of the London situation;[4] in the last decade equine and animal historians, food geographers, and American environmental urban historians, have reconstructed understanding of different aspects of 'the horse in the city' including transport.[5] They have shown the importance of the 'oat-powered engine' for the development of many facets of western society during the nineteenth century, including consumerism, industrialisation, and in larger centres, suburbanisation.

Even with this new attention, those wishing to investigate horse transport in urban areas in Britain now can do little more than cite national trends of horse populations or specific examples of location, type and scale. Although a sense of the general pattern of development of horse-powered transport in urban areas pervades the literature there has been no examination from an all-encompassing perspective. This approach would provide an accurate account of all forms of this activity, for all purposes, for a specific place at a particular date, with resultant indications about the day-to-day and long-term impact this form of transport had on the functions and structure of that settlement. This could lead to comparisons of studies in different locations and a general national pattern. The lack of a comprehensive historical picture may be because of the absence of detailed, accurate, horse population figures at regular intervals over the period in contrast with those provided by USA census returns from 1850 on. As a consequence, for any researcher exploring this topic there appears a daunting task of gathering data from many disparate sources, with the resultant complexity, incomparability, and inaccuracy; Turvey's 2005 review of earlier estimates of the nineteenth-century horse population of London illustrates this situation well.[6]

Is there a way of compensating for this lack of detailed data? This chapter describes an attempt from the discipline of building history to create a methodology that enables identification of the infrastructure in towns and cities of horse-powered transport of the nineteenth century; that is, the amount, its nature, and what still remains. Although based on information that is not as accurate as census data, this type of study could be of use to transport historians studying the nineteenth century and urban areas by enabling greater knowledge of the detail of this transport infrastructure. This, in turn, could increase and refine understanding of the role that horse transport played in the development and functioning of British towns and cities during the intense period of 40–50 years before 1910 when many existing urban settlements rapidly expanded. In addition, the consulted archival sources which relate to the material culture may be new to transport historians and could have a wider application across the discipline, for other transport and mobility forms of the nineteenth century.

National context: scale and trends

The changing extent of horse transport infrastructure during the period should reflect and indicate the importance of utilisation of this form of transport by society. The amount of infrastructure in urban areas at any date might be broadly assumed from the numbers of horses and vehicles involved, therefore a review of what is known about the national situation of these numbers, their trends during the nineteenth century and the causes of these trends is useful. The population of all horses in Britain (England, Wales, and Scotland) during the nineteenth century is not accurately known as the first national horse censuses were not taken until the 1910s (1910, 1912–13 and 1917).[7] However, in the 1970s Thompson constructed horse population estimates (1811–1911) from related official figures such as taxes (non-farm horses were taxed until 1873) and Agricultural Returns. These figures show an increase from about 1.3 million in 1811 to a peak of 3.3 million in 1901 then a decline to 3.0 million in 1911.[8]

The figures also show that the growth of the 'commercial' horse population, of which urban or town horses were the major part, from 251,000 in 1811 to a peak of 1.17 million in 1901, was much greater than the 'farm' or 'private or leisure' categories (nearly five times versus twice and thrice respectively). A major reason for the greater increase in the 'commercial' population, which was out of proportion to growth in the human population, was the increase of short-distance passenger and goods carriage traffic brought about by the development of the country-wide railway network from the mid-century onwards. The railway network made long-distance personal and goods transport cheaper and easier, and also the general rise in living standards over this period increased the demand for a greater variety of goods, thus, growing volumes of passengers and goods needed to be conveyed to and from stations and goods warehouses as well as being transported within areas of denser population. Although, of course, not all road journeys were connected to railway journeys this situation, along with the increase in size of urban populations, led to 'a rising per capita use of horses for business and pleasure'.[9]

Initially, there was anticipation that the new network of railway routes would reduce the number of horses used for carriage. In the 1830s railway advocates said 'the adoption of [railway] projects will enable 1 million horses to be dispensed with'.[10] This figure was possibly an exaggeration as in 1836, at the end of what was considered the 'golden-age' of long-distance stage-coaches (1820–1836), there were 150,000 horses employed (one for each mile of route) for an estimated 3,000–4,000 vehicles, of which 700 were mail coaches.[11] The total numbers involved in long-distance goods carriage at this time are not known. It is true that developments in railway transport had a great impact on long-distance goods and passenger transport via horse-power, an example of which is available from Doncaster, a major staging post on the Great North Road. In 1839, before the railway arrived, there were 258 horses available for coaches and waggons. Five years later this horse population was reduced to 60.[12] Mail-coach traffic greatly declined in the 1840s, the role transferring to the railways. Yet, in the face of lost business, horse-drawn transport operators adapted. One specific commercial response was that many long-distance road carriers, for example, Pickfords, switched to carrying goods to and from railway collection points. Some stage-coach routes became feeders to settlements where there were no railway lines.[13]

Thompson also provided town horse and national vehicle figures. He conjectured that town horse populations were two-thirds of the total 'non-farm' horses with a peak of about 1.2 million in the 1900s, about 37% of the estimated national population.[14] There had been a period of rapid growth from the 1850s, following the initial adjustment to the railways, as horse-bus services (mainly after 1865), and then horse-tram services (after the Tramways Act 1870) developed networks in larger urban areas, as well as the increasing goods carriage referred to previously. A tax on non-farm horses was removed in 1874 which boosted individual ownership for the middle classes as well. Thompson's figures for horse-drawn road vehicles (urban and rural) demonstrate the growth in horse-buses and horse-trams from 1871 to 1901 (3,500 to 31,000) and the subsequent sharper drop (to 2,500 in 1911).[15] Private carriages (taxed during whole nineteenth century) also reached peak numbers at that point (450,000),[16] whereas the national peak for carts, vans, and waggons was a decade later (832,000 in 1911)[17] although vehicle figures are less useful for indicating the amount of infrastructure as vehicles were often stored without shelter.

London's horse situation warrants specific mention as it was not just Britain's capital city but also the biggest city in the world in 1900 (6.5 million human inhabitants). Horse population figures have been summarised from different tax reports as 11,000 in the early part of the nineteenth-century in central London, over 22,000 by mid-century, over 70,000 for London as a whole by the mid-1860s and at least 200,000 by the end of the century; the lack of precision is due to the difficulties of finding reliable source figures as mentioned previously.[18] The range of uses for horse powered transport in the city was wide: Gordon provided a list of horse users during the early 1890s – buses, trams, cabs, railway companies (for waggons, goods, parcels, shunting, buses), carriers, Post Office (for mail), vestries (for refuse collection and street cleaning), brewers, the Queen, private carriages, fire brigades, coal merchants, undertakers, cavalry, police, private riding, other firms and job masters.[19] Omnibus companies grew to be one of the largest users of horses after the new vehicles and passenger system were first operated there in 1829; by 1901 they covered 242 route miles in the County of London, with the busiest thoroughfare at Hyde Park Corner with 606 buses per hour on 24 routes.[20]

After the horse population peak in about 1901 the town horse population declined (sharply after 1911) as new transport technologies and forms were introduced, particularly in urban mass-passenger transport, that is, steam or more commonly, electric trams, petrol motor buses and taxi cabs. The decline to zero use of horses for public transport took only about a decade in London.[21] An example of the rapid change is from The London

General Omnibus Company which used 16,714 horses in 1901 and 10 years later ran its last horse bus.[22] However, urban horse-drawn goods traffic did not decline as rapidly – the transition period was more complex. Total loss of the town horse was not envisaged for some time after the introduction of motor vehicles; in 1909 a report by a farm manager west of Manchester stated "demand for city dray horses in Lancashire (including Manchester) has certainly not been in any way affected by the introduction of motor vehicles", and in 1926 some managers in local distribution services were still debating the merits of the horse vs electric vs petrol motor.[23] A few town working horses remained in use into the 1940s and beyond, for example, by breweries, for house deliveries of food stuffs and coal, also by services such as the police, undertakers, and for refuse collection. The last working horse units in Manchester were sold off in 1963 by their carrier company partly because they were incompatible with parking meters.[24]

This summary of estimated knowledge of overall quantities of the power source and vehicle elements of horse transport sets the scene for a detailed investigation of the urban infrastructure – will this also follow the general trends outlined above? Can the extent and general location be determined for settlements of the period? What else can be revealed about the operation of horse transport in urban areas? Why are there few current traces of what appears to have been a ubiquitous transport activity at the end of the century?

Establishing the nature of the infrastructure

Almeroth-Williams has said in connection with eighteenth-century London working horses: 'Their constant need for shelter, fuelling, grooming, shoeing and healing persistently shaped the architecture and social organisation of the eighteenth-century metropolis. They were greedy consumers of urban infrastructures.'[25] Thus, an understanding of the activity of nineteenth-century horse transport in urban areas, and the requirements for its successful operation, was essential for the design of this exploratory study about the nature of its urban built infrastructure to ensure that all relevant elements were considered for inclusion. A comprehensive 'needs' analysis was undertaken and this identified requirements for the power source (horse) and also for any vehicle used as follows. After supply of horses from their rural origins there were requirements of accommodation, daily provision of provender (food and bedding) and water, treatment for ill-heath, maintenance, equipment, waste removal, and disposal at the end of working life. Any vehicles needed to be constructed and supplied, maintained, repaired, and accommodated.[26]

From this 'needs' approach a definition of horse transport built infrastructure was developed: that is, buildings located in an urban area with significant, but not exclusive, contact with horse transport of any type, for passengers or goods, regardless of origin (urban or rural). This definition includes buildings that provided accommodation for horses, provender, or vehicles, or housed the associated horse-related trades and maintenance activities. In the subsequent study, buildings for the associated human labour were excluded as these were thought to be not commonly distinctive from other human accommodation building types, and therefore not as readily identified from sources.

A variety of commonplace and exceptional building types was covered by the definition. By far the commonest was the stable, essential for all forms of horse transport, as it combined the functions of shelter and feeding with security of horses and their equipment. There was wide variation in stable buildings: of size and shape, materials and decoration, and in features such as ventilation, drainage, light, fittings, stall arrangement, and food and equipment storage method. Distinctive urban forms that developed in response to urban space constraints were the large underground and multi-storey commercial stables with ramps or lifts that developed around the country.[27] For London and a few other British cities a high-status domestic solution were mews, incorporating stables, coach-house, and staff accommodation near grand terraced houses.[28] This building form had first appeared in Covent Garden, London, in the early seventeenth century, but new construction in London declined after the 1860s, because of then even greater space constraints.[29]

Many businesses utilised medium to large (several hundred stalls) stables over the study period, from the older coaching inns (for permanent and temporary accommodation) to the depots for the new forms of intra-urban mass passenger transport, to those that were part of production and distribution in the growing retail activity, for example, breweries, department stores, and the Co-Op and, of course, the railways: it has been said a 'big railway terminus came to require about as much space for stabling as it did for its locomotive sheds'.[30] Carrier firms and job masters provided hired horses and vehicles for goods carriage from larger sites, and small private stables provided transport for a range of small businesses from the doctor to the coal merchant, as well as cabs. Municipal bodies had their own stables to enable the urban services of refuse disposal, street cleaning and paving, and street-lighting, for example. The fire service, police, cavalry, Post Office, and undertakers also required sizeable horse and vehicle accommodation. For individuals, who gained quicker access to the countryside near smaller towns by railways from major cities in the later nineteenth century, hunting stables were established near railway stations, either for day-hire or longer-term stabling. Also, for those living in towns and cities who wanted to own a horse, or a carriage and horses team but were not able to provide private accommodation, bait stabling was available, usually at a nearby livery stable, which also offered hire of horses and vehicles.

Apart from accommodation, the greatest resource requirement for an urban horse, in bulk and cost, was provender (food and bedding). This composed about 75% of the lifetime costs of a London dray horse, and was a cost whether the horse worked or not.[31] In 1909 the food allowances for urban working horses used by a brewery, railway carter, and a city corporation in the north-west of England, were all about 30 lb (13.5 kg) a day.[32] Hay supply was a year round necessity for most in urban settings that had no access to fresh grass, and hay meadows were a feature around large towns; 100 horses stabled in Dundee consumed about five tons a week.[33] Shoeing was also an ongoing essential maintenance requirement. On average a London working horse required two shoes a fortnight, with businesses that owned a medium-large number of horses having their own on-site smith. The waste from the horses needed to be removed from their accommodation and the streets; town horses each produced at least three to four tons per year.[34] Horse manure was a profitable resource for most of the nineteenth century with sales to local farmers, however, towards the end of the century, as the horse population grew and chemical fertilisers developed, the value of manure dropped. Businesses and town councils then had to arrange for short-term storage and pay for disposal as it became a public health nuisance. All of the above identified activity 'needs' required specific infrastructure in the form of buildings or designated areas for shelter, storage, and processing. Those related to provender supply were the large city feed mills, granaries and corn warehouses, and corn markets. Hay markets were usually large open areas which have left little material trace but fulfilled an essential function. There were tillage factories and warehouses (for processing and storing horse and other manure for use in agriculture), manure pits and stores, knacker's yards, coach and carriage building factories, horse and carriage bazaars and repositories; the latter enabled sales by auctions as opposed to open-air street bargaining. The trades associated with horse care and operation also required buildings: the harness makers and saddlers, wheelwrights, and the numerous blacksmiths and shoeing smiths, both industrial and public, along with the veterinary surgeons premises.

Using this information of the 'needs' of the activity of horse transport the next section describes a study that applied this understanding to enable precise identification of infrastructure in a specific place. Of course, this approach could be applied to other societal activities where the physical impact of the activity on a location is of interest.

Case study and method: Worksop, Nottinghamshire

To demonstrate the application of this 'needs' approach for the identification of horse transport's built infrastructure, a discrete geographical area was selected for a case study of horse transport buildings (1820–1920). Preliminary investigations indicated that selecting a smaller settlement, as opposed to a segment of a large city, would enable more straightforward location and consultation of available data sources. The market-town of Worksop, in north Nottinghamshire, with a human population of about 3,200 in 1801 and 21,000 in 1917, and with a river, canal (1777), railway station (1849), medieval market place, Norman castle site, and a ruined Abbey, appeared representative of many English settlements and so was considered a good choice for the formative study. The town's production specialities were malt-ing, timber processing industries, and tourism to the nearby 'Dukeries' area of four aristocratic estates with country houses, gardens and parks. It ser-viced an extensive agricultural hinterland and there were the usual country carrier routes, often linked with market day, running to and from the town to nearby villages until 1912, although coaching routes had disappeared by 1869. During the study period there was no extensive mass-passenger trans-port system within Worksop, only a few horse-buses running to the railway station half a mile north of the town centre, and little of the infrastructure was obvious at the outset of the study.[35]

Geographical boundaries for the study area were set around the town's centre and then, to isolate horse transport-related infrastructure, potential sources of information were identified that would aid identification, par-ticularly the location of individual sites and main building use; specific site data were collected from maps, trade directories, almanacs, census returns, building control plans, and various other primary sources, all with their own strengths and weaknesses in application. The usefulness of maps for this type of study depends on their scale and their original purpose, and hence, their differentiated detail. Ordnance Survey maps at large scale exist from the 1880s onwards and many towns with a population of over 4,000 were covered then by a 1:500 map with smithies (blacksmiths' forges) identi-fied. Earlier in the century many settlements were covered by enclosure and tithe maps, and possibly rental surveys for landowners; stables in the centre of Worksop were recorded in a rental survey as far back as 1635.[36] Medium to large stables, and other relevant large buildings may be labelled on maps created as a consequence of the Board of Health Act 1848. In Worksop such a map (1858) was adapted for use by the Worksop Gas Company (c1865) with an accompanying list of individual customers. For larger centres, in the late nineteenth century the Goad Fire Insurance maps indicate stables and other relevant buildings, for example, wheelwrights' workshops.[37]

The most comprehensive available data source for the case study area was the Valuation Office Survey conducted as a result of the Finance Act (1909–1910) for taxation purposes.[38] The Survey covered almost every par-cel of land in Great Britain in the years immediately after 1910 although some records have been destroyed subsequently. The associated documents comprise finalised annotated maps and field books held at the four coun-try national archives, with working copies of these held at some regional archives in England and Wales. This source enabled almost all land plots in the Worksop study area with horse transport related buildings to be counted and analysed, as the records for each land plot contained a range of information including occupier, plot and building use, and occasionally building materials and erection date, with the occasional plot diagram. The exceptions were inns and large industrial sites which were accounted for in other ways. For Worksop the surveyors recognised 10 main horse or vehicle accommodation types; these were stables of various stall sizes (with lofts or without), loose boxes (not usually in a separate building), carriage houses, coach houses (closed or open), trap houses, saddle-rooms, harness-rooms, cart sheds, although all these were not always separate, distinct, buildings.

Databases were created of all the relevant information from the 2100 land plot records of the Valuation Office Survey which were consulted along with those from the other primary sources and, where possible, logged on maps of selected dates throughout the period 1820–1920 so as to track changes and determine trends over time. Finally, the historic site locations were checked against recent maps, then verified by site visits to ascertain the current existence of some of the identified buildings. This past and present data collection was a necessary precursor for the analysis stage of the enquiry with an expected generation of new knowledge about nineteenth-century horse transport infrastructure and usage, and the state of the physical remains, for this urban area.

Study results

The 1910–1915 Valuation Office Survey supplied the most comprehensive data of all the sources so the analysis that follows is initially focused on this period. At that time Worksop did have some of the larger exceptional building types, for example, a corn exchange converted into a Town Hall, brewery stables for 60, one carriage factory and show room (the latter converted to a cinema in 1914) and a fire station; there were also five public blacksmiths, and a knacker's yard. Generally, horse transport buildings occurred on average on 10 in 100 plots in the study area, however, the range over the area was wide, from three in 100 plots to 27 in 100 plots. The town core plots (near the main street: Bridge St) had the highest concentrations, about one in five. Of the 230 plots (out of 2100) that contained the estimated 325 horse transport buildings, 90% had at least one stable. Where stable stallage size was known, the most common size was two stall (56%), and the average stallage per building was 3.26. There were limitations with the source data, however, an estimate of the town's stallage gave about 750; while some of this would have been for temporary accommodation it does give a rough indication of the number of horses used in the town. Vehicle accommodation contributed 25% of the buildings.

Detail about the users of horse transport post-1900 can be inferred from examining the existence of stables, and therefore horses, in relation to plot use. Some shopkeepers and those with perishable goods that were home-delivered, sold on the streets, or moved to other suppliers generally had stables, for example, grocers, butchers, bakers, milk dealers, fruiterers, and the knacker's yard. Many of these were single buildings located in the residential areas on the edge of the town's core. The bootmakers, tobacconists, a draper and a watchmaker had their shops and stables near the main street. Those who needed transport in the course of their daily work also had stables such as doctors (x 4), coal merchants (x 2), chimney sweep, builders (x 2), painters, and an insurance agent, as well as those who moved heavy, bulky, commodities such as a laundry, home furnishers, breweries, maltsters, mineral water bottlers, corn and hay dealers, and the coal warehouse at the canal wharf. In industry, the timber millers (x 2), wood turners, ironmongers (x 2), flour mill, and engineers used horses, as well as services such as the police, the late-century fire station, the water company, and the gas works, a school, two sports fields, the telegraph office, the newspaper publisher, and printer. Almost all of the 40 inns and beer-houses had stables in the early twentieth century, although they were often small (1–2 stall). Some hostelries shared their premises with another business possibly because of the convenience of sharing stables. Examples of this were bakers, blacksmiths and wheelwrights, cow houses, joiners, and a slaughterhouse with a butcher's shop nearby. Some private houses (possibly about 30) also shared a plot with stables and other horse buildings for no discernible business reason, perhaps these were for professional, managerial or leisure use as some of these were larger houses in the wealthier areas. The wealthier residents could afford horse transport for personal business transportation and leisure, but the poorer ones were still reliant on themselves and possibly bicycles. Collectively, the evidence above demonstrates that in the period 1910–1915 Worksop was still reliant on horse transport use for commercial purposes, services and personal transport, although in the latter area there were indications of change, for example, one doctor had converted the stable to a 'motor garage', a few others had a garage in addition to a stable.

In contrast to the information about transport users the information about trades associated with horse transport was mostly gathered from sources other than the 1910–1915 Valuation Office Survey, and is not as reliable as to location and number of buildings used. Most of these trades would have also serviced agricultural horses in surrounding areas so any changes to their horse transport market may have been buffered by this other market. Nonetheless, some useful information has been gathered that indicates changing horse use over time. Throughout most of the study period Worksop generally had 6–7 public blacksmith and shoeing smith businesses, 4–7 wheelwrights, 4–5 saddle or harness makers, 3 coach builders, 3 livery stables (including one for hunters), 2–3 veterinary surgeries, 3–5 corn millers or dealers, and 1–3 hay dealers although only a few existed on the same site for more than two decades. Most of the trades businesses operated out of single town centre site, however, corn and hay dealers may have had central offices with other storage areas elsewhere. Most of these businesses declined in number after 1900 (wheelwrights and saddlers started to decline from the 1860s, blacksmiths from 1915) although the number of livery stables and carrier companies increased. Nonetheless, in Worksop all the amenities for private or working horses were still available in the town into the 1920s, although declining in number for reasons such as competition from cheaper imports of horse gear and as overall horse use declined after 1910. The figures above therefore show that up until the 1920s even a small town required a number of horse transport related businesses and that their central location and accessibility was desirable.

Unfortunately, what would be of great interest for tracking the development of horse transport-related infrastructures – the number of individual carters in the town and their locations – was the hardest to glean from available data. For example, the 1861 census returns show 25 carters and waggoners (an increase from 15 in 1841), and the 1869 trade directory lists only six similar businesses. This example demonstrates a difficulty throughout the period, in that it is hard to differentiate between those who worked individually or for multi-employee companies. The latter included industrial sites, carrier companies and job masters (from about 1900 in Worksop), whilst the former could have been self-employed and servicing regular customers (possibly retail shops or small workshops) or working on-demand. One possibility for identification is that carters were connected with Valuation Office Survey (1910–1915) plots recorded with a warehouse and a stable but no other buildings or description.

Collection of data from over the study period has enabled an examination of the changes of in distribution of horse transport buildings within the urban area over time. Earlier on (1820s/1830s), all types of horse buildings were clustered around the market place, which is also where the main inns of the town were situated, for example, a veterinary surgeon, a fire engine shed next to a posting inn, and some trades buildings, for example, saddlers. From the 1860s, there was a noticeable move away from the main street of the trade buildings – new retail shops replaced the workshops. From the 1870s, the new medium-size stables for livery companies and hunting stables clustered particularly on the half mile route between the railway station and the edge of the town's commercial centre as this was the best location for gaining individual and group tourist business from the railway. About 1900 any individual stables sited away from the inner town or railway station were for a specific reason, for example, perishable goods trade to suburban residents. Also, by 1915 there were large villas on the main arterial roads and near the centre of the town with stables and carriage houses. Overall, the rise (after the 1860s) in the number of small stables, in particular, contributed to an increase in the density of buildings in the town's core. These trends show the infrastructure generated by changing transport requirements had impacts on the physical character of the town.

To aid understanding of what has happened to the infrastructure since the early twentieth century, and thus identification of remaining material, survival rates of buildings were determined by comparing the mapped historical data with current maps and fieldwork observations: for the buildings that existed in 1910–1915 the overall rate is 15–20%. Noticeably, this does not represent many of the smallest buildings – the one and two stall stables. Loose boxes, trap houses, and coach houses survived disproportionately highly, as did buildings with lofts or hay chambers. Cart sheds had the lowest survival rate of 3%. Analysis of plot and building use data indicated three influences on survival rates of urban horse transport buildings during and after the decline in urban horse transport from the early twentieth century onwards. In Worksop there were periods (1930s, 1950s and 1960s) of total clearance of segments of the town, sweeping all away in preparation for new construction of buildings and enhanced roads for new forms of transport, namely motor vehicles.

Partial clearance has been ongoing over the last 100 years in the urban core or historic town centre leading to 'outbuilding loss' – a situation where the main functional building on a land plot is kept, retaining the historic streetscape, but the outbuildings at the back are demolished. This has been a common occurrence with coaching inns, for example. Alternatively, some buildings have survived because their use changed to housing, storage, workshops, garages or offices, particularly those on the main route from the town centre to the railway station. In Worksop this change-of-use had started by 1915, the Survey records show stable conversions to a printer's machine room, warehouses, coal storage, stores, workshop, and a motor repair shop, although at the same time new stables were being built elsewhere in the town. However, it seems as well as the small buildings, many of the larger ones were demolished if no alternative use was found, for example, carriage factories and showrooms.

Assessment of research method, and implications

This new research, which comprised consideration of the 'needs' of operation of a societal transport activity and finding and interrogating sources of relevant data for a case study, has shown that it is possible to identify the urban built infrastructure of nineteenth- and early twentieth-century horse transport in a given area. It is possible to determine answers to the following enquiries – what there was, where it was, how much there was, and how much remains. The applied method enabled a large amount of previously unexamined primary source information to be amalgamated and analysed to indicate characteristics of the horse transport infrastructure for the urban area of Worksop, Nottinghamshire, particularly about 1910–1915. Findings for this date included the density of land plots with horse transport buildings which ranged from 3:100 to 27:100, dependant on location, with an average of 10:100. The total stallage for the town was estimated at about 750 and the wide range of horse transport users identified. The mapped data showed that the aspects of location, distribution and density of the infrastructure influenced the physical character of the town over the period and in some areas still do, with a current survival rate estimated at 15–20%.

However, the method outlined above does have weaknesses. When consulting the most accurate data-set (1910–1915 Valuation Office Survey) land plots are not equivalent to buildings, and interior function is not always equivalent to separate structure so analysis requires the researcher's understanding of, or best guess at, the surveyor's original meaning. Although presumably working to official guidance, if all the surveyors involved nationwide and the task they were undertaking are considered, it seems likely they did not necessarily complete the records in exactly the same way. The exclusion of detailed building use details for inns and larger industrial sites is regrettable and created a significant gap in the overall results, which could be only partially filled by other sources. Also, the information revealed about the operation of carters was scant and other sources would be needed to obtain a fuller picture. Another weak area was the integration of the locational and building use data from the 1910–1915 Survey records with data from other sources. Obviously, for examination of any other particular area, the comprehensiveness and accuracy of data for dates before 1910 will depend on the specific sources available.

The research method presented here has great potential, beyond the field of building history. The findings from studies using the same or similar methods could augment lines of enquiry for future transport historians, for example, investigations into the impact of changes in long-distance transport on short distance transport, the rise in accessibility of personal transportation (for business or leisure), the complexity of transport in urban areas in the nineteenth century (particularly retail supply), or the transition period from the dominance of horse power to the dominance of the petrol motor in urban areas.

Notes

1 T.C. Barker, "Urban Transport," in *Transport in Victorian Britain,* eds. M.J. Freeman and D.H. Aldcroft, (Manchester: Manchester University Press, 1988), 134.
2 F.M.L. Thompson, *Victorian England: The Horse Drawn Society* (London: Bedford College, University of London, 1970); F.M.L. Thompson, "Nineteenth-Century Horse Sense," *Economic History Review* 29, no. 1 (February 1976): 60–81; T.C. Barker, "The Delayed Decline of the Horse in the Twentieth Century," Keith Chivers, "The Supply of Horses in Nineteenth Century," and F.M.L. Thompson, "Horses and Hay 1830–1918," in F.M.L. Thompson, ed., *Horses in European Economic History A preliminary canter* (Reading: The British Agricultural History Society, 1983).
3 Thompson, "Nineteenth-Century," 66.
4 Ralph Turvey, "Horse Traction in Victorian London," *The Journal of Transport History* 26, no. 2 (2005): 38–59.
5 Peter Atkins, ed., *Animal Cities: Beastly Urban Histories* (Farnham: Ashgate, 2012); Susanna Forrest, *The Age of the Horse* (London: Atlantic Books, 2016); Clay McShane, and Joel Tarr, *The Horse in the City: Living Machines in the Nineteenth Century* (Baltimore: Johns Hopkins University Press, 2007); Ulrich Raulff, *Farewell to the Horse,* trans. Ruth Ahmedzai Kemp (London: Penguin Books, 2018); Hannah Veltan, *Beastly London: A History of Animals in the City* (London: Reaktion Books, 2013).
6 Turvey, "Horse Traction," 46–49.
7 G. Winton, *'Theirs Not To Reason Why': Horsing the British Army 1875–1925* (Solihull: Helion & Company, 2013), 154–156, 252; Keith Chivers, *The Shire Horse: A History of the Breed, the Society and the Men* (London: J.A. Allen, 1976), 742.

8 Thompson, "Nineteenth-Century," 80.

9 F.M.L. Thompson, "Horses and Hay 1830–1918," in *Horses in European Economic History A Preliminary Canter,* ed. F.M.L. Thompson (Reading: The British Agricultural History Society, 1983), 59.

10 F.M.L. Thompson, "Nineteenth-Century," 64.

11 John Copeland, *Roads and their Traffic 1750–1850* (Newton Abbot: David & Charles, 1968), 68 &184; Turvey, "Horse Traction," 42.

12 Philip S. Bagwell, *The Transport Revolution from 1770* (London: B T Batsford, 1974), 139.

13 John Copeland, *Roads and their traffic 1750-1850* (Newton Abbot: David & Charles, 1968), 184.

14 Thompson, "Horses and Hay," 59. Non-farm horses are those categorised in the 'commercial' or 'private or leisure' sectors.

15 Thompson, "Nineteenth-Century," 80.

16 Ibid.

17 Ibid., 72.

18 Turvey, "Horse Traction," 57.

19 William Gordon, *The Horse World of London* (London: Religious Tract Society, 1893).

20 G.A. Sekon, *Locomotion in Victorian London* (London: Oxford University Press, 1936), 201.

21 Theo Barker and Dorian Gerhold, *The Rise and Rise of Road Transport, 1700–1900* (London: Macmillan, 1993), 108.

22 Turvey, "Horse Traction," 45.

23 Stuart Heaton, "The City Dray Horse," *Journal of the Royal Agricultural Society* 70 (1909): 61–67; James Paterson, "Horse Transport and Motor Transport," *Journal of the Royal Society of Arts* 74, no. 3837 (June 4th, 1926): 689–702.

24 Anon (By our own reporter), "Last of Manchester's Cart Horses Auctioned – Archive, 1963," *The Guardian*, 17 April 2018, accessed June 25, 2019, www.theguardian.com/world/2018/apr/17/last-cart-horses-auctioned-manchester-1963

25 Thomas Almeroth-Williams, "The Brewery Horse and the Importance of Equine Power in Hanoverian London," *Urban History* 40, no. 3 (2013): 440.

26 Discussion of requirements of horse transport in Turvey, "Horse Traction"; Peter Atkins, ed., *Animal Cities*; Thompson, "Nineteenth-Century"; Thompson, *Victorian England.*

27 Several in London, and some noted during the research in Preston (4), Glasgow, Aberdeen, Arbroath, Leigh, Reading, York, Newcastle.

28 Giles Worsley, *The British Stable* (New Haven and London: Yale University Press for the Paul Mellon Centre for Studies in British Art, 2004), 103. The term 'mews' comes from the royal hawking buildings on the site of the present National Gallery in London, which were replaced in 1537 by the Royal Stables.

29 Thompson, *Victorian England,* 16.

30 Ibid., 13. Some railway horses assisted with movement of railway stock.

31 Turvey, "Horse Traction," 50.

32 Heaton, "The City," 65–66.

33 Edward Paget-Tomlinson, *The Railway Carriers: The history of Wordie & Co, Carriers, Hauliers and Store Keepers* (Lavenham: Terence Dalton with the Wordie Property Co., 1990), 60.

34 Thompson, "Nineteenth-Century," 77.

35 M.J. Jackson, *Worksop of Yesterday: The Town at the Turn of the Century* (Worksop: Worksop Archaeological and Local Historical Soc., 1969), 10.

36 John Harrison, *An Exact and Perfect Survey and View of the Manor of Worksop with the Priory Manor, situated in the County of Nottingham,* 1636, Sheffield City Archives ACM/W/26.

37 For example, for Manchester four issues from 1886 to 1902 cover different areas of the central city, with another set around railway stations for other NW towns c1900.
38 Some of the data for some counties is currently available online via web genealogy databases; www.glos1909survey.org.uk has a detailed explanation and copies of primary data including maps covering Gloucestershire; see also Anthea Jones, "Records of the Lloyd George survey of land values 1910: comparisons and insights from Gloucestershire," *The Local Historian* 43 (July 2014): 202–220.

Bibliography

Almeroth-Williams, Thomas. "The Brewery Horse and the Importance of Equine Power in Hanoverian London." *Urban History* 40 (2013): 416–441.

Anon. "Last of Manchester's Cart Horses Auctioned – Archive, 1963." *The Guardian*. April 17, 2018. Accessed June 25, 2019. www.theguardian.com/world/2018/apr/17/last-cart-horses-auctioned-manchester-1963/

Atkins, Peter. "The Charmed Circle." In *Animal Cities: Beastly Urban Histories,* edited by Peter Atkins, 53–76. Farnham: Ashgate, 2012.

———. "The Urban Blood and Guts Economy." In *Animal Cities: Beastly Urban Histories,* edited by Peter Atkins, 77–106. Farnham: Ashgate, 2012.

Bagwell, Philip S. *The Transport Revolution from 1770.* London: B T Batsford, 1974.

Barker, T.C. "The Delayed Decline of the Horse in the Twentieth Century." In *Horses in European Economic History A Preliminary Canter,* edited by F.M.L. Thompson, 101–112. Reading: The British Agricultural History Society, 1983.

———. "Urban Transport." In *Transport in Victorian Britain,* edited by M.J. Freeman and D.H. Aldcroft, 100–150. Manchester: Manchester University Press, 1988.

Barker, Theo and Dorian Gerhold. *The Rise and Rise of Road Transport, 1700–1900.* London: Macmillan, 1993.

Chivers, Keith. *The Shire Horse: A History of the Breed, the Society and the Men.* London: J.A. Allen, 1976.

———. "The Supply of Horses in Nineteenth Century." In *Horses in European Economic History A preliminary canter,* edited by F.M.L. Thompson, 31–49. Reading: The British Agricultural History Society, 1983.

Copeland, John. *Roads and their Traffic 1750–1850.* Newton Abbot: David & Charles, 1968.

Forrest, Susanna. *The Age of the Horse.* London: Atlantic Books, 2016

Gordon, William. *The Horse World of London.* London: Religious Tract Society, 1893.

Harrison, John. *An Exact and Perfect Survey and View of the Manor of Worksop with the Priory Manor, Situated in the County of Nottingham.* Sheffield City Archives ACM/W/26, 1636.

Heaton, Stuart. "The City Dray Horse." *Journal of the Royal Agricultural Society* 70 (1909): 61–67.

Horwood, Richard. *Plan of the Cities of London and Westminster the Borough of Southwark, and parts adjoining Shewing every House.* www.romanticlondon.org.

Jackson, M.J. *Worksop of Yesterday: The Town at the Turn of the Century.* Worksop: Worksop Archaeological and Local Historical Soc., 1969.

Jones, Anthea. "Records of the Lloyd George Survey of Land Values 1910: Comparisons and Insights from Gloucestershire." *The Local Historian* 43 (July 2014): 202–220.

McShane, Clay, and Joel Tarr. *The Horse in the City: Living Machines in the Nineteenth Century.* Baltimore: Johns Hopkins University Press, 2007.

Paget-Tomlinson, Edward. *The Railway Carriers: The History of Wordie & Co, Carriers, Hauliers and Store Keepers.* Lavenham: Terence Dalton with the Wordie Property Co., 1990.

Paterson, James. "Horse Transport and Motor Transport." *Journal of the Royal Society of Arts* 74, no. 3837 (June 4th, 1926): 689–702.

Raulff, Ulrich. *Farewell to the Horse.* Translated by Ruth Ahmedzai Kemp. London: Penguin Books, 2018.

Sekon, G.A. *Locomotion in Victorian London.* London: Oxford University Press, 1936.

Taylor, John. *Carriers Cosmographie.* London: Anne Griffin, 1637.Thompson, F.M.L. "Horses and Hay 1830–1918." In *Horses in European Economic History A preliminary canter,* edited by F.M.L. Thompson, 50–72. Reading: The British Agricultural History Society, 1983.

———. "Nineteenth-Century Horse Sense," *Economic History Review* 29 (1976): 60–81.

———. *Victorian England: The Horse Drawn Society.* London: Bedford College, University of London, 1970.

Turvey, Ralph. "Horse traction in Victorian London." *The Journal of Transport History* 26, no. 2 (2005): 38–59.

Veltan, Hannah. *Beastly London: A History of Animals in the City.* London: Reaktion Books, 2013.

Winton, Graham. *'Theirs Not To Reason Why': Horsing the British Army 1875–1925.* Solihull: Helion & Company, 2013.

Worsley, Giles. *The British Stable.* New Haven and London: Yale University Press for the Paul Mellon Centre for Studies in British Art, 2004.

11 Digital disasters

Crowdsourcing the railway accident

Mike Esbester

Introduction

On 10 November 1913, at 7.30pm, 'casual porter' Herbert French was putting sheets on wagons in the North Eastern Railway's goods warehouse in York. The wagons moved unexpectedly, catching French – though fortunately for him, he was injured rather than killed: his left thumb was pinched. Although a relatively minor injury, there was a state-sponsored investigation which amongst its conclusions found that foreman W Horsley:

> fully admits that not only immediately following this mishap, but frequently, he has given the shunters instructions to move waggons in the warehouse without knowing that his men were clear. [...] it is very evident that foreman Horsley has not exercised the care for the safety of his men that he should have done.[1]

French was just one of the nearly 30,000 railway employees who were either injured or killed in 1913 alone[2] – but about whom very little is known. His case represents some of the human costs of keeping the railway system running in the past but which have so far been largely overlooked by historical investigation – just as they were largely unknown to the public at the time.

This chapter opens up this new area for discussion in two ways. First, drawing on original archival research, it contributes a brief analysis of railway staff safety in Britain during the nineteenth and first half of the twentieth centuries. Using both quantitative and qualitative approaches, it examines how and why worker safety issues were obscured by other factors, and the key actors involved. These are important aspects in their own right, but also contribute to the increasing interest in the history of accidents, safety and risk more generally.[3] Second, the chapter moves beyond an empirical research contribution and advances the methodology of transport and mobility history by outlining the operation and implications of a digital crowd-sourcing project, working towards co-production between academics and partner experts. This is an area which has yet to be explored in a meaningful way within transport and mobility history and only in a

relatively limited way in wider historical methodology. The project underlying this chapter is therefore setting an agenda in the field of transport and
mobility history and in the discipline of history more widely.

The chapter starts by contextualising railway employee deaths and injuries, particularly in relation to passenger safety, between approximately 1830
and 1948. It argues that workers were systematically overlooked in favour of
passengers – both at the time (particularly by the state and public attention)
and in the existing historiography. In doing so, it focuses attention on staff
accidents, including on the steps taken to try to reduce or prevent employee
casualties. This includes a key initiative introduced by the railway industry
in the early twentieth century – safety education. Examining these factors
is an important means of redressing the relative paucity of historiographi-
cal attention directed at railway worker safety in the UK, and establishing
the area into which the 'Railway Work, Life & Death' project is making an
intervention.

The second half of the chapter will explore this project and how it contributes to the methodologies of transport and mobility history. It introduces the
project and considers the challenges and benefits it offers. This contributes
to the growing area of 'citizen science', the collaboration between different
'types' of researcher, sometimes framed as academic and non-academic,
though as will be argued in the conclusion, such a reductive binary fails to
recognise the existence of different forms of expertise. The argument engages with ideas about expertise and boundaries between historians, making a case for a more collaborative approach that breaks down potential
barriers to cooperation. In doing so, the project and this chapter draw from
and contribute to the emerging body of literature on crowd-sourcing in the
humanities and on the digital humanities more broadly.

Putting the worker into the railway accident

If the railway might be seen as emblematic of nineteenth-century British
modernity and as something over which early and mid-Victorian society ob-
sessed,[4] then the railway accident was surely its most visible and concerning feature. However, there was no such thing as *the* railway accident, for
there was not a single type of accident. From the 1840s, the state and others
made distinctions between accidents involving passenger trains, accidents
to workers, and accidents to others.[5] As Ralph Harrington, Peter Sinnema
and Wolfgang Schivelbusch amongst others have shown, accidents to passenger trains occupied the public gaze, at least as seen in the pages of the periodical press and newspapers of nineteenth century and in Parliamentary
and state discussion.[6] Historians and other analysts have replicated this, to
some extent, including medical humanities' consideration of the development of particular understandings of trauma like 'railway spine.'[7] Finally,
the railway accident as it appeared in popular culture was, for much if not
all of the period under consideration here, also focused on the passenger

crash. Nicholas Daly, Jill Matus and Matthew Wilson-Smith have all examined written and stage productions in which the passenger accident played a key role, for example.[8]

Other than as causes of accidents, or more occasionally as heroic (if doomed) figures like driver John Axon (who sacrificed his life in 1957 trying to stop a runaway train),[9] workers and worker accidents are relatively invisible, at the time and since. This might be considered surprising on two related grounds: first, the industry was the one of the largest employers in Britain by the turn of the nineteenth century, employing 575,834 people in 1901.[10] Second, if only the statistics are taken into account it might be questioned how it was possible to miss staff deaths and injuries: for example, in 1913, for every passenger casualty there were nine staff casualties.[11] However, a number of factors account for the relative invisibility of the railway worker.

Passenger crashes happened in public, or semi-public, spaces, were large-scale and relatively uncommon. They were seized upon by the press. They involved members of the public who had little control over the outcome of events, and struck across the class spectrum, raising the prominence of the passenger crash in Parliamentary and public discourses. By way of contrast, railway workers were culturally and politically invisible. In most cases, their accidents were hidden from the public gaze, in spaces inaccessible to non-employees; they happened in sufficiently large quantities that they were unexceptional, but also they tended to occur in ones and twos which were mundane and not newsworthy. Finally, for the entirety of the period covered by this chapter, workers were viewed as able to control, or at least influence, their fate; therefore, if they were involved in an accident, in most cases the companies, state agencies and many beyond simply saw it as a product of individual 'carelessness.'

Railway workers have not entirely been neglected by historical study. Specific work by Mike Esbester, Audrey Giles, Ewan Knox, and Rande Kostal means British railway staff safety has received some attention.[12] Some of this has involved statistical and empirical analysis, a significant part of highlighting an aspect of railway and labour history which needs to be exposed to light. This fits within a broader context of the history of labour and occupational safety and health, where workplace deaths and injuries have been hidden by the aspects noted above.[13] Significant work by the likes of Ronnie Johnston, Arthur McIvor and Mike Sanders has helped open the area out, both historiographically and in terms of literary critical approaches. In particular, these authors have explored everyday experiences of individuals, focusing on more subjective and cultural modes of analysis, including using previously neglected source bases (in this area) such as oral histories and literature.[14]

Railway work could be extremely dangerous, though this danger was not distributed evenly across all grades. Manual roles, such as track-laying and stock construction or operation, bore the greater part of the risk; comparatively, those in clerical roles were less routinely exposed to danger.

Table 11.1 Casualty and employment statistics, selected years

Year	Passenger casualties	Worker casualties	No. employed	% casualties/employed
1884	2,101	6,492	346,426	1.87%
1898	2,521	13,521	534141	2.53%
1913	3,791	29,710	643135	4.62%
1938	8,297	17,012	607278	2.80%

Taken from reports issued by the Railway Inspectorate for the respective years; General Report of the Board of Trade upon the Accidents that have occurred on the Railways of the United Kingdom During the Year 1884, 1898, 1913 (London, 1885, 1899, 1914) & Report to the Ministry of Transport upon the Accidents that have occurred on the Railways of the Great Britain for the Year 1938 (London, 1938).

The available statistics are problematic, as the way in which they were collected was changed from time to time, and as a result of the way that accidents to workshop staff were recorded in state reports it is impossible to obtain the numbers of railway workers involved. As a result, the statistics represent a minimum figure – the true total was rather greater. However, as Table 11.1 demonstrates, they at least give an impression of railway work's toll on the staff.

In 1900 the dangers faced by manual railway workers were compared to those faced in industries the state defined as 'dangerous trades', including mining. The latest statistics then available, for 1898, showed that for select grades on the railways, of every 1000 employed 31 were injured and 1.24 were killed. This was comparable with the 1.28 deaths per 1000 employed in coal mining and 0.96 per 1000 in metalliferous mining.[15] The casualty figures declined in absolute terms in the interwar period: for example, in 1938, the final full year for which statistics are available, there were just over 17,000 deaths and injuries, a decline of over 12,000 from 25 years previously. Nonetheless, the industry evidently remained dangerous.

Having established that large numbers of workers were killed and injured at work, it is helpful to consider what steps were taken to reduce or prevent staff casualties. This is one area, in particular, in which this chapter makes a new contribution, as to date accident prevention has not been examined in any depth. There were four main groups involved in staff safety matters: the workers, the trades unions, the railway companies, and the state. The first of these had relatively limited power to make significant changes; the workers, on the ground, were certainly restricted by the power imbalance with their employers. For the most part they could not alter their patterns or locations of work, or insist upon the use or provision of safety equipment (particularly those on piece rates, where things like machine guards to protect vulnerable fingers from moving parts might have slowed down production, losing them money). They might improvise defences against particular risks, as in the Wolverhampton works on the Great Western Railway in the early 1900s when men working on grinding wheels 'protected themselves against inhaling spray by draping a cloth over the lower part of their faces'.[16] However, such agency was generally circumscribed by the system within which the employees operated – one that was a product of decisions made by railway company managements.

From the 1870s the workers' representatives, the trades unions, gradually inserted themselves into the safety matrix. The key players in this regard were the all-grades Amalgamated Society of Railway Servants (ASRS, established 1871), which after a merger with two other unions became the National Union of Railwaymen (NUR) in 1913, and the Associated Society of Locomotive Enginemen and Firemen (established 1881). Recent historiography has explored how a variety of trades unions attempted to secure their members' interests through compensation for accidents and legal action as part of a 'mixed economy' of methods aimed at compelling organisations to improve safety.[17] The railway unions certainly adopted this strategy; in addition to legal and financial efforts, they also sponsored technical trials of safety appliances (for example, to improve couplings between wagons, at Darlington in 1882 and Nine Elms, London, in 1886).[18]

Perhaps most visibly, the unions campaigned on safety. Part of this was political, with the help of union-friendly or union-sponsored MPs like Michael Bass (Derby) and latterly railwaymen MPs like Jimmy Thomas (Derby) asking questions in Parliament and attempting to introduce legislation. Part of this was technical, making submissions and giving testimony to state enquiries, as well as raising concerns with the state department responsible for the railways, the Board of Trade and, from 1919, the Ministry of Transport. The growing power and influence of the unions via all of these routes as the nineteenth century progressed and into the twentieth century ensured that the unions had an increasing role to play in worker safety and in holding the railway companies to account.

After 1897, compensation became payable as a routine part of the accident process in most cases, so there was an increasing financial imperative, alongside the railway companies declining profitability.[19] These pressures were, however, keenly balanced against the potential costs of changes. These might have included changing the ways in which people worked to remove them from dangerous situations, or technological solutions (often suggested by the trades unions) – for example, in the late 1890s the costs of introducing automatic couplings on goods stock, to save workers from going between wagons to couple them, was put at 'several millions', a price the companies predictably deemed unacceptable and actively campaigned against.[20] As a result, the railway industry soon developed a relatively standard set of approaches to staff safety.

Integral were ideas that safety was a part of the relationship between management and staff, and external intervention in managerial prerogative was unacceptable. The companies fiercely guarded their right to manage labour, including so far as safety was concerned. The rule book and circular were key edicts, with rule 24(a) ordering workers to be safe and potentially subjecting them to disciplinary action if they did have an accident. Underpinning this was a view that virtually all accidents were a result of worker 'carelessness', and that only staff could make improvements by changing their behaviour. How far the rule book and circular were truly focused on worker safety rather than keeping the system running is debateable, so other techniques used since the early railway age included supervision of workers (though this was not always feasible, given the dispersed nature of the workforce) and provision of formal warning signs (rather than removing dangers).

Whilst these methods continued, and continue to this day, one innovation of the early twentieth century was the introduction of 'safety education' in 1913.[21] Introduced by the Great Western Railway, it was soon adopted by other companies across the UK. This was the industry's solution to mounting pressure to improve safety, largely led by the unions; it tried to show workers the right and wrong ways of doing their jobs, using the media to convey its messages. Photographs were prominent throughout (Figure 11.1). This enormously significant: for the first time it was attempted to make safety messages immediately accessible and comprehensible. Supplementing this was the tone of writing. Much of the material was very informal – something previously unknown in official communication. A variety of innovative techniques were used: articles in staff magazines, booklets, posters, competitions, psychological tricks and from the late 1930s, film. By way of example of the scale of this effort, after 1929, the Big Four railway companies collaborated to produce a series of 5 booklets, each aimed at different types of railway work (for example, workshop jobs or signal and telegraph work) and each of which was reprinted many times – at least 700,000 of them were distributed.

The attempt to make safety 'user-friendly' was crucial and provides perhaps the most lasting influence of the campaign. The introduction of the 'Safety Movement' (or 'safety first' campaign) was an important moment within Britain: this was the first dedicated and systematic safety campaign. Safety education soon spread far beyond the railways, including other workplaces and the whole of British society, including the formation in 1916 of the body that later became the Royal Society for the Prevention of Accidents.

The state role in the pre-1948 era was relatively tightly circumscribed. In relation to staff, for most of the nineteenth century the state followed a minimalist approach to intervention – adult male workers, in particular, were supposed to be able to look after themselves.[22] So, when the Railway Inspectorate was established in 1840, whilst it had a nominal staff safety role, it focused almost entirely on passenger accidents; it was not until 1877 that companies were compelled to report all staff accidents with anything approaching a degree of accuracy.[23] Legislative or regulative intervention on behalf of workers was limited, though key moments included the 1897

CHAPTER III.

NEEDLESS RISKS IN TRAFFIC WORKING.

1. Asking for Trouble.

LOOK at this picture. Probably there are few readers to whom the sight is a strange one. What does that mean? It means that the practice of riding on a shunting-pole is not uncommon. Everyone knows that it is forbidden. And why? Obviously because of its danger. Many an unfortunate fellow has attempted it to his peril. There is a man at Paddington who, nineteen years ago, lost both his legs through doing this. A sudden jerk of the vehicles threw him off the shunting-pole, which caught him in the back and knocked him down, and his legs were run over. A thoughtless moment entailed

2. Got It.

Figure 11.1 Typical page from an early safety education booklet; note the conversational tone and use of 'right' and 'wrong' photographs. The 'Safety' Movement (London, 1914), 12.

Workmen's Compensation Act, which included railway employees within its remit and provided, in most cases, for some degree of automatic financial redress in the event of accident. The 1900 Railway Employment (Prevention of Accidents) Act was a rare piece of legislation specific to railway employees. It produced some changes (such as better lighting in goods yards), but it could still hardly be said to have marked a massive change to the existing regime. Ultimately, the railway companies retained a great deal of control over employee safety issues until Nationalisation in 1948.

One key state aspect remains, which informs the remainder of this chapter's focus on the 'Railway Work, Life & Death' project: the Railway Inspectors within the Railway Department of the Board of Trade (from 1919 transferred to the Ministry of Transport). From 1894 a new category of Railway Inspector was appointed, dedicated to investigating staff accidents. They had limited powers, confined to investigating accidents after they had happened rather than (as the unions had argued) the power to investigate general conditions with a view to preventing accidents from occurring. They could also only make unenforceable recommendations, which the railway companies were under no obligation to adopt and on average only 3% of worker accidents were investigated in any given year. Despite this, they did manage to investigate many hundreds of accidents per year. From 1900 their reports were printed and circulated, forming a huge source-base – but one which has thus far been unindexed and available to researchers only in hardcopy at a number of locations. Unlocking the potential that these sources offered for a wide variety of researchers spurred the 'Railway Work, Life & Death' project.[24]

Working on staff accidents

The quantity of these reports made comprehensive exploration by an individual almost impossible. However, with the emerging trends in crowd-sourcing and 'citizen science', discussed below, a collaborative project bringing together a group of interested researchers had potential to provide a new resource enabling much wider use of the reports and new ways of analysing their data. It was also seen as an ideal way of testing the new, more collaborative methodologies in academic study of transport and mobility history, a field which had yet to see any significant engagement with crowd-sourcing.

Significant to this impetus was a diversity of voices who were interested in the sources, prompting action and becoming an integral part of the project ethos. Building on existing relationships, the initial collaboration emerged between Esbester and the National Railway Museum (NRM), following a family history conference held at the NRM in 2015 at which the idea of the project was put forward. This was significant, as the conference allowed early input into the project from family historians and genealogists amongst other stakeholders. Links were forged which have since proved extremely important in ensuring engagement with a range of family history groups and genealogists, including the support and advice offered by one key project ally, Jackie Depelle.

As part of the early discussions, key potential audiences for the work were identified as railway, transport, labour and socio-cultural historians (academic and beyond), museums and heritage professionals, family historians and genealogists, and the current rail industry. Karen Baker, NRM Librarian and project co-lead, and Esbester between them brought insight into the likely needs of the academic and museological stakeholders; for the remaining audiences representatives were involved in the set-up stages, including significant interaction with family historians, particularly over what data might most usefully be captured and how it could be presented. After a year of planning, including ethical opinion, the project started in late 2016 as a relatively small-scale, proof-of-concept venture, involving NRM volunteers; the outcomes of its first stage launched publicly in August 2017, with work continuing to date on further extensions and in late 2018 the Modern Records Centre at the University of Warwick (MRC) joining the project team as a collaborator. What follows outlines some key features of the project, including the rationale and planning process, ethics, operation (including challenges faced) and results.

From the outset, the potential was seen in crowd-sourcing (the idea that members of the public volunteer time and effort to assist in fields of scholarly enquiry, often to accumulate data by converting it from one format to another)[25] and 'citizen science' (a more analysis-focused approach and inclusive idea, in which participants are recognised as bringing different forms of expertise). With elements of both, perhaps the best known example is the 'Zooniverse' label (starting with a project to allow interested amateurs to help identify new galaxies from deep space photographs, subsequently expanding to include all sorts of participatory projects in the sciences, social sciences and arts and humanities).[26] As Sally Shuttleworth has demonstrated, citizen science is not a new phenomenon, but the advent of the internet has radically changed the scope, scale, and arguably democratic elements.[27] It would be entirely fair to ask *why* historical research might be conducted in this way. In the best outcome, there are benefits to all parties: the public gets access to material and is involved in research that might otherwise be hard to access, the profile of academic research is raised, sources are made available that might otherwise have taken years to deal with, there are social benefits for the volunteers, and all parties are involved, hopefully as co-creators.[28] This movement has gathered pace over approximately the last ten years, including in the arts, humanities and heritage sectors.[29]

In this sense, perhaps historians of transport and mobility have missed an opportunity so far, as relatively few digital history projects appear to exist. Two originating from the academic sphere concern car ownership in North Carolina, USA, between 1916 and 1919,[30] and medieval and early modern shipping trade routes,[31] though from the information available they do not appear to engage with crowd-sourcing methodologies. Two other projects from beyond the higher education sector have used forms of crowd-sourcing: the 'Crew List Index Project', an impressive volunteer project facilitating transcription of records of late nineteenth and early twentieth century British merchant seafarers.[32] Finally, and in relation to the UK railway industry, the 'Railways Archive' focuses on passenger accident cases, using a limited pool of volunteers to digitise and make available reports issued by the Railway Inspectorate from the 1840s to the present. However, their remit specifically excludes worker accidents (initially believing the reports did not exist).[33] The space was therefore open for a project which engaged with citizen science and crowd-sourcing methodologies on the topic of railway worker accidents.

Integral to the planning process was the rationale behind the project: particularly if volunteers were to be asked to spend time working on it, it was critical that there were significant outcomes for their efforts, as well as those of the co-leaders. Several areas of insight that the reports offered, and which making their contents more widely available would enhance, were identified. To those with railway and labour history interests, the reports would provide great detail about the experience of work on the railways in the past, and of course the risks to which individuals were exposed. For example, one 1923 report stated that:

> The practice of riding on the buffer [...] has been in operation [...] for many years, and in the past the management have not taken exception to it. The [site] and the methods of working are all dependent on some such method. [...] The practice [...] appears to be highly dangerous.[34]

This provides a sense not only of what was happening on the ground, but also how management was complicit in producing dangerous situations. Without the details found in these and other reports it would be difficult to reconstruct a sense of how workers were doing their jobs, and under what day-to-day conditions and constraints.

For family historians, it was identified that a resource allowing the accidents to be searched would allow people to find out more about family members who worked on the railways and had an accident, as the reports contained a wealth of biographical detail. As well as allowing people insight into the moment of the accident to an ancestor, the reports are name-rich, frequently including details such as an individual's job title, employer, age and working pattern and tasks undertaken. For museums, archives and heritage organisations, it was envisaged that the work would unlock holdings that were uncatalogued, allowing them both to answer queries from researchers and make holdings more accessible. The NRM was keen to use the stories contained within their records in future exhibitions and content. For rail enthusiasts and the general public, the project could provide new insight into the history of the railways, an extremely popular topic at the current time, and challenge people to consider not just the technological and engineering achievements, but the social impacts of the railways. Finally, the project would meet interest from within the current railway industry, which saw this sort of work as providing context for the present, as well as a non-threatening medium through which to discuss current safety-related issues; it would also allow the possibility of learning from the past, including by re-discovering institutional memory and by being reminded of past solutions to problems.

Evidently there were strong reasons why the project might make useful contributions, and support of the principle was forthcoming from the two partner institutions, albeit with the proviso that there was extremely limited budget available. As a result, and as a means of ensuring the work remained manageable, a small-scale, proof-of-concept project was to be the initial pilot. Coverage of 1911–1915 was chosen for a number of reasons, but particularly as a smaller scale cataloguing exercise at The National Archives of the UK (TNA) had covered the period up to 1910,[35] and the reports stopped being printed in June 1915, forming a natural endpoint.

Before the project could start it was both important and necessary to consider the ethical implications of working on this data in public and with the public. The contents of the reports do contain some graphic detail which might be considered upsetting, particularly if they related to someone known to the reader. They required and require respectful handling – though making their details available was positioned as one part of this respect, as doing so seeks to recognise the individual impacts of accidents which previously have only been considered en masse and as statistics. Whilst anonymising the cases was considered, retaining the names was crucial, both for the reason of recognising the individuals involved and to meet the needs of the family history communities. As the reports were publicly available at the time, this would not be bringing any new details into the public domain, albeit it was changing the ease and potential scale of access. Finally, it was essential that the project was acting ethically in relation to the volunteers. All of these aspects were scrutinised by the NRM's managing committees and a formal ethics application was made through the University of Portsmouth (UoP)'s ethics framework, receiving a favourable opinion.[36] This process was invaluable in allowing the project team to think through and receive guidance on the implications of the work, and steps to be taken to minimise any possibility of harm. This included our provision of guidance on respectful use of the data, given all those named were once living people and there may be descendants alive today, and transparency about steps to be taken if any concerns were raised about the inclusion of data.

Given the imperatives for a low-cost pilot project, the most feasible methodology it was possible to adopt involved a small group of NRM volunteers, around 16 in total – a version of 'targeted crowd-sourcing', in which a closed community of a limited scale was involved in the work.[37] Drawn from within the NRM's existing pool of volunteers, they were self-selecting and all were remotely based. This was well-suited to a project of this kind, with access to images of the relevant documents, but it imposed a particular mode of working and some challenges discussed below. The volunteers were supported by Craig Shaw, a volunteer himself but also the volunteer coordinator for this project, overseeing the interaction with the transcribers and undertaking a large degree of the quality control work. The volunteers were provided with digital copies of batches of accident reports and asked to summarise the data they contained and enter it into a standard spreadsheet template (which had been tested extensively beforehand). Once transcribed, the data was checked by at least three people, including Portsmouth-based volunteer Stuart Taylor, before being made available on the project website – which was set up and is maintained by Esbester's colleagues at the UoP. The work was time-consuming – between transcription and quality control well over 1,000 volunteer hours were logged – but it has produced much greater access to the information found within the reports.

This account of the project's genesis and operation belies significant challenges facing the manner of working and crowd-sourcing in general. Many of these are practical. In some cases, finding willing volunteers can pose challenges, though in this project's case the ready-made pool of NRM volunteers obviated this. The time commitment for all has meant relatively slow progress at times, as well as a big commitment for those involved. The lack of formal funding has influenced decisions – for example, there was no money to pay for a true database, and so spreadsheets were used instead. Fortunately, Esbester's access through the UoP to digital copies of the accident reports meant that digitisation costs were not faced, as they would have been prohibitively high. Similarly, although no formal budget was available for technical development and support, the UoP provided support in kind, via the time of Online Course Developers Scott Simmonds, Daren Cooper and James Hare and technicians Mark Jones and Tom Heard. Ensuring the accuracy of transcription has also been far from straightforward, and even with three people having checked the data to their best standard in the time available, some errors no doubt remain.[38]

Some of the challenges faced were philosophical, and tap into much wider contemporary debates. The first of these relates to ideas of how volunteers are involved in projects: whether as transcribers, simply undertaking large amounts of legwork for someone else, or as co-producers, actively involved in the research process and valued for their insight and the research questions they generated.[39] If projects are attempting co-production, then volunteers need to be involved as such, ideally from the planning stages – although that is difficult to do in practice, and unfortunately was not achieved in this pilot project. Involving remote volunteers magnifies these challenges, as they are never gathered together at any one time and place; nevertheless, over time and with the particular efforts of Shaw, the NRM's volunteer coordinator for this project, a sense of community has been developed, including several of the volunteers undertaking further research into the cases they had encountered during transcription and joining future public-facing events to discuss the project and their work.[40] All volunteers were encouraged to feed questions and ideas back to the project team, and to make use of their railway based knowledge in their work. As a result, whilst not fully co-production, the project has at least made efforts in the direction.

The final challenge is perhaps the deepest, and is ongoing: the perceived value of this kind of project to our institutions in the current context. With both universities and museums under increasing financial pressure, as well as the push to engage more widely (especially beyond 'traditional' audiences), projects like this might offer great potential. Yet every moment spent on them by institution staff is a moment not doing something else which might be more immediately obvious as income generation. To universities, 'impact' or engagement work is important – but difficult to make tangible in ways that fit with metrics of assessment. Publication and teaching are more clearly defined and quantifiable for exercises such as the Research Excellence Framework or in terms of career progression, so for academics who might get involved in public-facing crowd-sourcing and data generation projects, such as this one, there can be difficult choices about how to prioritise the finite amount of their time that is available.

By late 2018, the project has released its key dataset from the pilot – the database of nearly 4,000 individuals whose accidents between 1911 and June 1915 were investigated by the Railway Inspectors. This comprises tens of thousands of data points, searchable in a relatively easy-to-use interface, made freely available on the project website in August 2017. Other resources have been provided here, including a weekly blog which explores some of the cases, their wider context and their implications in more detail. Whilst metrics are notoriously unreliable, they still provide an indication of use – so at December 2018 the 2,902 downloads from all inhabited continents and over 23,000 website views worldwide suggest that the project is providing resources and content that are valuable. This has been supported by feedback from and interaction with stakeholders, whether in person at events or through the website and project Twitter account, which had accumulated nearly 1,100 followers in its first year. Whilst only limited as indicators of engagement in their own right, the interest and feedback has been important in supporting the volunteers and showing that their efforts are both appreciated and reaching a wide audience. It has also been crucial in making the case for further work: the concept has been proven successful and viable, both meeting existing demand from outside the project team for this work and demonstrating the potential value of this area, thereby generating demand for extending the project.

To this end, the initial pilot project has had sufficient impact to be able to secure support for several extensions, across multiple institutions. Many of the original NRM volunteers actively sought to continue with the project, and have been working on two new datasets. The first covers the Great Eastern Railway's Benevolent Fund book for 1913–1923 and details post-accident care disbursed to injured staff, giving greater insight into the lasting effects of workplace accidents and the history of disability and welfare. The second takes the same source base as the original project, the Railway Inspectors' reports, but for the inter-war period.

Concurrently, the project is working with TNA and a team of on-site volunteers to transcribe details found in railway company accident books, c.1897–1930. This will bring a different perspective on the accidents, many of which are expected to crossover with those found in the work carried out by NRM volunteers. Late in 2018 a collaboration started with the MRC, to bring in records from the ASRS/NUR from the 1870s to 1920s, providing a further alternative view on accidents. These links were forged at the 2015 conference at the NRM, and strengthened via a period of liaison and discussion initiated by Esbester and championed by both key colleagues, Chris Heather (TNA) and Helen Ford (MRC), in their respective institutions. Finding receptive and willing contacts within organisations has evidently been an important part of extending the project – as was the ability to demonstrate the viability of the methodology used in the original project work, how it had been received by people accessing the data, and the demand for further work.

These subsequent extensions have features more closely allied to co-production as outlined above, to involve volunteers more closely in the research process. This has been possible as the extensions are based on site at the two institutions, providing a focal point and a regular meeting slot, and enabling set-up sessions designed not just to discuss the practical methods of working but also to involve volunteers in setting a research agenda. It is anticipated that, across these extensions, potentially as many as 70,000 cases of accident may enter the dataset, creating a huge resource for all researchers and opening up possibilities of plotting long-term trends as well as identifying life stories of individuals or railway families who suffered multiple casualties.

Conclusion

The full implications of this work and this area are becoming clear, particularly in relation to the 'Railway Work, Life & Death' project as it reaches diverse audiences and is being used worldwide. This is expected to magnify in the coming years, both with the new data entering the database providing much greater coverage and as the various stakeholders make increasing use of the resources provided.

Underlying all of this is significant original research into the wider context and understandings of occupational safety and accidents on the railways, from the later nineteenth century to the mid-twentieth century. Explored in the first half of the chapter, this contributes to a range of fields of historical study, from transport and mobility history, the history of occupational safety and health and of accidents and risk, to history from below and social and cultural history. This has demonstrated how dangerous railway work could be, as well as the reasons for the relative invisibility of staff accidents. It also explored attitudes towards intervention held by key players: the workers, the trades unions, the state and the railway companies themselves. As might be expected, the first two of these were in favour of a more interventionist state and society including financial investment; the latter two were more inclined towards a hands-off approach, leaving private enterprise to manage risks. Finally, this section highlighted a significant innovation that started in the railway industry – safety education – which went on to have an impact on virtually all areas of British society after 1913.

Methodologically, the chapter has sought to move transport and mobility history forward, with its discussion of the 'Railway Work, Life & Death' project – also making a contribution to humanities crowd-sourcing and the digital humanities. By setting out key details of the project intentions, planning, operation and challenges – as well as its successes – it is hoped it will provide others with inspiration and practical insight into how crowd-sourced research might operate in their areas of specialism. As is clear, this is an area of great potential, but to date there has been relatively limited engagement, certainly within transport and mobility history and arguably within wider historical study. The project is therefore setting an agenda in the field and in the discipline more widely. One significant way in which it is doing so is by its engagement with a broad range of stakeholders.

There are significant benefits from this project for a number of groups, including academic researchers, by providing answers to questions about topics including the nature and experience of work on the railways and what actually happened in practice, changing understandings of occupational health and safety, and the relationships between employees, employers, unions and the state. It will, no doubt, raise new questions that have not been foreseen. The academic audience was, however, only one which was 'written into' the project at the outset, and it does not take priority over the others. Envisaged as significant users of the project were the museums and archives communities, particularly the original partner institution, the NRM. As it redevelops over the coming years, narratives and analysis from this project will inform display priorities and content. The family history and genealogical communities have taken up the project and made great use of it, as well as supporting it and its development. The name-rich data has provided a helpful source of new information, as well as wider context about ancestors' railway work, life and death.

This prompts a final point, about the nature of 'expertise' and where it is found. Each of the stakeholder groups noted above, and the volunteers, have brought their own types of expertise to the project, without which it would not be so rich nor a success.[41] Often these involve considerable and specific knowledge and research skills that the others involved do not possess – be it detailed insight into railway working practices, an ability to examine the wider family and community contexts to the individuals who suffered accidents, understanding of archival and museological practices, or the wider analytical and theoretical approaches to workplace safety and accidents.

The project has already brought together academic, museum, railway enthusiast and family history and genealogical partners, and will hopefully continue to bridge some of the gaps that have arisen between these groups in the past.[42] For too long an artificial divide has existed between these groups, something being critically examined and questioned by the work of Laura King, Tanya Evans, Peter Hobbins and others, in collaboration with partners particularly drawn from those who might self-identify as family historians or historians outside a formal academic environment.[43] For example, the recent 'Energy in Store' project, a collaboration between the Science Museum Group (SMG) and King's College London, sought to bring 'enthusiast experts' into the SMG's stores, to exchange knowledge and increase access and participation.[44] Such positive actions can help to re-orient attitudes and debate, and to increase mutual respect as well as challenge particular ways of thinking (on all sides). Even reframing the terms of reference – as the 'Railway Work, Life & Death' project has tried to do – to move away from a narrow conception of academic authority towards a more inclusive view of 'partner practitioners' or 'partner experts' is a significant step.[45]

This heterodoxy might be difficult to do for all, if they regard themselves/ 'their' discipline as the keepers of some sort of empirical or methodology orthodoxy, but if it can be done constructively and openly, there are great advantages for all. The challenges the areas noted – but particularly academic study of transport and mobility history and academic history more generally – face are significant, and moves to broaden dialogue, via collaborative crowd-sourcing and co-production projects, could be a vital and restorative means of crossing artificial barriers between academic and other partners, and of creating a much more shared sense of purpose as to interrogate the past.

Notes

1 *Railway Accidents. Summary of Accidents and Casualties reported to the Board of Trade by the several railway companies in the United Kingdom during the three months ending 31 December 1913* (London, 1914), 139.
2 *General Report to the Board of Trade upon the Accidents that have occurred on the Railways of the United Kingdom for 1913* (London: HMSO, 1914), 4.
3 Tom Crook and Mike Esbester, "Risk and the History of Governing Modern Britain, c.1800-2000," in *Governing Risks in Modern Britain. Danger, Safety and Accidents, c.1800-2000*, eds. T. Crook and M. Esbester (London: Palgrave Macmillan, 2016), 6–7.
4 Ian Carter, *Railways and Culture in Britain. The Epitome of Modernity* (Manchester: Manchester University Press, 2001); M. Freeman, *Railways and the Victorian Imagination* (New Haven: Yale University Press, 1999).
5 For example, trespassers or on level crossings; suicides were a more ambiguous area.
6 Ralph Harrington, "Railway Safety and Railway Slaughter: Railway Accidents, Government and Public in Victorian Britain," *Journal of Victorian Culture* 8, no. 2 (Autumn 2003): 187–207; Peter Sinnema, "Representing the Railway: Train

Accidents and Trauma in the *Illustrated London News*," *Victorian Periodicals Review* 31, no. 2 (Summer 1998): 142–168; Wolfgang Schivelbush, *The Railway Journey: The Industrialisation of Time and Space in the 19th Century* (Berkeley: University of California Press, 1986), 118–151.

7 Ralph Harrington, "The Railway Accident: Trains, Trauma and Technological Crisis in Nineteenth-Century Britain," in *Traumatic Pasts. History, Psychiatry, and Trauma in the Modern Age, 1870–1930*, eds. Mark S. Micale and Paul Lerner (Cambridge: Cambridge University Press, 2001), 31–56; Karen M. Odden, "'Able and Intelligent Medical Men Meeting Together': The Victorian Railway Crash, Medical Jurisprudence, and the Rise of Medical Authority," *Journal of Victorian Culture* 8, no. 1 (Spring 2003): 33–54; Schivelbush, *The Railway Journey*, 118–151.

8 Nicholas Daly, "Blood on the Tracks: Sensation Drama, the Railway, and the Dark Face of Modernity," *Victorian Studies* 42, no. 1 (Autumn 1998/1999): 47–76; Jill L. Matus, "Trauma, Memory, and Railway Disaster: The Dickensian Connection," *Victorian Studies* 43, no. 3 (Spring 2001): 413–436; M. Wilson-Smith, "Victorian Railway Accidents and the Melodramatic Imagination," *Modern Drama* 55, no. 4 (2012): 497–522.

9 Oliver Betts, "'By His Deeds You Shall Know Him, by the Work of his Hand...': The Engine Driver as Working-Class Hero," in *Railway Cultures*, eds., Christopher Leffler and Amanda Crawley (Sheffield: University of Sheffield and National Railway Museum, 2018), 41–49.

10 *General Report to the Board of Trade upon the Accidents that have occurred on the Railways of the United Kingdom for 1901* (London: HMSO 1902), 22.

11 Passengers: 3,791 casualties; workers: 29,247. *Return of Accidents and Casualties, as reported to the Board of Trade by the Railway Companies in the United Kingdom, during the year 1913* (London: HMSO 1914), 3, 26.

12 Mike Esbester, "Organizing Work: Company Magazines and the Discipline of Safety," *Management and Organizational History* 3, no. 3 (2008): 217–237; Mike Esbester, "Administration, Technology & Workplace Safety in the early Twentieth Century," *Jahrbuch für europäische Verwaltungsgeschichte* 20 (2008): 95–117; Audrey Giles, "Railway Accidents and Nineteenth-Century Legislation: "Misconduct, Want of Caution or Causes Beyond their Control?,"" *Labour History Review* 76, no. 2 (August 2011): 121–142; Ewan Knox, "Blood on the Tracks: Railway Employers and Safety in Late-Victorian and Edwardian Britain," *Historical Studies in Industrial Relations* 12 (Autumn 2001): 1–26; Rande W. Kostal, *Law and English Railway Capitalism 1825–1875* (Oxford: Clarendon Press, 1994).

13 Roger Cooter, and Bill Luckin, "Accidents in History: An Introduction," in *Accidents in History: Injuries, Fatalities and Social Relations*, eds., Roger Cooter and Bill Luckin (Atlanta: Rodopi, 1997), 1–16.

14 For example, Ronnie Johnston, and Arthur McIvor, "Dangerous Work, Hard Men and Broken Bodies: Masculinity in the Clydeside Heavy Industries, c.1930–1970s," *Labour History Review* 69, no. 2 (2004): 135–151; M. Sanders, "Manufacturing Accident: Industrialism and the Worker's Body in Early Victorian Fiction," *Victorian Literature and Culture* 28, no. 2 (2000): 313–329.

15 *Report*, Royal Commission on the Causes of Accidents, Fatal and Non-Fatal, to Servants of Railway Companies and of Truck Owners (London: HMSO, 1900), 11–12.

16 Harold Holcroft, *Locomotive Adventure. Fifty Years with Steam* (London: Allen, 1963), 36.

17 For example, Vicky Long, *The Rise and Fall of the Healthy Factory. The Politics of Industrial Health in Britain, 1914–60* (Basingstoke: Palgrave Macmillan, 2011); Arthur McIvor, *Working Lives in Britain since 1945* (Basingstoke: Palgrave Macmillan, 2013), 165.

18 Philip S. Bagwell, *The Railwaymen* (London: George Allen & Unwin, 1963), 99–105, 188.

19 Peter W.J. Bartrip, and Sandra Burman, *The Wounded Soldiers of Industry, Industrial Compensation Policy 1833–1897* (Oxford: Oxford University Press, 1983); Brian Mitchell, David Chambers, and Nick Crafts, "How Good Was Profitability of British Railways 1870–1912?," *Economic History Review* 64, no. 3 (2011): 798–831.

20 The figures were produced by the Railway Companies' Association in 1899, and cited in Knox, "Blood on the Tracks," 16.

21 Esbester, "Organizing Work"; Esbester, "Administration, Technology & Workplace Safety"; Mike Esbester, *The Birth of Modern Safety. Preventing Worker Accidents on Britain's Railways, 1871–1948* (London: Routledge, forthcoming).

22 For example, see P. Bartrip, "State Intervention in Mid-Nineteenth Century Britain: Fact or Fiction?," *Journal of British Studies* 23, no. 1 (Autumn 1983): 63–83; Andrew H. Yarmie, "British Employers' Resistance to "Grandmotherly" Government, 1850–80," *Social History* 9, no. 2 (May 1984): 141–169.

23 Following the report of the 1874 Royal Commission on Railway Accidents (London: HMSO, 1877).

24 See University of Portsmouth and National Railway Museum, "Home," *Railway Work, Life and Death project*, 2016-present, accessed June 25, 2019, www.railwayaccidents.port.ac.uk.

25 Stuart Dunn and Mark Hedges, *Connected Communities. Crowd-Sourcing in the Humanities. A Scoping Study* (2012); Stuart Dunn and Mark Hedges, "Crowd-sourcing as a Component of Humanities Research Infrastructures," *International Journal of Humanities and Arts Computing* 7, no. 1–2 (2013): 147–169.

26 "Welcome to the Zooniverse," *Zooniverse*, Undated, accessed December 4, 2018, www.zooniverse.org/.

27 Sally Shuttleworth, "Old Weather: Citizen Scientists in the 19th and 21st centuries," *Science Museum Group Journal* (Spring 2015), accessed December 4, 2018, https://ora.ox.ac.uk/objects/uuid:c6b21dad-d49d-4c32-b52b-cda932a0a928/download_file?file_format=pdf&safe_filename=Shuttleworth%2BOld%2B-Weather.pdf&type_of_work=Journal+article

28 T. Causer and V. Wallace, "Building a Volunteer Community: Results and Findings from *Transcribe Bentham*," *Digital Humanities Quarterly* 6, no. 2 (2012); See also, Caroline Williams, "The Impact of Volunteering in Archives," research report (March 2018); produced by the Archives & Records Association of the UK & Ireland.

29 An extremely helpful intervention is M. Ridge, *Crowd-sourcing our Cultural Heritage* (Abingdon: Routledge, 2014).

30 Run by Ross Bassett, North Carolina State University; at present no further details are publicly available.

31 Craig Lambert, "The Merchant Fleet of Late Medieval and Tudor England, 1400–1580," *University of Southampton*, Undated, December 4, 2018, http://medievalandtudorships.org/

32 *Crew List Index Project*, last modified June 25, 2019, accessed December 4, 2018, http://www.crewlist.org.uk/

33 *Railways Archive*, 2004-2019, accessed December 4, 2018, http://www.railwaysarchive.co.uk/

34 *Railway Accidents. Reports by the Inspecting Officers of Railways, Railway Employment Inspectors and Railway Employment Assistant Inspectors of Inquiries into accidents which occurred during the three months ending 30 June 1923* (London: HMSO, 1923), Appendix C, 19.

35 See: Chris Heather, "Railway Accident Reports: Unseen Victims," *The National Archives*, November 3, 2015, accessed December 4, 2018, https://blog.nationalarchives.gov.uk/blog/railway-accident-reports-unseen-victims/

36 UoP Faculty of Humanities and Social Sciences Ethics Committee, reference 16:17:08.
37 L.L. Dafis, L.M. Hughes, and R. James, "What's Welsh for "Crowdsourcing"? Citizen Science and Community Engagement at the National Library of Wales," in *Crowd-Sourcing*, ed. Mia Ridge (Farnham: Ashgate, 2014), 139–159.
38 On these and other challenges, see Ridge, *Crowd-sourcing*, 7.
39 Available from: Jon Voss, Gabriel Wolfenstein, and Kerri Young, "From Crowd-sourcing to Knowledge Communities: Creating Meaningful Scholarship through Digital Collaboration," *MW2015: Museums and the Web 2015*, February 1, 2015, accessed December 4, 2018, https://mw2015.museumsandtheweb.com/paper/from-crowdsourcing-to-knowledge-communities-creating-meaningful-scholarship-through-digital-collaboration/
40 For more on this from another project, see Causer and Wallace, "Building a Volunteer Community."
41 Ridge, *Crowd-sourcing*, 4.
42 Carter, *Railways and Culture*, 4–6.
43 Tanya Evans, *Fractured Families: Life On The Margins in Colonial New South Wales* (Sydney: UNSW Press, 2015); Laura King, "Living with Dying' project (AHRC funded, AH/P003478/1, 2016); see: "Living with Dying: Everyday Cultures of Dying within Family Life in Britain, 1900-50s," *University of Leeds*, accessed December 4, 2018, https://livingwithdying.leeds.ac.uk/; Peter Hobbins, *'An Intimate Pandemic: Fostering Community Histories of the 1918–19 Influenza Pandemic' Research Project (Australian Historical Association Funded, 2018)*. See also Tim Causer, and Melissa Terras, "Crowdsourcing Bentham: Beyond the Traditional Boundaries of Academic History," *International Journal of Humanities and Arts Computing* 8, no. 1 (April 2014): 46–64.
44 AHRC funded, AH/P013678/1, 2017: Integrating Forms of Care: building communities of practice around reserve collections; see "Energy in Store," *Science Museum Group*, July 2017–September 2018, accessed December 4, 2018 https://group.sciencemuseum.org.uk/our-work/research-public-history/energy-in-store/
45 I gratefully acknowledge the work of Peter Hobbins and discussions we have had for these terms and ideas.

Bibliography

Primary sources

Report. Royal Commission on Railway Accidents. London: HMSO, 1877.
General Report to the Board of Trade upon the Accidents That Have Occurred on the Railways of the United Kingdom for 1901. London: HMSO, 1902.
General Report to the Board of Trade upon the Accidents That Have Occurred on the Railways of the United Kingdom for 1913. London: HMSO, 1914.
Holcroft, H. *Locomotive Adventure. Fifty Years with Steam*. London: Allen, 1963.
Railway Accidents. Summary of Accidents and Casualties Reported to the Board of Trade by the Several Railway Companies in the United Kingdom during the Three Months Ending 31 December 1913. London: HMSO, 1914.
Return of Accidents and Casualties, as Reported to the Board of Trade by the Railway Companies in the United Kingdom, during the Year 1913. London: HMSO, 1914.
Railway Accidents. Reports by the Inspecting Officers of Railways, Railway Employment Inspectors and Railway Employment Assistant Inspectors of Inquiries into Accidents Which Occurred during the Three Months Ending 30 June 1923. London: HMSO, 1923.
Report, Royal Commission on the Causes of Accidents, Fatal and Non-Fatal, to Servants of Railway Companies and of Truck Owners. London: HMSO, 1900.

Secondary sources

Bagwell, Philip S. *The Railwaymen.* London: George Allen & Unwin, 1963.

Bartrip, P. "State Intervention in Mid-Nineteenth Century Britain: Fact or Fiction?" *Journal of British Studies* 23, no. 1 (Autumn 1983): 63–83.

Betts, O. "'By His Deeds You Shall Know Him, by the Work of his Hand...': The Engine Driver as Working-Class Hero." In *Railway Cultures,* edited by C. Leffler and A. Crawley Jackson, 41–49. Sheffield: University of Sheffield and National Railway Museum, 2018.

Carter, Ian. *Railways and Culture in Britain. The Epitome of Modernity.* Manchester: Manchester University Press, 2001.

Causer, T., and V. Wallace. "Building a Volunteer Community: Results and Findings from *Transcribe Bentham.*" *Digital Humanities Quarterly* 6, no. 2 (2012). http://www.digitalhumanities.org/dhq/vol/6/2/000125/000125.html

Causer, Tim, and Melissa Terras. "Crowdsourcing Bentham: Beyond the Traditional Boundaries of Academic History." *International Journal of Humanities and Arts Computing* 8, no. 1 (April 2014): 46–64.

Cooter, R., and Vill Luckin. "Accidents in History: An Introduction.' In *Accidents in History: Injuries, Fatalities and Social Relations,* edited by R. Cooter and B. Luckin, 1–16. Atlanta: Rodopi, 1997.

Crew List Index Project. Last modified June 25, 2019. Accessed December 4, 2018. www.crewlist.org.uk/

Crook, Tom, and Mike Esbester. "Risk and the History of Governing Modern Britain, c.1800–2000." In *Governing Risks in Modern Britain. Danger, Safety and Accidents, c.1800–2000,* edited by Tim Crook and Mike Esbester, 1–26. London: Palgrave Macmillan, 2016.

Dafis, L.L., L.M. Hughes, and R. James. "What's Welsh for "Crowdsourcing"? Citizen Science and Community Engagement at the National Library of Wales." In *Crowd-Sourcing,* edited by Mia Ridge, 139–159. Farnham: Ashgate, 2014.

Daly, N. "Blood on the Tracks: Sensation Drama, the Railway, and the Dark Face of Modernity." *Victorian Studies* 42, no. 1 (Autumn 1998/1999): 47–76.

Dunn, Stuart, and Mark Hedges. *Connected Communities. Crowd-Sourcing in the Humanities. A scoping study.* Swindon: Arts & Humanities Research Council, 2012. https://ahrc.ukri.org/documents/project-reports-and-reviews/connected-communities/crowd-sourcing-in-the-humanities/.

——— "Crowd-sourcing as a Component of Humanities Research Infrastructures." *International Journal of Humanities and Arts Computing* 7, nos. 1–2 (2013): 147–169.

"Energy in Store." *Science Museum Group.* July 2017–September 2018. Accessed December 4, 2018. https://group.sciencemuseum.org.uk/our-work/research-public-history/energy-in-store/.

Esbester, Mike. *The Birth of Modern Safety. Preventing Worker Accidents on Britain's Railways, 1871–1948.* London: Routledge, forthcoming.

———. "Organizing Work: Company Magazines and the Discipline of Safety." *Management and Organizational History* 3, no. 3 (2008): 217–237.

———. "Administration, Technology & Workplace Safety in the early Twentieth Century." *Jahrbuch für europäische Verwaltungsgeschichte* 20 (2008): 95–117.

Evans, Tanya. *Fractured Families: Life On The Margins in Colonial New South Wales.* Sydney: UNSW Press, 2015.

Freeman, Michael. *Railways and the Victorian Imagination.* New Haven: Yale University Press, 1999.

Giles, Audrey. "Railway Accidents and Nineteenth-Century Legislation: "Misconduct, Want of Caution or Causes Beyond their Control?"" *Labour History Review* 76, no. 2 (August 2011): 121–142.

Harrington, Ralph. "Railway Safety and Railway Slaughter: Railway Accidents, Government and Public in Victorian Britain." *Journal of Victorian Culture* 8, no. 2 (Autumn 2003): 187–207.

———. "The Railway Accident: Trains, Trauma and Technological Crisis in Nineteenth-Century Britain." In *Traumatic Pasts. History, Psychiatry, and Trauma in the Modern Age, 1870–1930*, edited by Mark S. Micale and Paul Lerner, 31–56. Cambridge: Cambridge University Press, 2001.

Johnston, Ronnie, and Arthur McIvor. "Dangerous Work, Hard Men and Broken Bodies: Masculinity in the Clydeside heavy Industries, c.1930–1970s." *Labour History Review* 69, no. 2 (2004): 135–151

Knox, Ewan. "Blood on the Tracks: Railway Employers and Safety in Late-Victorian and Edwardian Britain." *Historical Studies in Industrial Relations* 12 (Autumn 2001): 1–26.

Kostal, Rande W. *Law and English Railway Capitalism 1825–1875*. Oxford: Oxford University Press, 1994.

Lambert, Craig. "The Merchant Fleet of Late Medieval and Tudor England, 1400–1580." *University of Southampton*. Undated. Accessed December 4, 2018. http://medievalandtudorships.org/

Long, Vicky. *The Rise and Fall of the Healthy Factory. The Politics of Industrial Health in Britain, 1914–60*. Basingstoke: Palgrave Macmillan, 2011.

Matus, Jill L. "Trauma, Memory, and Railway Disaster: The Dickensian Connection," *Victorian Studies* 43, no. 3 (Spring 2001): 413–436.

McIvor, Arthur. *Working Lives in Britain since 1945*. Basingstoke: Palgrave Macmillan, 2013.

Mitchell, Brian, David Chambers, and Nick Crafts. "How Good was Profitability of British Railways 1870–1912?" *Economic History Review* 64, no. 3 (2011): 798–831.

Odden, Karen M. "'Able and Intelligent Medical Men Meeting Together": The Victorian Railway Crash, Medical Jurisprudence, and the Rise of Medical Authority." *Journal of Victorian Culture* 8, no. 1 (Spring 2003): 33–54.

Railways Archive. 2004–2019. Accessed December 4, 2018. www.railwaysarchive.co.uk/.

Ridge, Mia. *Crowd-sourcing our Cultural Heritage*. Abingdon: Routledge, 2014.

Sanders, M. "Manufacturing Accident: Industrialism and the Worker's Body in Early Victorian Fiction." *Victorian Literature and Culture* 28, no. 2 (2000): 313–329.

Schivelbush, Wolfgang. *The Railway Journey: The Industrialisation of Time and Space in the 19th Century*. Berkeley: University of California Press, 1986.

Shuttleworth, Sally. "Old Weather: Citizen Scientists in the 19th and 21st Centuries," *Science Museum Group Journal*. Spring 2015. Accessed December 4, 2018. https://ora.ox.ac.uk/objects/uuid:c6b21dad-d49d-4c32-b52b-cda932a0a928/download_file?file_format=pdf&safe_filename=Shuttleworth%2BOld%2B-Weather.pdf&type_of_work=Journal+article.

Sinnema, Peter. "Representing the Railway: Train Accidents and Trauma in the *Illustrated London News*." *Victorian Periodicals Review* 31, no. 2 (Summer 1998): 142–168.

University of Portsmouth and National Railway Museum. "Home," *Railway Work, Life and Death project*. 2016-present. Accessed June 25, 2019. www.railwayaccidents.port.ac.uk.

Voss, Jon, Gabriel Wolfenstein, and Kerri Young. "From Crowdsourcing to Knowledge Communities: Creating Meaningful Scholarship through Digital Collaboration" *MW2015: Museums and the Web 2015*. February 1, 2015. Accessed December 4, 2018. https://mw2015.museumsandtheweb.com/paper/from-crowdsourcing-to-knowledge-communities-creating-meaningful-scholarship-through-digital-collaboration/

Williams, Caroline. "The Impact of Volunteering in Archives." Research report produced by the Archives & Records Association of the UK & Ireland. March 2018.

Wilson-Smith, M. "Victorian Railway Accidents and the Melodramatic Imagination." *Modern Drama* 55, no. 4 (2012): 497–522.

Yarmie, Andrew H. "British Employers' Resistance to "Grandmotherly" Government, 1850–80." *Social History* 9, no. 2 (May 1984): 141–169.

Index